23 Things They Don't Tell You about Capitalism

23 Things They Don't Tell You about Capitalism

HA-JOON CHANG

BLOOMSBURY PRESS

NEW YORK • BERLIN • LONDON • SYDNEY

Published by Bloomsbury Press, New York

All papers used by Bloomsbury Press are natural, recyclable products made from wood grown in well-managed forests. The manufacturing processes conform to the environmental regulations of the country of origin.

LIBRARY OF CONGRESS CATALOGING-IN-PUBLICATION DATA HAS BEEN APPLIED FOR.

ISBN: 978-1-60819-166-6 (hardcover)

First published in Great Britain in 2010 by Allen Lane, an imprint of Penguin Books
First published in the United States by Bloomsbury Press in 2011

3 5 7 9 10 8 6 4

Printed in the United States of America by Quad/Graphics, Fairfield, Pennsylvania

To Hee-Jeong, Yuna, and Jin-Gyu

7 Ways to Read *23 Things They Don't Tell You about Capitalism*

Way 1. If you are not even sure what capitalism is, read:
Things 1, 2, 5, 8, 13, 16, 19, 20, and 22

Way 2. If you think politics is a waste of time, read:
Things 1, 5, 7, 12, 16, 18, 19, 21, and 23

Way 3. If you have been wondering why your life does not seem to get better despite ever-rising income and ever-advancing technologies, read:
Things 2, 4, 6, 8, 9, 10, 17, 18, and 22

Way 4. If you think some people are richer than others because they are more capable, better educated and more enterprising, read:
Things 3, 10, 13, 14, 15, 16, 17, 20, and 21

Way 5. If you want to know why poor countries are poor and how they can become richer, read:
Things 3, 6, 7, 8, 9, 10, 11, 12, 15, 17, and 23

Way 6. If you think the world is an unfair place but there is nothing much you can do about it, read:
Things 1, 2, 3, 4, 5, 11, 13, 14, 15, 20, and 21

Way 7. Read the whole thing in the following order . . .

Contents

Acknowledgements

I have benefited from many people in writing this book. Having played such a pivotal role in bringing about my previous book, *Bad Samaritans*, which focused on the developing world, Ivan Mulcahy, my literary agent, gave me constant encouragement to write another book with a broader appeal. Peter Ginna, my editor at Bloomsbury USA, not only provided valuable editorial feedback but also played a crucial role in setting the tone of the book by coming up with the title, *23 Things They Don't Tell You about Capitalism*, while I was conceptualizing the book. William Goodlad, my editor at Allen Lane, took the lead in the editorial work and did a superb job in getting everything just right.

Many people read chapters of the book and provided helpful comments. Duncan Green read all the chapters and gave me very useful advice, both content-wise and editorially. Geoff Harcourt and Deepak Nayyar read many of the chapters and provided sagacious advice. Dirk Bezemer, Chris Cramer, Shailaja Fennell, Patrick Imam, Deborah Johnston, Amy Klatzkin, Barry Lynn, Kenia Parsons, and Bob Rowthorn read various chapters and gave me valuable comments.

Without the help of my capable research assistants, I could not have got all the detailed information on which the book is built. I thank, in alphabetical order, Bhargav Adhvaryu, Hassan Akram, Antonio Andreoni, Yurendra Basnett, Muhammad Irfan, Veerayooth Kanchoochat, and Francesca Reinhardt, for their assistance.

I also would like to thank Seung-il Jeong and Buhm Lee for providing me with data that are not easily accessible.

Last but not least, I thank my family, without whose support and love the book would not have been finished. Hee-Jeong, my wife, not only gave me strong emotional support while I was writing the book but also read all the chapters and helped me formulate my arguments in a more coherent and user-friendly way. I was extremely pleased to see that, when I floated some of my ideas to Yuna, my daughter, she responded with a surprising intellectual maturity for a 14-year-old. Jin-Gyu, my son, gave me some very interesting ideas as well as a lot of moral support for the book. I dedicate this book to the three of them.

Introduction

The global economy lies in tatters. While fiscal and monetary stimulus of unprecedented scale has prevented the financial melt-down of 2008 from turning into a total collapse of the global economy, the 2008 global crash still remains the second-largest economic crisis in history, after the Great Depression. At the time of writing (March 2010), even as some people declare the end of the recession, a sustained recovery is by no means certain. In the absence of financial reforms, loose monetary and fiscal policies have led to new financial bubbles, while the real economy is starved of money. If these bubbles burst, the global economy could fall into another ('double-dip') recession. Even if the recovery is sustained, the aftermath of the crisis will be felt for years. It may be several years before the corporate and the household sectors rebuild their balance sheets. The huge budget deficits created by the crisis will force governments to reduce public investments and welfare entitlements significantly, negatively affecting economic growth, poverty and social stability – possibly for decades. Some of those who lost their jobs and houses during the crisis may never join the economic mainstream again. These are frightening prospects.

This catastrophe has ultimately been created by the free-market ideology that has ruled the world since the 1980s. We have been told that, if left alone, markets will produce the most efficient and just outcome. Efficient, because individuals know best how to utilize the resources they command, and just, because the competitive market process ensures that individuals are rewarded according to their productivity. We have been told that business should be given maximum freedom. Firms, being closest to the market, know what is best for their businesses. If we let them do what they want, wealth creation will be maximized, benefiting the rest of society as well. We were told that government intervention in the markets would only reduce their efficiency. Government intervention is often designed to limit the very scope of wealth creation for misguided egalitarian reasons. Even when it is not, governments cannot improve on market outcomes, as they have neither the necessary information nor the incentives to make good business decisions. In sum, we were told to put all our trust in the market and get out of its way.

Following this advice, most countries have introduced free-market policies over the last three decades – privatization of state-owned industrial and financial firms, deregulation of finance and industry, liberalization of international trade and investment, and reduction in income taxes and welfare payments. These policies, their advocates admitted, may temporarily create some problems, such as rising inequality, but ultimately they will make everyone better off by creating a more dynamic and wealthier society. The rising tide lifts all boats together, was the metaphor.

The result of these policies has been the polar opposite of what was promised. Forget for a moment the financial meltdown, which will scar the world for decades to come. Prior to that, and unbeknown to most people, free-market policies had resulted in slower growth, rising inequality and heightened instability in most countries. In many rich countries, these problems were masked by huge credit expansion; thus the fact that US wages had remained stagnant and working hours increased since the 1970s was conveniently fogged over by the heady brew of credit-fuelled consumer boom. The problems were bad enough in the rich countries, but they were even more serious for the developing world. Living standards in Sub-Saharan Africa have stagnated for the last three decades, while Latin America has seen its per capita growth rate fall by two-thirds during the period. There were some developing countries that grew fast (although with rapidly rising inequality) during this period, such as China and India, but these are precisely the countries that, while partially liberalizing, have refused to introduce full-blown free-market policies.

Thus, what we were told by the free-marketeers – or, as they are often called, neo-liberal economists – was at best only partially true and at worst plain wrong. As I will show throughout this book, the 'truths' peddled by free-market ideologues are based on lazy assumptions and blinkered visions, if not necessarily self-serving notions. My aim in this book is to tell you some essential truths about capitalism that the free-marketeers won't.

This book is not an anti-capitalist manifesto. Being critical of free-market ideology is not the same as being against capitalism. Despite its problems and limitations, I believe that capitalism is still the best economic system that humanity has invented. My criticism is of a particular version of capitalism that has dominated the world in the last three decades, that is, free-market capitalism. This is not the only way to run capitalism, and certainly not the best, as the record of the last three decades shows. The book shows that there are ways in which capitalism should, and can, be made better.

Even though the 2008 crisis has made us seriously question the way in which our economies are run, most of us do not pursue such questions because we think that they are ones for the experts. Indeed they are – at one level. The precise answers do require knowledge on many technical issues, many of them so complicated that the experts themselves disagree on them. It is then natural that most of us simply do not have the time or the necessary training to learn all the technical details before we can pronounce our judgements on the effectiveness of TARP (Troubled Asset Relief Program), the necessity of G20, the wisdom of bank nationalization or the appropriate levels of executive salaries. And when it comes to things like poverty in Africa, the workings of the World Trade Organization, or the capital adequacy rules of the Bank for International Settlements, most of us are frankly lost.

However, it is *not* necessary for us to understand all the technical details in order to understand what is going on in the world and exercise what I call an 'active economic citizenship' to demand the right courses of action from those in decision-making positions. After all, we make judgements about all sorts of other issues despite lacking technical expertise. We don't need to be expert epidemiologists in order to know that there should be hygiene standards in food factories, butchers and restaurants. Making judgements about economics is no different: once you know the key principles and basic facts, you can make some robust judgements without knowing the technical details. The only prerequisite is that you are willing to remove those rose-tinted glasses that neo-liberal ideologies like you to wear every day. The glasses make the world look simple and pretty. But lift them off and stare at the clear harsh light of reality.

Once you know that there is really no such thing as a free market, you won't be deceived by people who denounce a regulation on the grounds that it makes the market 'unfree' (*see Thing 1*). When you learn that large and active governments can promote, rather than dampen, economic dynamism, you will see that the widespread distrust of government is unwarranted (*see Things 12 and 21*). Knowing that we do *not* live in a post-industrial knowledge economy will make you question the wisdom of neglecting, or even implicitly welcoming, industrial decline of a country, as some governments have done (*see Things 9 and 17*). Once you realize that trickle-down economics does not work, you will see the excessive tax cuts for the rich for what they are – a simple upward redistribution of income, rather than a way to make all of us richer, as we were told (*see Things 13 and 20*).

What has happened to the world economy was no accident or the outcome of an irresistible force of history. It is not because of some iron law of the market that wages have been stagnating and working hours rising for most Americans, while the top managers and bankers vastly increased their incomes (*see Things 10 and 14*). It is not simply because of unstoppable progress in the technologies of communications and transportation that we are exposed to increasing forces of international competition and have to worry about job security (*see Things 4 and 6*). It was not inevitable that the financial sector got more and more detached from the real economy in the last three decades, ultimately creating the economic catastrophe we are in today (*see Things 18 and 22*). It is not mainly because of some unalterable structural factors – tropical climate, unfortunate location, or bad culture – that poor countries are poor (*see Things 7 and 11*).

Human decisions, especially decisions by those who have the power to set the rules, make things happen in the way they happen, as I will explain. Even though no single decision-maker can be sure that her actions will always lead to the desired results, the decisions that have been made are not in some sense inevitable. We do not live in the best of all possible worlds. If different decisions had been taken, the world would have been a different place. Given this, we need to ask whether the decisions that the rich and the powerful take are based on sound reasoning and robust evidence. Only when we do that can we demand right actions from corporations, governments and international organizations. Without our active economic citizenship, we will always be the victims of people who have greater ability to make decisions, who tell us that things happen because they have to and therefore that there is nothing we can do to alter them, however unpleasant and unjust they may appear.

This book is intended to equip the reader with an understanding of how capitalism really works and how it can be made to work better. It is, however, not an 'economics for dummies'. It is attempting to be both far less and far more.

It is less than economics for dummies because I do not go into many of the technical details that even a basic introductory book on economics would be compelled to explain. However, this neglect of technical details is not because I believe them to be beyond my readers. 95 per cent of economics is common sense made complicated, and even for the remaining 5 per cent, the essential reasoning, if not all the technical details, can be explained in plain terms. It is simply because I believe that the best way to learn economic principles is by using them to understand problems that interest the reader the most. Therefore, I introduce technical details only when they become relevant, rather than in a systematic, textbook-like manner.

But while completely accessible to non-specialist readers, this book is a lot more than economics for dummies. Indeed, it goes much deeper than many advanced economics books in the sense that it questions many received economic theories and empirical facts that those books take for granted. While it may sound daunting for a non-specialist reader to be asked to question theories that are supported by the 'experts' and to suspect empirical facts that are accepted by most professionals in the field, you will find that this is actually a lot easier than it sounds, once you stop assuming that what most experts believe must be right.

Most of the issues I discuss in the book do not have simple answers. Indeed, in many cases, my main point is that there is no simple answer, unlike what free-market economists want you to believe. However, unless we confront these issues, we will not perceive how the world really works. And unless we understand that, we won't be able to defend our own interests, not to speak of doing greater good as active economic citizens.

Thing 1
There is no such thing as a free market

What they tell you

Markets need to be free. When the government interferes to dictate what market participants can or cannot do, resources cannot flow to their most efficient use. If people cannot do the things that they find most profitable, they lose the incentive to invest and innovate. Thus, if the government puts a cap on house rents, landlords lose the incentive to maintain their properties or build new ones. Or, if the government restricts the kinds of financial products that can be sold, two contracting parties that may both have benefited from innovative transactions that fulfil their idiosyncratic needs cannot reap the potential gains of free contract. People must be left 'free to choose', as the title of free-market visionary Milton Friedman's famous book goes.

What they don't tell you

The free market doesn't exist. Every market has some rules and boundaries that restrict freedom of choice. A market looks free only because we so unconditionally accept its underlying restrictions that we fail to see them. How 'free' a market is cannot be objectively defined. It is a political definition. The usual claim by free-market economists that they are trying to defend the market from politically motivated interference by the government is false. Government is always involved and those free-marketeers are as politically motivated as anyone. Overcoming the myth that there is such a thing as an objectively defined 'free market' is the first step towards understanding capitalism.

Labour ought to be free

In 1819 new legislation to regulate child labour, the Cotton Factories Regulation Act, was tabled in the British Parliament. The proposed regulation was incredibly 'light touch' by modern standards. It would ban the employment of young children – that is, those under the age of nine. Older children (aged between ten and sixteen) would still be allowed to work, but with their working hours restricted to twelve per day (yes, they were really going soft on those kids). The new rules applied only to cotton factories, which were recognized to be exceptionally hazardous to workers' health.

The proposal caused huge controversy. Opponents saw it as undermining the sanctity of freedom of contract and thus destroying the very foundation of the free market. In debating this legislation, some members of the House of Lords objected to it on the grounds that 'labour ought to be free'. Their argument said: the children want (and need) to work, and the factory owners want to employ them; what is the problem?

Today, even the most ardent free-market proponents in Britain or other rich countries would not think of bringing child labour back as part of the market liberalization package that they so want. However, until the late nineteenth or the early twentieth century, when the first serious child labour regulations were introduced in Europe and North America, many respectable people judged child labour regulation to be against the principles of the free market.

Thus seen, the 'freedom' of a market is, like beauty, in the eyes of the beholder. If you believe that the right of children not to have to work is more important than the right of factory owners to be able to hire whoever they find most profitable, you will not see a ban on child labour as an infringement on the freedom of the labour market. If you believe the opposite, you will see an 'unfree' market, shackled by a misguided government regulation.

We don't have to go back two centuries to see regulations we take for granted (and accept as the 'ambient noise' within the free market) that were seriously challenged as undermining the free market, when first introduced. When environmental regulations (e.g., regulations on car and factory emissions) appeared a few decades ago, they were opposed by many as serious infringements on our freedom to choose. Their opponents asked: if people want to drive in more polluting cars or if factories find more polluting production methods more profitable, why should the government prevent them from making such choices? Today, most people accept these regulations as 'natural'. They believe that actions that harm others, however unintentionally (such as pollution), need to be restricted. They also understand that it is sensible to make careful use of our energy resources, when many of them are non-renewable. They may believe that reducing human impact on climate change makes sense too.

If the same market can be perceived to have varying degrees of freedom by different people, there is really no objective way to define how free that market is. In other words, the free market is an illusion. If some markets *look* free, it is only because we so totally accept the regulations that are propping them up that they become invisible.

Piano wires and kungfu masters

Like many people, as a child I was fascinated by all those gravity-defying kungfu masters in Hong Kong movies. Like many kids,

I suspect, I was bitterly disappointed when I learned that those masters were actually hanging on piano wires.

The free market is a bit like that. We accept the legitimacy of certain regulations so totally that we don't see them. More carefully examined, markets are revealed to be propped up by rules – and many of them.

To begin with, there is a huge range of restrictions on what can be traded; and not just bans on 'obvious' things such as narcotic drugs or human organs. Electoral votes, government jobs and legal decisions are not for sale, at least openly, in modern economies, although they were in most countries in the past. University places may not usually be sold, although in some nations money can buy them – either through (illegally) paying the selectors or (legally) donating money to the university. Many countries ban trading in firearms or alcohol. Usually medicines have to be explicitly licensed by the government, upon the proof of their safety, before they can be marketed. All these regulations are potentially controversial – just as the ban on selling human beings (the slave trade) was one and a half centuries ago.

There are also restrictions on who can participate in markets. Child labour regulation now bans the entry of children into the labour market. Licences are required for professions that have significant impacts on human life, such as medical doctors or lawyers (which may sometimes be issued by professional associations rather than by the government). Many countries allow only companies with more than a certain amount of capital to set up banks. Even the stock market, whose under-regulation has been a cause of the 2008 global recession, has regulations on who can trade. You can't just turn up in the New York Stock Exchange (NYSE) with a bag of shares and sell them. Companies must fulfil listing requirements, meeting stringent auditing standards over a certain number of years, before they can offer their shares for trading. Trading of shares is only conducted by licensed brokers and traders.

Conditions of trade are specified too. One of the things that surprised me when I first moved to Britain in the mid 1980s was that one could demand a full refund for a product one didn't like, even if it wasn't faulty. At the time, you just couldn't do that in Korea, except in the most exclusive department stores. In Britain, the consumer's right to change her mind was considered more important than the right of the seller to avoid the cost involved in returning unwanted (yet functional) products to the manufacturer. There are many other rules regulating various aspects of the exchange process: product liability, failure in delivery, loan default, and so on. In many countries, there are also necessary permissions for the location of sales outlets – such as restrictions on street-vending or zoning laws that ban commercial activities in residential areas.

Then there are price regulations. I am not talking here just about those highly visible phenomena such as rent controls or minimum wages that free-market economists love to hate.

Wages in rich countries are determined more by immigration control than anything else, including any minimum wage legislation. How is the immigration maximum determined? Not by the 'free' labour market, which, if left alone, will end up replacing 80–90 per cent of native workers with cheaper, and often more productive, immigrants. Immigration is largely settled by politics. So, if you have any residual doubt about the massive role that the government plays in the economy's free market, then pause to reflect that all our wages are, at root, politically determined (*see Thing 3*).

Following the 2008 financial crisis, the prices of loans (if you can get one or if you already have a variable rate loan) have become a lot lower in many countries thanks to the continuous slashing of interest rates. Was that because suddenly people didn't want loans and the banks needed to lower their prices to shift them? No, it was the result of political decisions to boost demand by cutting interest rates. Even in normal times, interest rates are set in most countries by the central bank, which means that political considerations creep in. In other words, interest rates are also determined by politics.

If wages and interest rates are (to a significant extent) politically determined, then all the other prices are politically determined, as they affect all other prices.

Is free trade fair?

We see a regulation when we don't endorse the moral values behind it. The nineteenth-century high-tariff restriction on free trade by the US federal government outraged slave-owners, who at the same time saw nothing wrong with trading people in a free market. To those who believed that people can be owned, banning trade in slaves was objectionable in the same way as restricting trade in manufactured goods. Korean shopkeepers of the 1980s would probably have thought the requirement for 'unconditional return' to be an unfairly burdensome government regulation restricting market freedom.

This clash of values also lies behind the contemporary debate on free trade vs. fair trade. Many Americans believe that China is engaged in international trade that may be free but is not fair. In their view, by paying workers unacceptably low wages and making them work in inhumane conditions, China competes unfairly. The Chinese, in turn, can riposte that it is unacceptable that rich countries, while advocating free trade, try to impose artificial barriers to China's exports by attempting to restrict the import of 'sweatshop' products. They find it unjust to be prevented from exploiting the only resource they have in greatest abundance – cheap labour.

Of course, the difficulty here is that there is no objective way to define 'unacceptably low wages' or 'inhumane working conditions'. With the huge international gaps that exist in the level of economic development and living standards, it is natural that what is a starvation wage in the US is a handsome wage in China (the average being 10 per cent that of the US) and a fortune in India (the average being 2 per cent that of the US). Indeed, most fair-trade-minded Americans would not have bought things made by their own grandfathers, who worked extremely long hours under inhumane conditions. Until the beginning of the twentieth century, the average work week in the US was around sixty hours. At the time (in 1905, to be more precise), it was a country in which the Supreme Court declared unconstitutional a New York state law limiting the working days of bakers to ten hours, on the grounds that it 'deprived the baker of the liberty of working as long as he wished'.

Thus seen, the debate about fair trade is essentially about moral values and political decisions, and not economics in the usual sense. Even though it is about an economic issue, it is not something economists with their technical tool kits are particularly well equipped to rule on.

All this does *not* mean that we need to take a relativist position and fail to criticize anyone because anything goes. We can (and I do) have a view on the acceptability of prevailing labour standards in China (or any other country, for that matter) and try to do something about it, without believing that those who have a different view are wrong in some absolute sense. Even though China cannot afford American wages or Swedish working conditions, it certainly can improve the wages and the working conditions of its workers. Indeed, many Chinese don't accept the prevailing conditions and demand tougher regulations. But economic theory (at least free-market economics) cannot tell us what the 'right' wages and working conditions should be in China.

I don't think we are in France any more

In July 2008, with the country's financial system in meltdown, the US government poured $200 billion into Fannie Mae and Freddie Mac, the mortgage lenders, and nationalized them. On witnessing this, the Republican Senator Jim Bunning of Kentucky famously denounced the action as something that could only happen in a 'socialist' country like France.

France was bad enough, but on 19 September 2008, Senator Bunning's beloved country was turned into the Evil Empire itself by his own party leader. According to the plan announced that day by President George W. Bush and subsequently named TARP (Troubled Asset Relief Program), the US government was to use at least $700 billion of taxpayers' money to buy up the 'toxic assets' choking up the financial system.

President Bush, however, did not see things quite that way. He argued that, rather than being 'socialist', the plan was simply a continuation of the American system of free enterprise, which 'rests on the conviction that the federal government should interfere in the market place only when necessary'. Only that, in his view, nationalizing a huge chunk of the financial sector was just one of those necessary things.

Mr Bush's statement is, of course, an ultimate example of political double-speak – one of the biggest state interventions in human history is dressed up as another workaday market process. However, through these words Mr Bush exposed the flimsy foundation on which the myth of the free market stands. As the statement so clearly reveals, what is a necessary state intervention consistent with free-market capitalism is really a matter of opinion. There is no scientifically defined boundary for free market.

If there is nothing sacred about any particular market boundaries that happen to exist, an attempt to change them is as legitimate as the attempt to defend them. Indeed, the history of capitalism has been a constant struggle over the boundaries of the market.

A lot of the things that are outside the market today have been removed by political decision, rather than the market process itself – human beings, government jobs, electoral votes, legal decisions, university places or uncertified medicines. There are still attempts to buy at least some of these things illegally (bribing government officials, judges or voters) or legally (using expensive lawyers to win a lawsuit, donations to political parties, etc.), but, even though there have been movements in both directions, the trend has been towards less marketization.

For goods that are still traded, more regulations have been introduced over time. Compared even to a few decades ago, now we have much more stringent regulations on who can produce what (e.g., certificates for organic or fair-trade producers), how they can be produced (e.g., restrictions on pollution or carbon emissions), and how they can be sold (e.g., rules on product labelling and on refunds).

Furthermore, reflecting its political nature, the process of re-drawing the boundaries of the market has sometimes been marked by violent conflicts. The Americans fought a civil war over free trade in slaves (although free trade in goods – or the tariffs issue – was also an important issue).[1] The British government fought the Opium War against China to realize a free trade in opium. Regulations on free market in child labour were implemented only because of the struggles by social reformers, as I discussed earlier. Making free markets in government jobs or votes illegal has been met with stiff resistance by political parties who bought votes and dished out government jobs to reward loyalists. These practices came to an end only through a combination of political activism, electoral reforms and changes in the rules regarding government hiring.

Recognizing that the boundaries of the market are ambiguous and cannot be determined in an objective way lets us realize that economics is not a science like physics or chemistry, but a political exercise. Free-market economists may want you to believe that the correct boundaries of the market can be scientifically determined, but this is incorrect. If the boundaries of what you are studying cannot be scientifically determined, what you are doing is not a science.

Thus seen, opposing a new regulation is saying that the status quo, however unjust from some people's point of view, should not be changed. Saying that an existing regulation should be abolished is saying that the domain of the market should be expanded, which means that those who have money should be given more power in that area, as the market is run on one-dollar-one-vote principle.

So, when free-market economists say that a certain regulation should not be introduced because it would restrict the 'freedom' of a certain market, they are merely expressing a political opinion that they reject the rights that are to be defended by the proposed law. Their ideological cloak is to pretend that their politics is not really political, but rather is an objective economic truth, while other people's politics *is* political. However, they are as politically motivated as their opponents.

Breaking away from the illusion of market objectivity is the first step towards understanding capitalism.

Thing 2
Companies should *not* be run in the interest of their owners

What they tell you

Shareholders own companies. Therefore, companies should be run in their interests. It is not simply a moral argument. The shareholders are not guaranteed any fixed payments, unlike the employees (who have fixed wages), the suppliers (who are paid specific prices), the lending banks (who get paid fixed interest rates), and others involved in the business. Shareholders' incomes vary according to the company's performance, giving them the greatest incentive to ensure the company performs well. If the company goes bankrupt, the shareholders lose everything, whereas other 'stakeholders' get at least something. Thus, shareholders bear the risk that others involved in the company do not, incentivizing them to maximize company performance. When you run a company for the shareholders, its profit (what is left after making all fixed payments) is maximized, which also maximizes its social contribution.

What they don't tell you

Shareholders may be the owners of corporations but, as the most mobile of the 'stakeholders', they often care the least about the long-term future of the company (unless they are so big that they cannot really sell their shares without seriously disrupting the business). Consequently, shareholders, especially but not exclusively the smaller ones, prefer corporate strategies that maximize short-term profits, usually at the cost of long-term investments, and maximize the dividends from those profits, which even further weakens the long-term prospects of the company by reducing the amount of retained profit that can be used for re-investment. Running the company for the shareholders often reduces its long-term growth potential.

Karl Marx defends capitalism

You have probably noticed that many company names in the English-speaking world come with the letter L – PLC, LLC, Ltd, etc. The letter L in these acronyms stands for 'limited', short for 'limited liability' – public *limited* company (PLC), *limited* liability company (LLC) or simply *limited* company (Ltd). Limited liability means that investors in the company will lose only what they have invested (their 'shares'), should it go bankrupt.

However, you may not have realized that the L word, that is, limited liability, is what has made modern capitalism possible. Today, this form of organizing a business enterprise is taken for granted, but it wasn't always like that.

Before the invention of the limited liability company in sixteenth-century Europe – or the joint-stock company, as it was known in its early days – businessmen had to risk everything when they started a venture. When I say everything, I really mean everything – not just personal property (unlimited liability meant that a failed businessman had to sell all his personal properties to repay all the debts) but also personal freedom (they could go to a debtors' prison, should they fail to honour their debts). Given this, it is almost a miracle that anyone was willing to start a business at all.

Unfortunately, even after the invention of limited liability, it was in practice very difficult to use it until the mid nineteenth century – you needed a royal charter in order to set up a limited liability company (or a government charter in a republic). It was believed that those who were managing a limited liability company without owning it 100 per cent would take excessive risks, because part of the money they were risking was not their own. At the same time, the non-managing investors in a limited liability company would also become less vigilant in monitoring the managers, as their risks were capped (at their respective investments). Adam Smith, the father of economics and the patron saint of free-market capitalism, opposed limited liability on these grounds. He famously said that the 'directors of [joint stock] companies . . . being the managers rather of other people's money than of their own, it cannot well be expected that they would watch over it with the same anxious vigilance with which the partners in a private copartnery [i.e., partnership, which demands unlimited liability] frequently watch over their own'.[1]

Therefore, countries typically granted limited liability only to exceptionally large and risky ventures that were deemed to be of national interest, such as the Dutch East India Company set up in 1602 (and its arch-rival, the British East India Company) and the notorious South Sea Company of Britain, the speculative bubble surrounding which in 1721 gave limited liability companies a bad name for generations.

By the mid nineteenth century, however, with the emergence of large-scale industries such as railways, steel and chemicals, the need for limited liability was felt increasingly acutely. Very few people had a big enough fortune to start a steel mill or a railway singlehandedly, so, beginning with Sweden in 1844 and followed by Britain in 1856, the countries of Western Europe and North America made limited liability generally available – mostly in the 1860s and 70s.

However, the suspicion about limited liability lingered on. Even

as late as the late nineteenth century, a few decades after the introduction of generalized limited liability, small businessmen in
Britain 'who, being actively in charge of a business as well as its
owner, sought to limit responsibility for its debts by the device of
incorporation [limited liability]' were frowned upon, according
to an influential history of Western European entrepreneurship.[2]

Interestingly, one of the first people who realized the significance of limited liability for the development of capitalism was
Karl Marx, the supposed arch-enemy of capitalism. Unlike many
of his contemporary free-market advocates (and Adam Smith
before them), who opposed limited liability, Marx understood how
it would enable the mobilization of large sums of capital that were
needed for the newly emerging heavy and chemical industries by
reducing the risk for individual investors. Writing in 1865, when
the stock market was still very much a side-show in the capitalist
drama, Marx had the foresight to call the joint-stock company
'capitalist production in its highest development'. Like his free-
market opponents, Marx was aware of, and criticized, the tendency
for limited liability to encourage excessive risk-taking by managers.
However, Marx considered it to be a side-effect of the huge material progress that this institutional innovation was about to bring.
Of course, in defending the 'new' capitalism against its free-market
critics, Marx had an ulterior motive. He thought the joint-stock
company was a 'point of transition' to socialism in that it separated
ownership from management, thereby making it possible to eliminate capitalists (who now do not manage the firm) without
jeopardizing the material progress that capitalism had achieved.

The death of the capitalist class

Marx's prediction that a new capitalism based on joint-stock
companies would pave the way for socialism has not come true.

However, his prediction that the new institution of generalized limited liability would put the productive forces of capitalism on to a new plane proved extremely prescient.

During the late nineteenth and early twentieth centuries limited liability hugely accelerated capital accumulation and technological progress. Capitalism was transformed from a system made up of Adam Smith's pin factories, butchers and bakers, with at most dozens of employees and managed by a sole owner, into a system of huge corporations hiring hundreds or even thousands of employees, including the top managers themselves, with complex organizational structures.

Initially, the long-feared managerial incentive problem of limited liability companies – that the managers, playing with other people's money, would take excessive risk – did not seem to matter very much. In the early days of limited liability, many large firms were managed by a charismatic entrepreneur – such as Henry Ford, Thomas Edison or Andrew Carnegie – who owned a significant chunk of the company. Even though these part-owner-managers could abuse their position and take excessive risk (which they often did), there was a limit to that. Owning a large chunk of the company, they were going to hurt themselves if they made an overly risky decision. Moreover, many of these part-owner-managers were men of exceptional ability and vision, so even their poorly incentivized decisions were often superior to those made by most of those well-incentivized full-owner-managers.

However, as time wore on, a new class of professional managers emerged to replace these charismatic entrepreneurs. As companies grew in size, it became more and more difficult for anyone to own a significant share of them, although in some European countries, such as Sweden, the founding families (or foundations owned by them) hung on as the dominant shareholders, thanks to the legal allowance to issue new shares with smaller (typically 10 per cent, sometimes even 0.1 per cent) voting rights.

With these changes, professional managers became the dominant players and the shareholders became increasingly passive in determining the way in which companies were run.

From the 1930s, the talk was increasingly of the birth of managerial capitalism, where capitalists in the traditional sense – the 'captains of industry', as the Victorians used to call them – had been replaced by career bureaucrats (private sector bureaucrats, but bureaucrats nonetheless). There was an increasing worry that these hired managers were running the enterprises in their own interests, rather than in the interests of their legal owners, that is, the shareholders. When they should be maximizing profits, it was argued, these managers were maximizing sales (to maximize the size of the company and thus their own prestige) and their own perks, or, worse, engaged directly in prestige projects that add hugely to their egos but little to company profits and thus its value (measured essentially by its stock market capitalization).

Some accepted the rise of the professional managers as an inevitable, if not totally welcome, phenomenon. Joseph Schumpeter, the Austrian-born American economist who is famous for his theory of entrepreneurship (*see Thing 15*), argued in the 1940s that, with the growing scale of companies and the introduction of scientific principles in corporate research and development, the heroic entrepreneurs of early capitalism would be replaced by bureaucratic professional managers. Schumpeter believed this would reduce the dynamism of capitalism, but thought it inevitable. Writing in the 1950s, John Kenneth Galbraith, the Canadian-born American economist, also argued that the rise of large corporations managed by professional managers was unavoidable and therefore that the only way to provide 'countervailing forces' to those enterprises was through increased government regulation and enhanced union power.

However, for decades after that, more pure-blooded advocates of private property have believed that managerial incentives need to be designed in such a way that the managers maximize profits. Many fine brains had worked on this 'incentive design' problem, but the 'holy grail' proved elusive. Managers could always find a way to observe the letter of the contract but not the spirit, especially when it is not easy for shareholders to verify whether poor profit performance by a manager was the result of his failure to pay enough attention to profit figures or due to forces beyond his control.

The holy grail or an unholy alliance?

And then, in the 1980s, the holy grail was found. It was called the principle of shareholder value maximization. It was argued that professional managers should be rewarded according to the amount they can give to shareholders. In order to achieve this, it was argued, first profits need to be maximized by ruthlessly cutting costs – wage bills, investments, inventories, middle-level managers, and so on. Second, the highest possible share of these profits needs to be distributed to the shareholders – through dividends and share buybacks. In order to encourage managers to behave in this way, the proportion of their compensation packages that stock options account for needs to be increased, so that they identify more with the interests of the shareholders. The idea was advocated not just by shareholders, but also by many professional managers, most famously by Jack Welch, the long-time chairman of General Electric (GE), who is often credited with coining the term 'shareholder value' in a speech in 1981.

Soon after Welch's speech, shareholder value maximization became the zeitgeist of the American corporate world. In the beginning, it seemed to work really well for both the managers and the shareholders. The share of profits in national income, which had shown a downward trend since the 1960s, sharply rose in the mid 1980s and has shown an upward trend since then.[3] And the shareholders got a higher share of that profit as dividends, while seeing the value of their shares rise. Distributed profits as a share of total US corporate profit stood at 35–45 per cent between the 1950s and the 1970s, but it has been on an upward trend since the late 70s and now stands at around 60 per cent.[4] The managers saw their compensation rising through the roof (*see Thing 14*), but shareholders stopped questioning their pay packages, as they were happy with ever-rising share prices and dividends. The practice soon spread to other countries – more easily to countries like Britain, which had a corporate power structure and managerial culture similar to those of the US, and less easily to other countries, as we shall see below.

Now, this unholy alliance between the professional managers and the shareholders was all financed by squeezing the other stakeholders in the company (which is why it has spread much more slowly to other rich countries where the other stakeholders have greater relative strength). Jobs were ruthlessly cut, many workers were fired and re-hired as non-unionized labour with lower wages and fewer benefits, and wage increases were suppressed (often by relocating to or outsourcing from low-wage countries, such as China and India – or the threat to do so). The suppliers, and their workers, were also squeezed by continued cuts in procurement prices, while the government was pressured into lowering corporate tax rates and/or providing more sub-sidies, with the help of the threat of relocating to countries with lower corporate tax rates and/or higher business subsidies. As a result, income inequality soared (*see Thing 13*) and in a seemingly endless corporate boom (ending, of course, in 2008), the vast majority of the American and the British populations could share in the (apparent) prosperity only through borrowing at un-precedented rates.

The immediate income redistribution into profits was bad

enough, but the ever-increasing share of profit in national income since the 1980s has not been translated into higher investments either (*see Thing 13*). Investment as a share of US national output has actually fallen, rather than risen, from 20.5 per cent in the 1980s to 18.7 per cent since then (1990–2009). It may have been acceptable if this lower investment rate had been compensated for by a more efficient use of capital, generating higher growth. However, the growth rate of per capita income in the US fell from around 2.6 per cent per year in the 1960s and 70s to 1.6 per cent during 1990–2009, the heyday of shareholder capitalism. In Britain, where similar changes in corporate behaviour were happening, per capita income growth rates fell from 2.4 per cent in the 1960s–70s, when the country was allegedly suffering from the 'British Disease', to 1.7 per cent during 1990–2009. So running companies in the interest of the shareholders does not even benefit the economy in the average sense (that is, ignoring the upward income redistribution).

This is not all. The worst thing about shareholder value maximization is that it does not even do the company itself much good. The easiest way for a company to maximize profit is to reduce expenditure, as increasing revenues is more difficult – by cutting the wage bill through job cuts and by reducing capital expenditure by minimizing investment. Generating higher profit, however, is only the beginning of shareholder value maximization. The maximum proportion of the profit thus generated needs to be given to the shareholders in the form of higher dividends. Or the company uses part of the profits to buy back its own shares, thereby keeping the share prices up and thus indirectly redistributing even more profits to the shareholders (who can realize higher capital gains should they decide to sell some of their shares). Share buybacks used to be less than 5 per cent of US corporate profits for decades until the early 1980s, but have kept rising since then and reached an epic proportion of 90 per cent in 2007 and an absurd 280 per cent in 2008.[5] William Lazonick, the American business economist, estimates that, had GM not spent the $20.4 billion that it did in share buybacks between 1986 and 2002 and put it in the bank (with a 2.5 per cent after-tax annual return), it would have had no problem finding the $35 billion that it needed to stave off bankruptcy in 2009.[6] And in all this binge of profits, the professional managers benefit enormously too, as they own a lot of shares themselves through stock options.

All this damages the long-run prospect of the company. Cutting jobs may increase productivity in the short run, but may have negative long-term consequences. Having fewer workers means increased work intensity, which makes workers tired and more prone to mistakes, lowering product quality and thus a company's reputation. More importantly, the heightened inse-curity, coming from the constant threat of job cuts, discourages workers from investing in acquiring company-specific skills, eroding the company's productive potential. Higher dividends and greater own-share buybacks reduce retained profits, which are the main sources of corporate investment in the US and other rich capitalist countries, and thus reduce investment. The impacts of reduced investment may not be felt in the short run, but in the long run make a company's technology backward and threaten its very survival.

But wouldn't the shareholders care? As owners of the company, don't they have the most to lose, if their company declines in the long run? Isn't the whole point of someone being an owner of an asset – be it a house, a plot of land or a company – that she cares about its long-run productivity? If the owners are letting all this happen, defenders of the status quo would argue, it must be because that is what they want, however insane it may look to outsiders.

Unfortunately, despite being the legal owners of the company, shareholders are the ones who are least committed among the various stakeholders to the long-term viability of the company. This is because they are the ones who can exit the company most easily – they just need to sell their shares, if necessary at a slight loss, as long as they are smart enough not to stick to a lost cause for too long. In contrast, it is more difficult for other stakeholders, such as workers and suppliers, to exit the company and find another engagement, because they are likely to have accumulated skills and capital equipment (in the case of the suppliers) that are specific to the companies they do business with. Therefore, they have a greater stake in the long-run viability of the company than most shareholders. This is why maximizing shareholder value is bad for the company, as well as the rest of the economy.

The dumbest idea in the world

Limited liability has allowed huge progress in human productive power by enabling the amassing of huge amounts of capital, exactly because it has offered shareholders an easy exit, thereby reducing the risk involved in any investment. However, at the same time, this very ease of exit is exactly what makes the shareholders unreliable guardians of a company's long-term future.

This is why most rich countries outside the Anglo-American world have tried to reduce the influence of free-floating shareholders and maintain (or even create) a group of long-term stakeholders (including some shareholders) through various formal and informal means. In many countries, the government has held sizeable share ownership in key enterprises – either directly (e.g., Renault in France, Volkswagen in Germany) or indirectly through ownership by state-owned banks (e.g., France, Korea) – and acted as a stable shareholder. As mentioned above, countries like Sweden allowed differential voting rights for different classes of shares, which enabled the founding families to retain significant control over the corporation while raising additional capital. In some countries, there are formal representations by workers, who have a greater long-term orientation than floating shareholders, in company management (e.g., the presence of union representatives on company supervisory boards in Germany). In Japan, companies have minimized the influence of floating shareholders through cross-shareholding among friendly companies. As a result, professional managers and floating shareholders have found it much more difficult to form the 'unholy alliance' in these countries, even though they too prefer the shareholder-value-maximization model, given its obvious benefits to them.

Being heavily influenced, if not totally controlled, by longer-term stakeholders, companies in these countries do not as easily sack workers, squeeze suppliers, neglect investment and use profits for dividends and share buybacks as American and British companies do. All this means that in the long run they may be more viable than the American or the British companies. Just think about the way in which General Motors has squandered its absolute dominance of the world car industry and finally gone bankrupt while being on the forefront of shareholder value maximization by constantly downsizing and refraining from investment (*see Thing 18*). The weakness of GM management's short-term-oriented strategy has been apparent at least from the late 1980s, but the strategy continued until its bankruptcy in 2009, because it made both the managers and the shareholders happy even while debilitating the company.

Running companies in the interests of floating shareholders is not only inequitable but also inefficient, not just for the national economy but also for the company itself. As Jack Welch recently confessed, shareholder value is probably the 'dumbest idea in the world'.

Thing 3
Most people in rich countries are paid more than they should be

What they tell you

In a market economy, people are rewarded according to their productivity. Bleeding-heart liberals may find it difficult to accept that a Swede gets paid fifty times what an Indian gets paid for the same job, but that is a reflection of their relative productivities. Attempts to reduce these differences artificially – for example, by introducing minimum wage legislation in India – lead only to unjust and inefficient rewarding of individual talents and efforts. Only a free labour market can reward people efficiently and justly.

What they don't tell you

The wage gaps between rich and poor countries exist not mainly because of differences in individual productivity but mainly because of immigration control. If there were free migration, most workers in rich countries could be, and would be, replaced by workers from poor countries. In other words, wages are largely politically determined. The other side of the coin is that poor countries are poor not because of their poor people, many of whom can out-compete their counterparts in rich countries, but because of their rich people, most of whom cannot do the same. This does not, however, mean that the rich in the rich countries can pat their own backs for their individual brilliance.

Their high productivities are possible only because of the historically inherited collective institutions on which they stand. We should reject the myth that we all get paid according to our individual worth, if we are to build a truly just society.

Drive straight on . . . or dodge the cow (and the rickshaw as well)

A bus driver in New Delhi gets paid around 18 rupees an hour. His equivalent in Stockholm gets paid around 130 kronas, which was, as of summer 2009, around 870 rupees. In other words, the Swedish driver gets paid nearly fifty times that of his Indian equivalent.

Free-market economics tells us that, if something is more expensive than another comparable product, it must be because it is better. In other words, in free markets, products (including labour services) get paid what they deserve. So, if a Swedish driver – let's call him Sven – is paid fifty times more than an Indian driver – let's call him Ram – it must be because Sven is fifty times more productive as a bus driver than Ram is.

In the short run, some (although not all) free-market economists may admit, people may pay an excessively high price for a product because of a fad or a craze. For example, people paid ludicrous prices for those 'toxic assets' in the recent financial boom (that has turned into the biggest recession since the Great Depression) because they were caught in a speculative frenzy. However, they would argue, this kind of thing cannot last for long, as people figure out the true value of things sooner or later (*see Thing 16*). Likewise, even if an underqualified worker somehow manages to get a well-paid job through deceit (e.g., fabricating a certificate) or bluffing in an interview, he will soon be fired and replaced, because it will quickly become apparent that he does not have the productivity to justify his wage. So, the reasoning goes, if Sven is getting paid fifty times what Ram is paid, he must be producing fifty times more output than Ram.

But is this what is really going on? To begin with, is it possible that someone drives fifty times better than another? Even if we somehow manage to find a way to measure quantitatively the quality of driving, is this kind of productivity gap in driving possible? Perhaps it is, if we compare professional racing drivers like Michael Schumacher or Lewis Hamilton with some particularly uncoordinated eighteen-year-old who has just passed his driving test. However, I simply cannot envisage how a regular bus driver can drive fifty times better than another.

Moreover, if anything, Ram would likely be a much more skilled driver than Sven. Sven may of course be a good driver by Swedish standards, but has he ever had to dodge a cow in his life, which Ram has to do regularly? Most of the time, what is required of Sven is the ability to drive straight (OK, give or take a few evasive manoeuvres to deal with drunken drivers on Saturday nights), while Ram has to negotiate his way almost every minute of his driving through bullock carts, rickshaws and bicycles stacked three metres high with crates. So, according to free-market logic, Ram should be paid more than Sven, not the other way round.

In response, a free-market economist might argue that Sven gets paid more because he has more 'human capital', that is, skills and knowledge accumulated through education and training. Indeed, it is almost certain that Sven has graduated from high school, with twelve years of schooling under his belt, whereas Ram probably can barely read and write, having completed only five years of education back in his village in Rajahstan.

However, little of Sven's additional human capital acquired in his extra seven years of schooling would be relevant for bus driving (*see Thing 17*). He does not need any knowledge of human chromosomes or Sweden's 1809 war with Russia in order to drive his bus well. So Sven's extra human capital cannot explain why he is paid fifty times more than Ram is.

The main reason that Sven is paid fifty times more than Ram is, to put it bluntly, protectionism – Swedish workers are protected from competition from the workers of India and other poor countries through immigration control. When you think about it, there is no reason why all Swedish bus drivers, or for that matter the bulk of the workforce in Sweden (and that of any other rich country), could not be replaced by some Indians, Chinese or Ghanaians. Most of these foreigners would be happy with a fraction of the wage rates that Swedish workers get paid, while all of them would be able to perform the job at least equally well, or even better. And we are not simply talking about low-skill workers such as cleaners or street-sweepers. There are huge numbers of engineers, bankers and computer programmers waiting out there in Shanghai, Nairobi or Quito, who can easily replace their counterparts in Stockholm, Linköping and Malmö. However, these workers cannot enter the Swedish labour market because they cannot freely migrate to Sweden due to immigration control. As a result, Swedish workers can command fifty times the wages of Indian workers, despite the fact that many of them do not have productivity rates that are higher than those of Indian workers.

Elephant in the room

Our story of bus drivers reveals the existence of the proverbial elephant in the room. It shows that the living standards of the huge majority of people in rich countries critically depend on the existence of the most draconian control over their labour markets – immigration control. Despite this, immigration control is invisible to many and deliberately ignored by others, when they talk about the virtues of the free market.

I have already argued (*see Thing 1*) that there really is no such thing as a free market, but the example of immigration control reveals the sheer extent of market regulation that we have in supposedly free-market economies but fail to see.

While they complain about minimum wage legislation, regulations on working hours, and various 'artificial' entry barriers into the labour market imposed by trade unions, few economists even mention immigration control as one of those nasty regulations hampering the workings of the free labour market. Hardly any of them advocates the abolition of immigration control. But, if they are to be consistent, they should also advocate free immigration. The fact that few of them do once again proves my point in *Thing 1* that the boundary of the market is politically determined and that free-market economists are as 'political' as those who want to regulate markets.

Of course, in criticizing the inconsistency of free-market economists about immigration control, I am *not* arguing that immigration control should be abolished – I don't need to do that because (as you may have noticed by now) I am not a free-market economist.

Countries have the right to decide how many immigrants they accept and in which parts of the labour market. All societies have limited capabilities to absorb immigrants, who often have very different cultural backgrounds, and it would be wrong to demand that a country goes over that limit. Too rapid an inflow of immigrants will not only lead to a sudden increase in competition for jobs but also stretch the physical and social infrastructures, such as housing and healthcare, and create tensions with the resident population. As important, if not as easily quantifiable, is the issue of national identity. It is a myth – a necessary myth, but a myth nonetheless – that nations have immutable national identities that cannot be, and should not be, changed. However, if there are too many immigrants coming in at the same time, the receiving society will have problems creating a new national identity, without which it may find it difficult to maintain social cohesion.

This means that the speed and the scale of immigration need to be controlled.

This is not to say that the current immigration policies of the rich countries cannot be improved. While any society's ability to absorb immigrants is limited, it is not as if the total population is fixed. Societies can decide to be more, or less, open to immigrants by adopting different social attitudes and policies towards immigration. Also in terms of the composition of the immigrants, most rich countries are accepting too many 'wrong' people from the point of view of the developing countries. Some countries practically sell their passports through schemes in which those who bring in more than a certain amount of 'investment' are admitted more or less immediately. This scheme only adds to the capital shortage that most developing countries are suffering from. The rich countries also contribute to the brain drain from developing countries by more willingly accepting people with higher skills. These are people who could have contributed more to the development of their own countries than unskilled immigrants, had they remained in their home countries.

Are poor countries poor because of their poor people?

Our story about the bus drivers not only exposes the myth that everyone is getting paid fairly, according to her own worth in a free market, but also provides us with an important insight into the cause of poverty in developing countries.

Many people think that poor countries are poor because of their poor people. Indeed, the rich people in poor countries typically blame their countries' poverty on the ignorance, laziness and passivity of their poor. If only their fellow countrymen worked like the Japanese, kept time like the Germans and were inventive like the Americans – many of these people would tell you, if you would listen – their country would be a rich one.

Arithmetically speaking, it is true that poor people are the ones that pull down the average national income in poor countries. Little do the rich people in poor countries realize, however, that their countries are poor not because of their poor but because of themselves. To go back to our bus driver example, the primary reason why Sven is paid fifty times more than Ram is that he shares his labour market with other people who are way more than fifty times more productive than their Indian counterparts.

Even if the average wage in Sweden is about fifty times higher than the average wage in India, most Swedes are certainly *not* fifty times more productive than their Indian counterparts. Many of them, including Sven, are probably less skilled. But there are some Swedes – those top managers, scientists and engineers in world-leading companies such as Ericsson, Saab and SKF – who are hundreds of times more productive than their Indian equivalents, so Sweden's average national productivity ends up being in the region of fifty times that of India.

In other words, poor people from poor countries are usually able to hold their own against their counterparts in rich countries. It is the rich from the poor countries who cannot do that. It is their low relative productivity that makes their countries poor, so their usual diatribe that their countries are poor because of all those poor people is totally misplaced. Instead of blaming their own poor people for dragging the country down, the rich of the poor countries should ask themselves why they cannot pull the rest of their countries up as much as the rich of the rich countries do.

Finally, a word of warning to the rich of the rich countries, lest they become smug, hearing that their own poor are paid well only because of immigration control and their own high productivity.

Even in sectors where rich country individuals are genuinely more productive than their counterparts in poor countries, their productivity is in great part due to the system, rather than the individuals themselves. It is not simply, or even mainly, because they are cleverer and better educated that some people in rich countries are hundreds of times more productive than their counterparts in poor countries. They achieve this because they live in economies that have better technologies, better organized firms, better institutions and better physical infrastructure – all things that are in large part products of collective actions taken over generations (*see Things 15 and 17*). Warren Buffet, the famous financier, put this point beautifully, when he said in a television interview in 1995: 'I personally think that society is responsible for a very significant percentage of what I've earned. If you stick me down in the middle of Bangladesh or Peru or someplace, you'll find out how much this talent is going to produce in the wrong kind of soil. I will be struggling thirty years later. I work in a market system that happens to reward what I do very well – disproportionately well.'

So we are actually back to where we started. What an individual is paid is *not* fully a reflection of her worth. Most people, in poor and rich countries, get paid what they do only because there is immigration control. Even those citizens of rich countries who cannot be easily replaced by immigrants, and thus may be said to be really being paid their worth (although they may not – *see Thing 14*), are as productive as they are only because of the socio-economic system they are operating in. It is not simply because of their individual brilliance and hard work that they are as productive as they are.

The widely accepted assertion that, only if you let markets be, will everyone be paid correctly and thus fairly, according to his worth, is a myth. Only when we part with this myth and grasp the political nature of the market and the collective nature of individual productivity will we be able to build a more just society in which historical legacies and collective actions, and not just individual talents and efforts, are properly taken into account in deciding how to reward people.

Thing 4
The washing machine has changed the world more than the internet has

What they tell you

The recent revolution in communications technologies, represented by the internet, has fundamentally changed the way in which the world works. It has led to the 'death of distance'. In the 'borderless world' thus created, old conventions about national economic interests and the role of national governments are invalid. This technological revolution defines the age we live in. Unless countries (or companies or, for that matter, individuals) change at corresponding speeds, they will be wiped out. We – as individuals, firms or nations – will have to become ever more flexible, which requires greater liberalization of markets.

What they don't tell you

In perceiving changes, we tend to regard the most recent ones as the most revolutionary. This is often at odds with the facts. Recent progress in telecommunications technologies is not as revolutionary as what happened in the late nineteenth century – wired telegraphy – in relative terms. Moreover, in terms of the consequent economic and social changes, the internet revolution has (at least as yet) not been as important as the washing machine and other household appliances, which, by vastly reducing the amount of work needed for household chores, allowed women to enter the labour market and virtually abolished professions like domestic service. We should not 'put the telescope backward' when we look into the past and underestimate the old and overestimate the new. This leads us to make all sorts of wrong decisions about national economic policy, corporate policies and our own careers.

Everyone has a maid in Latin America

According to an American friend, the Spanish textbook that she used in her school in the 1970s had a sentence saying (in Spanish, of course) that 'everyone in Latin America has a maid'.

When you think about it, this is a logical impossibility. Do maids also have maids in Latin America? Perhaps there is some kind of maid exchange scheme that I have not heard of, where maids take turns in being each other's maids, so that all of them can have a maid, but I don't think so.

Of course, one can see why an American author could come up with such a statement. A far higher proportion of people in poor countries have maids than in rich countries. A schoolteacher or a young manager in a small firm in a rich country would not dream of having a live-in maid, but their counterparts in a poor country are likely to have one – or even two. The figures are difficult to come by, but, according to ILO (International Labour Organisation) data, 7–8 per cent of the labour force in Brazil and 9 per cent of that in Egypt are estimated to be employed as domestic servants. The corresponding figures are 0.7 per cent in Germany, 0.6 per cent in the US, 0.3 per cent in England and Wales, 0.05 per cent in Norway and as low as 0.005 per cent in Sweden (the figures are all for the 1990s, except for those of Germany and Norway, which are for the 2000s).[1] So, in proportional terms, Brazil has 12–13 times more domestic servants than the US does and Egypt has 1,800 times more than Sweden. No wonder that many Americans think 'everyone' has a maid in Latin America and a Swede in Egypt feels that the country is practically overrun with domestic servants.

The interesting thing is that the share of the labour force working as domestic servants in today's rich countries used to be similar to what you find in the developing countries today. In the US, around 8 per cent of those who were 'gainfully employed' in 1870 were domestic servants. The ratio was also around 8 per cent in Germany until the 1890s, although it started falling quite fast after that. In England and Wales, where the 'servant' culture survived longer than in other countries due to the strength of the landlord class, the ratio was even higher – 10–14 per cent of the workforce was employed as domestic servants between 1850 and 1920 (with some ups and downs). Indeed, if you read Agatha Christie novels up to the 1930s, you would notice that it is not just the press baron who gets murdered in his locked library who has servants but also the hard-up old middle-class spinster, even though she may have just one maid (who gets mixed up with a good-for-nothing garage mechanic, who turns out to be the illegitimate son of the press baron, and also gets murdered on p. 111 for being foolish enough to mention something that she was not supposed to have seen).

The main reason why there are so much fewer (of course, in proportional terms) domestic servants in the rich countries – although obviously not the only reason, given the cultural differences among countries at similar levels of income, today and in the past – is the higher relative price of labour. With economic development, people (or rather the labour services they offer) become more expensive in relative terms than 'things' (*see also Thing 9*). As a result, in rich countries, domestic service has become a luxury good that only the rich can afford, whereas it is still cheap enough to be consumed even by lower-middle-class people in developing countries.

Enter the washing machine

Now, whatever the movements in the relative prices of 'people' and 'things', the fall in the share of people working as domestic servants would not have been as dramatic as it has been in the rich countries over the last century, had there not been the supply of a host of household technologies, which I have represented by the washing machine. However expensive (in relative terms) it may be to hire people who can wash clothes, clean the house, heat the house, cook and do the dishes, they would still have to be hired, if these things could not be done by machines. Or you would have to spend hours doing these things yourselves.

Washing machines have saved mountains of time. The data are not easy to come by, but a mid 1940s study by the US Rural Electrification Authority reports that, with the introduction of the electric washing machine and electric iron, the time required for washing a 38 lb load of laundry was reduced by a factor of nearly 6 (from 4 hours to 41 minutes) and the time taken to iron it by a factor of more than 2.5 (from 4.5 hours to 1.75 hours).[2] Piped water has meant that women do not have to spend hours fetching water (for which, according to the United Nations Development Program, up to two hours per day are spent in some developing countries). Vacuum cleaners have enabled us to clean our houses more thoroughly in a fraction of the time that was needed in the old days, when we had to do it with broom and rags. Gas/electric kitchen stoves and central heating have vastly reduced the time needed for collecting firewood, making fires, keeping the fires alive, and cleaning after them for heating and cooking purposes. Today many people in rich countries even have the dishwasher, whose (future) inventor a certain Mr I. M. Rubinow, an employee of the US Department of Agriculture, said would be 'a true benefactor of mankind' in his article in the *Journal of Political Economy* in 1906.

The emergence of household appliances, as well as electricity, piped water and piped gas, has totally transformed the way women, and consequently men, live. They have made it possible for far more women to join the labour market. For example, in the US, the proportion of married white women in prime working ages (35–44 years) who work outside the home rose from a few per cent in the late 1890s to nearly 80 per cent today.[3] It has also changed the female occupational structure dramatically by allowing society to get by with far fewer people working as domestic servants, as we have seen above – for example, in the 1870s, nearly 50 per cent of women employed in the US were employed as 'servants and waitresses' (most of whom we can take to have been servants rather than waitresses, given that eating out was not yet big business).[4] Increased labour market participation has definitely raised the status of women at home and in society, thus also reducing preference for male children and increasing investment in female education, which then further increases female labour market participation. Even those educated women who in the end choose to stay at home with their children have higher status at home, as they can make credible threats that they can support themselves should they decide to leave their partners. With outside employment opportunities, the opportunity costs of children have risen, making families have fewer children. All of these have changed the traditional family dynamics. Taken together, they constitute really powerful changes.

Of course, I am not saying that these changes have happened only – or even predominantly – because of changes in household technologies. The 'pill' and other contraceptives have had a powerful impact on female education and labour market participation by allowing women to control the timing and the frequency of their childbirths. And there are non-technological causes. Even with the same household technologies, countries can have quite different female labour market participation ratios and different occupation structures, depending on things like social conventions regarding the acceptability of middle-class women working (poor women have always worked), tax incentives for paid work and child rearing, and the affordability of childcare. Having said all this, however, it is still true that, without the washing machine (and other labour-saving household technologies), the scale of change in the role of women in society and in family dynamics would not have been nearly as dramatic.

The washing machine beats the internet

Compared to the changes brought about by the washing machine (and company), the impact of the internet, which many think has totally changed the world, has not been as fundamental – at least so far. The internet has, of course, transformed the way people spend their out-of-work hours – surfing the net, chatting with friends on Facebook, talking to them on Skype, playing electronic games with someone who's sitting 5,000 miles away, and what not. It has also vastly improved the efficiency with which we can find information about our insurance policies, holidays, restaurants, and increasingly even the price of broccoli and shampoo.

However, when it comes to production processes, it is not clear whether the impacts have been so revolutionary. To be sure, for some, the internet has profoundly changed the way in which they work. I know that by experience. Thanks to the internet, I have been able to write a whole book with my friend and sometime co-author, Professor Ilene Grabel, who teaches in Denver, Colorado, with only one face-to-face meeting and one or two phone calls.[5] However, for many other people, the internet has not had much impact on productivity. Studies have struggled to find the positive impact of the internet on overall productivity – as Robert

Solow, the Nobel laureate economist, put it, 'the evidence is everywhere but in numbers'.

You may think that my comparison is unfair. The household appliances that I mention have had at least a few decades, sometimes a century, to work their magic, whereas the internet is barely two decades old. This is partly true. As the distinguished historian of science, David Edgerton, said in his fascinating book *The Shock of the Old – Technology and Global History Since 1900*, the maximum use of a technology, and thus the maximum impact, is often achieved decades after the invention of the technology. But even in terms of its immediate impact, I doubt whether the internet is the revolutionary technology that many of us think it is.

The internet is beaten by the telegraph

Just before the start of the trans-Atlantic wired telegraph service in 1866, it took about three weeks to send a message to the other side of the 'pond' – the time it took to cross the Atlantic by sail ships. Even going 'express' on a steamship (which did not become prevalent until the 1890s), you had to allow two weeks (the record crossings of the time were eight to nine days).

With the telegraph, the transmission time for, say, a 300-word message was reduced to 7 or 8 minutes. It could even be quicker still. The *New York Times* reported on 4 December 1861 that Abraham Lincoln's State of the Union address of 7,578 words was transmitted from Washington, DC to the rest of the country in 92 minutes, giving an average of 82 words per minute, which would have allowed you to send the 300-word message in less than 4 minutes. But that was a record, and the average was more like 40 words per minute, giving us 7.5 minutes for a 300-word message. A reduction from 2 weeks to 7.5 minutes is by a factor of over 2,500 times.

The internet reduced the transmission time of a 300-word message from 10 seconds on the fax machine to, say, 2 seconds, but this is only a reduction by a factor of 5. The speed reduction by the internet is greater when it comes to longer messages – it can send in 10 seconds (considering that it has to be loaded), say, a 30,000-word document, which would have taken more than 16 minutes (or 1,000 seconds) on the fax machine, giving us an acceleration in transmission speed of 100 times. But compare that to the 2,500-time reduction achieved by the telegraph.

The internet obviously has other revolutionary features. It allows us to send pictures at high speed (something that even telegraph or fax could not do and thus relied on physical transportation). It can be accessed in many places, not just in post offices. Most importantly, using it, we can search for particular information we want from a vast number of sources. However, in terms of sheer acceleration in speed, it is nowhere near as revolutionary as the humble wired (not even wireless) telegraphy.

We vastly overestimate the impacts of the internet only because it is affecting us now. It is not just us. Human beings tend to be fascinated by the newest and the most visible technologies. Already in 1944, George Orwell criticized people who got over-excited by the 'abolition of distance' and the 'disappearance of frontiers' thanks to the aeroplane and the radio.

Putting changes into perspective

Who cares if people think wrongly that the internet has had more important impacts than telegraphy or the washing machine? Why does it matter that people are more impressed by the most recent changes?

It would not matter if this distortion of perspectives was just a matter of people's opinions. However, these distorted perspectives have real impacts, as they result in misguided use of scarce resources.

The fascination with the ICT (Information and Communication Technology) revolution, represented by the internet, has made some rich countries – especially the US and Britain – wrongly conclude that making things is so 'yesterday' that they should try to live on ideas. And as I explain in *Thing 9*, this belief in 'post-industrial society' has led those countries to unduly neglect their manufacturing sector, with adverse consequences for their economies.

Even more worryingly, the fascination with the internet by people in rich countries has moved the international community to worry about the 'digital divide' between the rich countries and the poor countries. This has led companies, charitable foundations and individuals to donate money to developing countries to buy computer equipment and internet facilities. The question, however, is whether this is what the developing countries need the most. Perhaps giving money for those less fashionable things such as digging wells, extending electricity grids and making more affordable washing machines would have improved people's lives more than giving every child a laptop computer or setting up internet centres in rural villages. I am not saying that those things are *necessarily* more important, but many donors have rushed into fancy programmes without carefully assessing the relative long-term costs and benefits of alternative uses of their money.

In yet another example, a fascination with the new has led people to believe that the recent changes in the technologies of communications and transportation are so revolutionary that now we live in a 'borderless world', as the title of the famous book by Kenichi Ohmae, the Japanese business guru, goes.[6] As a result, in the last twenty years or so, many people have come to believe that whatever change is happening today is the result of monumental technological progress, going against which will be like trying to turn the clock back. Believing in such a world, many governments have dismantled some of the very necessary regulations on cross-border flows of capital, labour and goods, with poor results (for example, *see Things 7 and 8*). However, as I have shown, the recent changes in those technologies are not nearly as revolutionary as the corresponding changes of a century ago. In fact, the world was a lot more globalized a century ago than it was between the 1960s and the 1980s despite having much inferior technologies of communication and transportation, because in the latter period governments, especially the powerful governments, believed in tougher regulations of these cross-border flows. What has determined the degree of globalization (in other words, national openness) is politics, rather than technology. However, if we let our perspective be distorted by our fascination with the most recent technological revolution, we cannot see this point and end up implementing the wrong policies.

Understanding technological trends is very important for correctly designing economic policies, both at the national and the international levels (and for making the right career choices at the individual level). However, our fascination with the latest, and our under-valuation of what has already become common, can, and has, led us in all sorts of wrong directions. I have made this point deliberately provocatively by pitting the humble washing machine against the internet, but my examples should have shown you that the ways in which technological forces have shaped economic and social developments under capitalism are much more complex than is usually believed.

Thing 5
Assume the worst about people and you get the worst

What they tell you

Adam Smith famously said: 'It is not from the benevolence of the butcher, the brewer, or the baker that we expect our dinner, but from their regard to their own interest.' The market beautifully harnesses the energy of selfish individuals thinking only of themselves (and, at most, their families) to produce social harmony. Communism failed because it denied this human instinct and ran the economy assuming everyone to be selfless, or at least largely altruistic. We have to assume the worst about people (that is, they only think about themselves), if we are to construct a durable economic system.

What they don't tell you

Self-interest is a most powerful trait in most human beings. However, it's not our only drive. It is very often not even our primary motivation. Indeed, if the world were full of the self-seeking individuals found in economics textbooks, it would grind to a halt because we would be spending most of our time cheating, trying to catch the cheaters, and punishing the caught. The world works as it does only because people are not the totally self-seeking agents that free-market economics believes them to be. We need to design an economic system that, while acknowledging that people are often selfish, exploits other human motives to the full and gets the best out of people. The likelihood is that, if we assume the worst about people, we will get the worst out of them.

How (not) to run a company

In the mid 1990s, I was attending a conference in Japan on the 'East Asian growth miracle', organized by the World Bank. On one side of the debate were people like myself, arguing that government intervention had played a positive role in the East Asian growth story by going against market signals and protecting and subsidizing industries such as automobiles and electronics. On the other side, there were economists supporting the World Bank, who argued that government intervention had at best been an irrelevant sideshow or at worst done more harm than good in East Asia. More importantly, they added, even if it were true that the East Asian miracle owed something to government intervention, that does not mean that policies used by the East Asian countries can be recommended to other countries. Government officials who make policies are (like all of us) self-seeking agents, it was pointed out, more interested in expanding their own power and prestige rather than promoting national interests. They argued that government intervention worked in East Asia only because they had exceptionally selfless and capable bureaucrats for historical reasons (which we need not go into here). Even some of the economists who were supporting an active role for government conceded this point.

Listening to this debate, a distinguished-looking Japanese gentleman in the audience raised his hand. Introducing himself as one of the top managers of Kobe Steel, the then fourth-largest steel producer in Japan, the gentleman chided the economists for misunderstanding the nature of modern bureaucracy, be it in the government or in the private sector.

The Kobe Steel manager said (I am, of course, paraphrasing him): 'I am sorry to say this, but you economists don't understand how the real world works. I have a PhD in metallurgy and have been working in Kobe Steel for nearly three decades, so I know a thing or two about steel-making. However, my company is now so large and complex that even I do not understand more than half the things that are going on within it. As for the other managers – with backgrounds in accounting and marketing – they really haven't much of a clue. Despite this, our board of directors routinely approves the majority of projects submitted by our employees, because we believe that our employees work for the good of the company. If we assumed that everyone is out to promote his own interests and questioned the motivations of our employees all the time, the company would grind to a halt, as we would spend all our time going through proposals that we really don't understand. You simply cannot run a large bureaucratic organization, be it Kobe Steel or your government, if you assume that everyone is out for himself.'

This is merely an anecdote, but it is a powerful testimony to the limitations of standard economic theory, which assumes that self-interest is the only human motivation that counts. Let me elaborate.

Selfish butchers and bakers

Free-market economics starts from the assumption that all economic agents are selfish, as summed up in Adam Smith's assessment of the butcher, the brewer and the baker. The beauty of the market system, they contend, is that it channels what seems to be the worst aspect of human nature – self-seeking, or greed, if you like – into something productive and socially beneficial.

Given their selfish nature, shopkeepers will try to over-charge you, workers will try their best to goof off from work, and professional managers will try to maximize their own salaries and prestige rather than profits, which go to the shareholders rather than themselves. However, the power of the market will put strict limits to, if not completely eliminate, these behaviours: shopkeepers won't cheat you if they have a competitor around the corner; workers would not dare to slack off if they know they can be easily replaced; hired managers will not be able to fleece the shareholders if they operate in a vibrant stock market, which will ensure that managers who generate lower profits, and thus lower share prices, risk losing their jobs through takeover.

To free-market economists, public officials – politicians and government bureaucrats – pose a unique challenge in this regard. Their pursuit of self-interest cannot be restrained to any meaningful degree because they are not subject to market discipline. Politicians do face some competition from each other, but elections happen so infrequently that their disciplinary effects are limited. Consequently, there is plenty of scope for them to pursue policies that heighten their power and wealth, at the cost of national welfare. When it comes to the career bureaucrats, the scope for self-seeking is even greater. Even if their political masters, the politicians, try to make them implement policies that cater to electoral demands, they can always obfuscate and manipulate the politicians, as was so brilliantly depicted in the BBC comedy series *Yes, Minister* and its sequel, *Yes, Prime Minister*. Moreover, unlike the politicians, these career bureaucrats have high job security, if not lifetime tenure, so they can wait out their political masters by simply delaying things. This is the crux of the concerns that the World Bank economists were expressing in the meeting in Japan that I mentioned at the beginning of this *Thing*.

Therefore, free-market economists recommend, the portion of the economy controlled by politicians and bureaucrats should be minimized. Deregulation and privatization, in this view, are not only economically efficient but also politically sensible in that they minimize the very possibility that public officials can use the state as a vehicle to promote their own self-interests, at the cost of the general public. Some – the so-called 'New Public Management' school – go even further and recommend that the management of the government itself should be exposed to greater market forces: a more aggressive use of performance-related pay and short-term contracts for bureaucrats; more frequent contracting-out of government services; a more active exchange of personnel between the public and the private sectors.

We may not be angels, but . . .

The assumption of self-seeking individualism, which is at the foundation of free-market economics, has a lot of resonance with our personal experiences. We have all been cheated by unscrupulous traders, be it the fruit seller who put some rotten plums at the bottom of the paper bag or the yoghurt company that vastly exaggerated the health benefits of it products. We know too many corrupt politicians and lazy bureaucrats to believe that all public servants are solely serving the public. Most of us, myself included, have goofed off from work ourselves and some of us have been frustrated by junior colleagues and assistants who find all kinds of excuses not to put in serious work. Moreover, what we read in the news media these days tells us that professional managers, even the supposed champions of shareholder interest such as Jack Welch of GE and Rick Wagoner of GM, have not really been serving the best interests of the shareholders (*see Thing 2*).

This is all true. However, we also have a lot of evidence – not just anecdotes but systematic evidence – showing that self-interest is not the only human motivation that matters even in our economic life. Self-interest, to be sure, is one of the most important, but we have many other motives – honesty, self-respect, altruism, love, sympathy, faith, sense of duty, solidarity, loyalty, public-spiritedness, patriotism, and so on – that are sometimes even more important than self-seeking as the driver of our behaviours.[1]

Our earlier example of Kobe Steel shows how successful companies are run on trust and loyalty, rather than suspicion and self-seeking. If you think this is a peculiar example from a country of 'worker ants' that suppresses individuality against human nature, pick up any book on business leadership or any autobiography by a successful businessman published in the West and see what they say. Do they say that you have to suspect people and watch them all the time for slacking and cheating? No, they probably talk mostly about how to 'connect' with the employees, change the way they see things, inspire them, and promote teamwork among them. Good managers know that people are not tunnel-visioned self-seeking robots. They know that people have 'good' sides and 'bad' sides and that the secret of good management is in magnifying the former and toning down the latter.

Another good example to illustrate the complexity of human motivation is the practice of 'work to rule', where workers slow down output by strictly following the rules that govern their tasks. You may wonder how workers can hurt their employer by working according to the rule. However, this semi-strike method – known also as 'Italian strike' (and as '*sciopero bianco*', or 'white strike', by Italians themselves) – is known to reduce output by 30 –50 per cent. This is because not everything can be specified in employment contracts (rules) and therefore all production processes rely heavily on the workers' goodwill to do extra things that are not required by their contracts or exercise initiatives and take shortcuts in order to expedite things, when the rules are too cumbersome. The motivations behind such non-selfish behaviours by workers are varied – fondness of their jobs, pride in their workmanship, self-respect, solidarity with their colleagues, trust in their top managers or loyalty to the company. But the bottom line is that companies, and thus our economy, would grind to a halt if people acted in a totally selfish way, as they are assumed to do in free-market economics.

Not realizing the complex nature of worker motivation, the capitalists of the early mass-production era thought that, by totally depriving workers of discretion over the speed and the intensity of their work and thus their ability to shirk, the conveyor belt would maximize their productivity. However, as those capitalists soon found out, the workers reacted by becoming passive, un-thinking and even uncooperative, when they were deprived of their autonomy and dignity. So, starting with the Human Relations School that emerged in the 1930s, which highlighted the need for good communications with, and among, workers, many managerial approaches have emerged that emphasize the complexity of human motivation and suggest ways to bring the best out of workers. The pinnacle of such an approach is the so-called 'Japanese production system' (sometimes known as the 'Toyota production system'), which exploits the goodwill and creativity of the workers by giving them responsibilities and trusting them as moral agents. In the Japanese system, workers are given a considerable degree of control over the production line. They are also encouraged to make suggestions for improving the production process. This approach has enabled Japanese firms to achieve such production efficiency and quality that now many non-Japanese companies are imitating them. By *not* assuming the worst about their workers, the Japanese companies have got the best out of them.

Moral behaviour as an optical illusion?

So, if you look around and think about it, the world seems to be full of moral behaviours that go against the assumptions of free-market economists. When they are confronted with these behaviours, free-market economists often dismiss them as 'optical illusions'. If people look as if they are behaving morally, they argue, it is only because the observers do not see the *hidden* rewards and sanctions that they are responding to.

According to this line of reasoning, people always remain self-seekers. If they behave morally, it is not because they believe in the moral code itself but because behaving in that way maximizes rewards and minimizes punishments for them personally. For example, if traders refrain from cheating even when there is no legal compulsion or when there are no competitors ready to take away their businesses, it does not mean that they believe in honesty. It is because they know that having a reputation as an honest trader brings in more customers. Or many tourists who behave badly would not do the same at home, not because they suddenly become decent people when they go back home but because they do not have the anonymity of a tourist and therefore are afraid of being criticized or shunned by people they know and care about.

There is some truth in this. There *are* subtle rewards and sanctions that are not immediately visible and people do respond to them. However, this line of reasoning does not work in the end.

The fact is that, even when there are no hidden reward-and-sanction mechanisms at work, many of us behave honestly. For example, why do we – or at least those of us who are good runners – not run away without paying after a taxi ride?[2] The taxi driver cannot really chase us far, as he cannot abandon his car for too long. If you are living in a big city, there is virtually no chance that you will meet the same driver again, so you need not even be afraid of the taxi driver retaliating in some way in the future. Given all this, it is quite remarkable that so few people run away without paying after a taxi ride. To take another example, on a foreign holiday some of you may have come across a garage mechanic or a street vendor who did not cheat you, even when there really was no way for you to reward her by spreading her reputation for honest dealings – particularly difficult when you cannot even spell the Turkish garage's name or when your Cambodian noodle lady, whose name you cannot remember anyway, may not even trade in the same place every day.

More importantly, in a world populated by selfish individuals, the invisible reward/sanction mechanism *cannot* exist. The problem is that rewarding and punishing others for their behaviours costs time and energy only to the individuals taking the action, while their benefits from improved behavioural standards accrue to everyone. Going back to our examples above, if you, as a taxi driver, want to chase and beat up a runaway customer, you may have to risk getting fined for illegal parking or even having your taxi broken into. But what is the chance of you benefiting from an improved standard of behaviour by that passenger, who you may not meet ever again? It would cost you time and energy to spread the good word about that Turkish garage, but why should you do that if you will probably never visit that part of the world ever again? So, as a self-seeking individual, you wait for someone foolish enough to spend his time and energy in administering private justice to wayward taxi passengers or honest out-of-the-way garages, rather than paying the costs yourself. However, if everyone were a self-interested individual like you, everyone would do as you do. As a result, no one would reward and punish others for their good or bad behaviour. In other words, those invisible reward/sanction mechanisms that free-market economists say create the optical illusion of morality can exist only because we are *not* the selfish, amoral agents that those economists say we are.

Morality is not an optical illusion. When people act in a non-selfish way – be it not cheating their customers, working hard despite no one watching them, or resisting bribes as an underpaid public official – many, if not all, of them do so because they genuinely believe that that is the right thing to do. Invisible rewards and sanctions mechanisms do matter, but they cannot explain all – or, in my view, even the majority of – non-selfish behaviours, if only for the simple reason that they would not exist if we were entirely selfish. Contrary to Mrs Thatcher's assertion that 'there is no such thing as society. There are individual men and women, and there are families', human beings have never existed as atomistic selfish agents unbound by any society. We are born into societies with certain moral codes and are socialized into 'internalizing' those moral codes.

Of course, all this is not to deny that self-seeking is one of the most important human motivations. However, if everyone were really only out to advance his own interest, the world would have already ground to a halt, as there would be so much cheating in trading and slacking in production. More importantly, if we design our economic system based on such an assumption, the result is likely to be lower, rather than higher, efficiency. If we did that, people would feel that they are not trusted as moral agents and refuse to act in moral ways, making it necessary for us to spend a huge amount of resources monitoring, judging and punishing people. If we assume the worst about people, we will get the worst out of them.

Thing 6
Greater macroeconomic stability has *not* made the world economy more stable

What they tell you

Until the 1970s, inflation was the economy's public enemy number one. Many countries suffered from disastrous hyperinflation experiences. Even when it did not reach a hyperinflationary magnitude, the economic instability that comes from high and fluctuating inflation discouraged investment and thus growth. Fortunately, the dragon of inflation has been slain since the 1990s, thanks to much tougher attitudes towards government budget deficits and the increasing introduction of politically independent central banks that are free to focus single-mindedly on inflation control. Given that economic stability is necessary for long-term investment and thus growth, the taming of the beast called inflation has laid the basis for greater long-term prosperity.

What they don't tell you

Inflation may have been tamed, but the world economy has become considerably shakier. The enthusiastic proclamations of our success in controlling price volatility during the last three decades have ignored the extraordinary instability shown by economies around the world during that time. There have been a huge number of financial crises, including the 2008 global financial crisis, destroying the lives of many through personal indebtedness, bankruptcy and unemployment. An excessive focus on inflation has distracted our attention away from issues of full employment and economic growth. Employment has been made more unstable in the name of 'labour market flexibility', destabilizing many people's lives. Despite the assertion that price stability is the precondition of growth, the policies that were intended to bring lower inflation have produced only anaemic growth since the 1990s, when inflation is supposed to have finally been tamed.

That's where the money is — or is it?

In January 1923, French and Belgian troops occupied the Ruhr region of Germany, known for its coal and steel. This was because, during 1922, the Germans seriously fell behind the reparation payments demanded of them by the Versailles Treaty, which had concluded the First World War.

Had they wanted money, however, the French and the Belgians should have occupied the banks – after all, 'that's where the money is', as the famous American bank robber Willie Sutton allegedly said, when asked why he robbed banks – rather than a bunch of coal mines and steel mills. Why didn't they do that? It was because they were worried about German inflation.

Since the summer of 1922, inflation in Germany had been getting out of control. The cost of living index rose by sixteen times in six months in the second half of 1922. Of course, the hyperinflation was at least in part caused by the onerous reparation demands by the French and the Belgians, but once it started, it was entirely rational for the French and the Belgians to occupy the Ruhr in order to make sure that they were paid their war reparations in goods, such as coal and steel, rather than in worthless paper, whose value would diminish rapidly.

They were right to do so. German inflation got completely out of control after the occupation of the Ruhr, with prices rising by another 10 billion times (yes, billion, not thousand or even million) until November 1923, when Rentenmark, the new currency, was introduced.

The German hyperinflation has left big and long-lasting marks on the evolution of German, and world, history. Some claim, with justification, that the experience of hyperinflation laid the grounds for the rise of the Nazis by discrediting the liberal institutions of the Weimar Republic. Those who take this view are then implicitly saying that the 1920s German hyperinflation was one of the main causes of the Second World War. The German trauma from the hyperinflation was such that the Bundesbank, the West German central bank after the Second World War, was famous for its excessive aversion to loose monetary policy. Even after the birth of the European single currency, the euro, and the consequent *de facto* abolition of national central banks in the Eurozone countries, Germany's influence has made the European Central Bank (ECB) stick to tight monetary policy even in the face of persistently high unemployment, until the 2008 world financial crisis forced it to join other central banks around the world in an unprecedented relaxation of monetary policy. Thus, when talking about the consequences of the German hyperinflation, we are talking about a shockwave lasting nearly a century after the event and affecting not just German, but other European, and world, histories.

How bad is inflation?

Germany is not the only country that has experienced hyper-inflation. In the financial press Argentina has become a byword for hyperinflation in modern times, but the highest rate of inflation it experienced was *only* around 20,000 per cent. Worse than the German one was the Hungarian inflation right after the Second World War and that in Zimbabwe in 2008 in the last days of President Robert Mugabe's dictatorship (now he shares power with the former opposition).

Hyperinflation undermines the very basis of capitalism, by turning market prices into meaningless noises. At the height of the Hungarian inflation in 1946, prices doubled every fifteen hours, while prices doubled every four days in the worst days of the German hyperinflation of 1923. Price signals should not be absolute guides, as I argue throughout this book, but it is impossible to have a decent economy when prices rise at such rates. Moreover, hyperinflation is often the result or the cause of political disasters, such as Adolf Hitler or Robert Mugabe. It is totally understandable why people desperately want to avoid hyperinflation.

However, not all inflation is hyperinflation. Of course, there are people who fear that any inflation, if left alone, would escalate into a hyperinflation. For example, in the early 2000s, Mr Masaru Hayami, the governor of the central bank of Japan, famously refused to ease money supply on the ground that he was worried about the possibility of a hyperinflation – despite the fact that his country was at the time actually in the middle of a deflation (falling prices). But there is actually no evidence that this is inevitable – or even likely. No one would argue that hyperinflation is desirable, or even acceptable, but it is highly questionable whether all inflation is a bad thing, whatever the rate is.

Since the 1980s, free-market economists have managed to convince the rest of the world that economic stability, which they define as very low (ideally zero) inflation, should be attained at all costs, since inflation is bad for the economy. The target inflation rate they recommended has been something like 1–3 per cent, as suggested by Stanley Fischer, a former economics professor at MIT and the chief economist of the IMF between 1994 and 2001.[1]

However, there is actually no evidence that, at low levels, inflation is bad for the economy. For example, even studies done by some free-market economists associated with institutions such as the University of Chicago or the IMF suggest that, below 8–10 per cent, inflation has no relationship with a country's economic growth rate.[2] Some other studies would even put the threshold higher – 20 per cent or even 40 per cent.[3]

The experiences of individual countries also suggest that fairly high inflation is compatible with rapid economic growth. During the 1960s and 70s, Brazil had an average inflation rate of 42 per cent but was one of the fastest-growing economies in the world, with its per capita income growing at 4.5 per cent a year. During the same period, per capita income in South Korea was growing at 7 per cent per year, despite having an annual average rate of inflation of nearly 20 per cent, which was actually higher than that found in many Latin American countries at the time.[4]

Moreover, there is evidence that excessive anti-inflationary policies can actually be harmful for the economy. Since 1996, when Brazil – having gone through a traumatic phase of rapid inflation, although not quite of hyperinflationary magnitude – started to control inflation by raising real interest rates (nominal interest rates minus the rate of inflation) to some of the highest levels in the world (10–12 per cent per year), its inflation fell to 7.1 per cent per year but its economic growth also suffered, with a per capita income growth rate of only 1.3 per cent per year. South Africa has also had a similar experience since 1994, when it started giving inflation control top priority and jacked up interest rates to the Brazilian levels mentioned above.

Why is this? It is because the policies that are aimed to reduce inflation actually reduce investment and thus economic growth, if taken too far. Free-market economists often try to justify their highly hawkish attitude towards inflation by arguing that economic stability encourages savings and investment, which in turn encourage economic growth. So, in trying to argue that macroeconomic stability, defined in terms of low inflation, was a key factor in the rapid growth of the East Asian economies (a proposition that does not actually apply to South Korea, as seen above), the World Bank argues in its 1993 report: 'Macroeconomic stability encourages long-term planning and private investment and, through its impact on real interest rates and the real value of financial assets, helped to increase financial savings.' However, the truth of the matter is that policies that are needed to bring down inflation to a very low – low single-digit – level discourage investment.

Real interest rates of 8, 10 or 12 per cent mean that potential investors would not find non-financial investments attractive, as few such investments bring profit rates higher than 7 per cent.[5] In this case, the only profitable investment is in high-risk, high-return financial assets. Even though financial investments can drive growth for a while, such growth cannot be sustained, as those investments have to be ultimately backed up by viable long-term investments in real sector activities, as so vividly shown by the 2008 financial crisis (*see Thing 22*).

So, free-market economists have deliberately taken advantage of people's justified fears of hyperinflation in order to push for excessive anti-inflationary policies, which do more harm than good. This is bad enough, but it is worse than that. Anti-inflationary policies have not only harmed investment and growth but they have failed to achieve their supposed aim – that is, enhancing economic stability.

False stability

Since the 1980s, but especially since the 1990s, inflation control has been at the top of policy agendas in many countries. Countries were urged to check government spending, so that budget deficits would not fuel inflation. They were also encouraged to give political independence to the central bank, so that it could raise interest rates to high levels, if necessary against popular protests, which politicians would not be able to resist.

The struggle took time, but the beast called inflation has been tamed in the majority of countries in recent years. According to the IMF data, between 1990 and 2008, average inflation rate fell in 97 out of 162 countries, compared to the rates in the 1970s and 80s. The fight against inflation was particularly successful in the rich countries: inflation fell in all of them. Average inflation for the OECD countries (most of which are rich, although not all rich countries belong to the OECD) fell from 7.9 per cent to 2.6 per cent between the two periods (70s–80s vs. 90s–00s). The world, especially if you live in a rich country, has become more stable – or has it?

The fact is that the world has become more stable only if we regard low inflation as the sole indicator of economic stability, but it has *not* become more stable in the way most of us experience it.

One sense in which the world has become more unstable during the last three decades of free-market dominance and strong anti-inflationary policies is the increased frequency and extent of financial crises. According to a study by Kenneth Rogoff, a former chief economist of the IMF and now a professor at Harvard University, and Carmen Reinhart, a professor at the University of Maryland, virtually no country was in banking crisis between the end of the Second World War and the mid 1970s, when the world was much more unstable than today, when measured by inflation. Between the mid 1970s and the late 1980s, when inflation accelerated in many countries, the proportion of countries with banking crises rose to 5–10 per cent, weighted by their share of world income, seemingly confirming the inflation-centric view of the world. However, the proportion of countries with banking crises shot up to around 20 per cent in the mid 1990s, when we are supposed to have finally tamed the beast called inflation and attained the elusive goal of economic stability. The ratio then briefly fell to zero for a few years in the mid 2000s, but went up again to 35 per cent following the 2008 global financial crisis (and is likely to rise even further at the time of writing, that is, early 2010).[6]

Another sense in which the world has become more unstable during the last three decades is that job insecurity has increased for many people during this period. Job security has always been low in developing countries, but the share of insecure jobs in the so-called 'informal sector' – the collection of unregistered firms which do not pay taxes or observe laws, including those providing job security – has increased in many developing countries during the period, due to premature trade liberalization that destroyed a lot of secure 'formal' jobs in their industries. In the rich countries, job insecurity increased during the 1980s too, due to rising (compared to the 1950s–70s) unemployment, which was in large part a result of restrictive macroeconomic policies that put inflation control above everything else. Since the 1990s, unemployment has fallen, but job insecurity has still risen, compared to the pre-1980s period.

There are many reasons for this. First, the share of short-term jobs has risen in the majority of rich countries, although not hugely as some people think. Second, while those who keep their job may stay in the same job almost (although not quite) as long as their pre-1980s counterparts used to, a higher proportion of employment terminations have become involuntary, at least in some countries (especially the US). Third, especially in the UK and the US, jobs that had been predominantly secure even until the 1980s – managerial, clerical and professional jobs – have become insecure since the 1990s. Fourth, even if the job itself has remained secure, its nature and intensity have become subject to more frequent and bigger changes – very often for the worse. For example, according to a 1999 study for the Joseph Rowntree Foundation, the British social reform charity named after the famous Quaker philanthropist businessman, nearly two-thirds of British workers said they had experienced an increase in the speed or the intensity of work over the preceding five-year period. Last but not least, in many (although not all) rich countries, the welfare state has been cut back since the 1980s, so people feel more insecure, even if the objective probability of job loss is the same.

The point is that price stability is only one of the indicators of economic stability. In fact, for most people, it is not even the most important indicator. The most destabilizing events in most people's lives are things like losing a job (or having it radically redefined) or having their houses repossessed in a financial crisis, and not rising prices, unless they are of a hyperinflationary magnitude (hand on heart, can you really tell the difference between a 4 per cent inflation and a 2 per cent one?). This is why taming inflation has not quite brought to most people the sense of stability that the anti-inflationary warriors had said it would.

Now, the coexistence of price stability (that is, low inflation) and the increase in non-price forms of economic instability, such as more frequent banking crises and greater job insecurity, is not a coincidence. All of them are the results of the same free-market policy package.

In the study cited above, Rogoff and Reinhart point out that the share of countries in banking crises is very closely related to the degree of international capital mobility. This increased international mobility is a key goal for free-market economists, who believe that a greater freedom of capital to move across borders would improve the efficiency of the use of capital (*see Thing 22*). Consequently, they have pushed for capital market opening across the world, although recently they have been softening their position in this regard in relation to developing countries.

Likewise, increased job insecurity is a direct consequence of free-market policies. The insecurity manifested in high unemployment in the rich countries in the 1980s was the result of stringent anti-inflationary macroeconomic policies. Between the 1990s and the outbreak of the 2008 crisis, even though unemployment fell, the chance of involuntary job termination increased, the share of short-term jobs rose, jobs were more frequently redefined and work intensified for many jobs – all as a result of changes in labour market regulations that were intended to increase labour market flexibility and thus economic efficiency.

The free-market policy package, often known as the neo-liberal policy package, emphasizes lower inflation, greater capital mobility and greater job insecurity (euphemistically called greater labour market flexibility), essentially because it is mainly geared towards the interests of the holders of financial assets. Inflation control is emphasized because many financial assets have nominally fixed rates of return, so inflation reduces their real returns. Greater capital mobility is promoted because the main source of the ability for the holders of financial assets to reap higher returns than the holders of other (physical and human) assets is their ability to move around their assets more quickly (*see Thing 22*). Greater labour market flexibility is demanded because, from the point of view of financial investors, making hiring and firing of the workers easier allows companies to be restructured more quickly, which means that they can be sold and bought more readily with better short-term balance sheets, bringing higher financial returns (*see Thing 2*).

Even if they have increased financial instability and job insecurity, policies aimed at increasing price stability may be partially justified, had they increased investment and thus growth, as the inflation hawks had predicted. However, the world economy has grown much more slowly during the post-1980s low-inflation era, compared to the high-inflation period of the 1960s and 70s, not least because investment has fallen in most countries (*see Thing 13*). Even in the rich countries since the 1990s, where inflation has been completely tamed, per capita income growth fell from 3.2 per cent in the 1960s and 70s to 1.4 per cent during 1990–2009.

All in all, inflation, at low to moderate levels, is not as dangerous as free-market economists make it out to be. Attempts to bring inflation down to very low levels have reduced investment and growth, contrary to the claim that the greater economic stability that lower inflation brings will encourage investment and thus growth. More importantly, lower inflation has not even brought genuine economic stability to most of us. Liberalizations of capital and labour markets that form integral parts of the free-market policy package, of which inflation control is a key element, have increased financial instability and job insecurity, making the world more unstable for most of us. To add insult to injury, the alleged growth-enhancing impact of inflation control has not materialized.

Our obsession with inflation should end. Inflation has become the bogeyman that has been used to justify policies that have mainly benefited the holders of financial assets, at the cost of long-term stability, economic growth and human happiness.

Thing 7
Free-market policies rarely make poor countries rich

What they tell you

After their independence from colonial rule, developing countries tried to develop their economies through state intervention, sometimes even explicitly adopting socialism. They tried to develop industries such as steel and automobiles, which were beyond their capabilities, artificially by using measures such as trade protectionism, a ban on foreign direct investment, industrial subsidies, and even state ownership of banks and industrial enterprises. At an emotional level this was understandable, given that their former colonial masters were all capitalist countries pursuing free-market policies. However, this strategy produced at best stagnation and at worst disaster. Growth was anaemic (if not negative) and the protected industries failed to 'grow up'. Thankfully, most of these countries have come to their senses since the 1980s and come to adopt free-market policies. When you think about it, this was the right thing to do from the beginning. All of today's rich countries, with the exception of Japan (and possibly Korea, although there is debate on that), have become rich through free-market policies, especially through free trade with the rest of the world. And developing countries that have more fully embraced such policies have done better in the recent period.

What they don't tell you

Contrary to what is commonly believed, the performance of developing countries in the period of state-led development was superior to what they have achieved during the subsequent period of market-oriented reform. There were some spectacular failures of state intervention, but most of these countries grew much faster, with more equitable income distribution and far fewer financial crises, during the 'bad old days' than they have done in the period of market-oriented reforms. Moreover, it is also *not* true that almost all rich countries have become rich through free-market policies. The truth is more or less the opposite. With only a few exceptions, all of today's rich countries, including Britain and the US – the supposed homes of free trade and free market – have become rich through the combinations of protectionism, subsidies and other policies that today they advise the developing countries not to adopt. Free-market policies have made few countries rich so far and will make few rich in the future.

Two basket cases

Here are the profiles of two developing countries. You are an economic analyst trying to assess their development prospects. What would you say?

Country A: Until a decade ago, the country was highly protectionist, with an average industrial tariff rate well above 30 per cent. Despite the recent tariff reduction, important visible and invisible trade restrictions remain. The country has heavy restrictions on cross-border flows of capital, a state-owned and highly regulated banking sector, and numerous restrictions on foreign ownership of financial assets. Foreign firms producing in the country complain that they are discriminated against through differential taxes and regulations by local governments. The country has no elections and is riddled with corruption. It has opaque and complicated property rights. In particular, its protection of intellectual property rights is weak, making it the pirate capital of the world. The country has a large number of state-owned enterprises, many of which make large losses but are propped up by subsidies and government-granted monopoly rights.

Country B: The country's trade policy has literally been the most protectionist in the world for the last few decades, with an average industrial tariff rate at 40–55 per cent. The majority of the population cannot vote, and vote-buying and electoral fraud are widespread. Corruption is rampant, with political parties selling government jobs to their financial backers. The country has never recruited a single civil servant through an open, competitive process. Its public finances are precarious, with records of government loan defaults that worry foreign investors. Despite this, it discriminates heavily against foreign investors. Especially in the banking sector, foreigners are prohibited from becoming directors while foreign shareholders cannot even exercise their voting rights unless they are resident in the country. It does not have a competition law, permitting cartels and other forms of monopoly to grow unchecked. Its protection of intellectual property rights is patchy, particularly marred by its refusal to protect foreigners' copyrights.

Both these countries are up to their necks in things that are supposed to hamper economic development – heavy protectionism, discrimination against foreign investors, weak protection of property rights, monopolies, lack of democracy, corruption, lack of meritocracy, and so on. You would think that they are both headed for developmental disasters. But think again.

Country A is China today – some readers may have guessed that. However, few readers would have guessed that *Country B* is the USA – that is, around 1880, when it was somewhat poorer than today's China.

Despite all the supposedly anti-developmental policies and institutions, China has been one of the world's most dynamic and successful economies over the last three decades, while the USA in the 1880s was one of the fastest-growing – and rapidly becoming one of the richest – countries in the world. So the economic superstars of the late nineteenth century (USA) and of today (China) have both followed policy recipes that go almost totally against today's neo-liberal free-market orthodoxy.

How is this possible? Hasn't the free-market doctrine been distilled out of two centuries of successful development experiences by today's two dozen rich countries? In order to answer these questions, we need to go back in history.

Dead presidents don't talk

Some Americans call their dollar bills 'dead presidents', or 'dead prez'. Not quite accurately. They are all dead all right, but not all the politicians whose portraits adorn the dollar bills are former presidents of the US.

Benjamin Franklin – who features on the best-known paper money in human history, the \$100 bill – never was president. However, he could well have been. He was the oldest of the Founding Fathers and arguably the most revered politician of the new-born country. Although he was too old and George Washington's political stature too great for him to run for the first presidency in 1789, Franklin was the only person who could possibly have challenged Washington for the job.

The real surprise in the pantheon of presidents on the greenback is Alexander Hamilton, who features on the $10 bill. Like Franklin, Hamilton was never a president of the US. But unlike Franklin, whose life story has become American legend, he was, well, not Franklin. Hamilton was a mere Treasury Secretary, even though he was the very first one. What is he doing among the presidents?

Hamilton is there because, unbeknown to most Americans today, he is the architect of the modern American economic system. Two years after becoming Treasury Secretary in 1789 at the outrageously young age of thirty-three, Hamilton submitted to the Congress the *Report on the Subject of Manufactures*, where he set out the economic development strategy for his young country. In the report, he argued that 'industries in their infancy', like the American ones, need to be protected and nurtured by government before they can stand on their own feet. Hamilton's report was not *just* about trade protectionism – he also argued for public investment in infrastructure (such as canals), development of the banking system, promotion of a government bond market – but protectionism was at the heart of his strategy. Given his views, were Hamilton finance minister of a developing country today, he would have been heavily criticized by the US Treasury Department for his heresy. His country might even have been refused a loan from the IMF and the World Bank.

The interesting thing, however, is that Hamilton was not alone in this. All the other 'dead presidents' would have met with the same disapproval from the US Treasury, the IMF, the World Bank and other defenders of the free-market faith today.

On the $1 bill is the first president, George Washington. At his inauguration ceremony, he insisted on wearing American clothes – specially woven in Connecticut for the occasion – rather than higher-quality British ones. Today, this would have been a violation of the proposed WTO rule on transparency in government procurement. And let's not forget that Washington was the one who appointed Hamilton as Treasury Secretary, and in full knowledge of what his view on economic policy was – Hamilton was Washington's aide-de-camp during the American War of Independence and his closest political ally after that.

On the $5 bill, we have Abraham Lincoln, a well-known protectionist, who during the Civil War raised tariffs to their highest level ever.[1] On the $50 bill, we have Ulysses Grant, the Civil War hero-turned president. In defiance of the British pressure on the USA to adopt free trade, he once remarked that 'within 200 years, when America has gotten out of protection all that it can offer, it too will adopt free trade'.

Benjamin Franklin did not share Hamilton's infant industry doctrine, but he insisted on high tariff protection for another reason. At the time, the existence of almost-free land in the US made it necessary for American manufacturers to offer wages around four times higher than the European average, as otherwise the workers would have run away to set up farms (this was no idle threat, given that many of them were farmers in their previous lives) (*see Thing 10*). Therefore, Franklin argued, the American manufacturers could not survive unless they were protected from low-wage competition – or what is known as 'social dumping' today – from Europe. This is exactly the logic that Ross Perot, the billionaire-turned-politician, used in order to oppose the NAFTA (North American Free Trade Agreement) in the 1992 presidential election campaign – a logic that 18.9 per cent of the American voters were happy to endorse.

But surely, you may say, Thomas Jefferson (on the rarely seen $2 bill) and Andrew Jackson (on the $20 bill), the patron saints of American free-market capitalism, would have passed the 'US Treasury Test'?

Thomas Jefferson may have been against Hamilton's protectionism but, unlike Hamilton, who supported the patent system, he argued strongly against patents. Jefferson believed that ideas are 'like air' and therefore should not be owned by anyone. Given the emphasis that most of today's free-market economists put on the protection of patents and other intellectual property rights, his views would have gone down like a lead balloon among them.

Then how about Andrew Jackson, that protector of the 'common man' and fiscal conservative (he paid off all federal government debts for the first time in US history)? Unfortunately for his fans, even he would not pass the test. Under Jackson, average industrial tariffs were in the region of 35–40 per cent. He was also notoriously anti-foreign. When in 1836 he cancelled the licence for the semi-public (second) Bank of the USA (it was 20 per cent owned by the US federal government), one of the main excuses was that it was 'too much' owned by foreign (mainly British) investors. And how much was too much? Only 30 per cent. If some developing country president today cancelled the licence for a bank because it was 30 per cent owned by the Americans, it would send the US Treasury into a fit.

So there we go. Every day, tens of millions of Americans go through the day paying for their taxis and buying their sandwiches with a Hamilton or a Lincoln, getting their change with Washingtons, not realizing that these revered politicians are nasty protectionists that most of their country's news media, conservative and liberal alike, love to lambast. New York bankers and Chicago university professors tut-tut through articles criticizing the anti-foreign antics of Hugo Chavez, the Venezuelan president, in copies of the *Wall Street Journal* bought with an Andrew Jackson, without realizing that he was far more anti-foreign than Chavez.

The dead presidents don't talk. But if they could, they would tell Americans and the rest of the world how the policies that their successors promote today are the exact opposite of what they used in order to transform a second-rate agrarian economy dependent on slave labour into the world's greatest industrial power.

Do as I say, not as I did

When reminded of the protectionist past of the US, free-market economists usually retort that the country succeeded despite, rather than because of, protectionism. They say that the country was destined to grow fast anyway, because it had been exceptionally well endowed with natural resources and received a lot of highly motivated and hard-working immigrants. It is also said that the country's large internal market somewhat mitigated the negative effects of protectionism, by allowing a degree of competition among domestic firms.

But the problem with this response is that, dramatic as it may be, the US is not the only country that has succeeded with policies that go against the free-market doctrine. In fact, as I shall elaborate below, most of today's rich countries have succeeded with such policies.[2] And, when they are countries with very different conditions, it is not possible to say that they all shared some special conditions that cancelled out the negative impacts of protectionism and other 'wrong' policies. The US may have benefited from a large domestic market, but then how about tiny Finland or Denmark? If you think the US benefited from abundance of natural resources, how do you explain the success of countries such as Korea and Switzerland that had virtually no natural resources to speak of? If immigration was a positive factor for the US, how about all those other countries – from Germany to Taiwan – that lost some of their best people to the US and other New World countries? The 'special conditions' argument simply does not work.

Britain, the country which many people think invented free trade, built its prosperity on the basis of policies similar to those that Hamilton promoted. This was not a coincidence. Although Hamilton was the first person to *theorize* the 'infant industry' argument, many of his policies were copied from Robert Walpole, the so-called first British Prime Minister, who ran the country between 1721 and 1742.

During the mid eighteenth century, Britain moved into the woollen manufacturing industry, the high-tech industry of the time that had been dominated by the Low Countries (what are Belgium and the Netherlands today), with the help of tariff protection, subsidies, and other supports that Walpole and his successors provided to the domestic woollen manufacturers. The industry soon provided Britain's main source of export earnings, which enabled the country to import the food and raw materials that it needed to launch the Industrial Revolution in the late eighteenth and the early nineteenth centuries. Britain adopted free trade only in the 1860s, when its industrial dominance was absolute. In the same way in which the US was the most protectionist country in the world during most of its phase of ascendancy (from the 1830s to the 1940s), Britain was one of the world's most protectionist countries during much of its own economic rise (from the 1720s to the 1850s).

Virtually all of today's rich countries used protectionism and subsidies to promote their infant industries. Many of them (especially Japan, Finland and Korea) also severely restricted foreign investment. Between the 1930s and the 1980s, Finland used to classify all enterprises with more than 20 per cent foreign ownership officially as 'dangerous enterprises'. Several of them (especially France, Austria, Finland, Singapore and Taiwan) used state-owned enterprises to promote key industries. Singapore, which is famous for its free-trade policies and welcoming attitudes towards foreign investors, produces over 20 per cent of its output through state-owned enterprises, when the international average is around 10 per cent. Nor did today's rich countries protect foreigners' intellectual property rights very well, if at all – in many of them it was legal to patent someone else's invention as long as that someone else was a foreigner.

There were exceptions of course. The Netherlands, Switzerland (until the First World War) and Hong Kong used little protectionism, but even these countries did not follow today's orthodox doctrines. Arguing that patents are artificial monopolies that go against the principle of free trade (a point which is strangely lost on most of today's free-trade economists), the Netherlands and Switzerland refused to protect patents until the early twentieth century. Even though it did not do it on such principled grounds, Hong Kong was until recently even more notorious for its violation of intellectual property rights than the former countries. I bet you know someone – or at least have a friend who knows someone – who has bought pirated computer software, a fake Rolex watch or an 'unofficial' Calvin & Hobbes T-shirt from Hong Kong.

Most readers may find my historical account counter-intuitive. Having been repeatedly told that free-market policies are the best for economic development, they would find it mysterious how most of today's countries could use all those supposedly bad policies – such as protectionism, subsidies, regulation and state ownership of industry – and still become rich.

The answer lies in the fact that those bad policies were in fact good policies, given the stage of economic development in which those countries were at the time, for a number of reasons. First is Hamilton's infant industry argument, which I explain in greater detail in the chapter 'My six-year-old son should get a job' in my earlier book *Bad Samaritans*. For the same reason why we send our children to school rather than making them compete with adults in the labour market, developing countries need to protect and nurture their producers before they acquire the capabilities to compete in the world market unassisted. Second, in the earlier stages of development, markets do not function very well for various reasons – poor transport, poor flow of information, the small size of the market that makes manipulation by big actors easier, and so on. This means that the government needs to regulate the market more actively and sometimes even deliberately create some markets. Third, in those stages, the government needs to do many things itself through state-owned enterprises because there are simply not enough capable private sector firms that can take up large-scale, high-risk projects (*see Thing 12*).

Despite their own history, the rich countries make developing countries open their borders and expose their economies to the full forces of global competition, using the conditions attached to their bilateral foreign aid and to the loans from international financial institutions that they control (such as the IMF and the World Bank) as well as the ideological influence that they exercise through intellectual dominance. In promoting policies that they did not use when they were developing countries themselves, they are saying to the developing countries, 'Do as I say, not as I did.'

A pro-growth doctrine that reduces growth

When the historical hypocrisy of the rich countries is pointed out, some defenders of the free market come back and say: 'Well, protectionism and other interventionist policies may have worked in nineteenth-century America or mid twentieth-century Japan, but haven't the developing countries monumentally screwed up when they tried such policies in the 1960s and 70s?' What may have worked in the past, they say, is not necessarily going to work today.

The truth is that developing countries did not do badly at all during the 'bad old days' of protectionism and state intervention in the 1960s and 70s. In fact, their economic growth performance during the period was far superior to that achieved since the 1980s under greater opening and deregulation.

Since the 1980s, in addition to rising inequality (which was to be expected from the pro-rich nature of the reforms – *see Thing 13*), most developing countries have experienced a significant deceleration in economic growth. Per capita income growth in the developing world fell from 3 per cent per year in the 1960s and 70s to 1.7 per cent during the 1980–2000 period, when there was the greatest number of free-market reforms. During the 2000s, there was a pick-up in the growth of the developing world, bringing the growth rate up to 2.6 per cent for the 1980–2009 period, but this was largely due to the rapid growth of China and India – two giants that, while liberalizing, did *not* embrace neo-liberal policies.

Growth performances in regions that have faithfully followed the neo-liberal recipe – Latin America and Sub-Saharan Africa – have been much inferior to what they had in the 'bad old days'. In the 1960s and 70s, Latin America grew at 3.1 per cent in per capita terms. Between 1980 and 2009, it grew at a rate just above one-third that – 1.1 per cent. And even that rate was partly due to the rapid growth of countries in the region that had explicitly rejected neo-liberal policies sometime earlier in the 2000s – Argentina, Ecuador, Uruguay and Venezuela. Sub-Saharan Africa grew at 1.6 per cent in per capita terms during the 'bad old days', but its growth rate was only 0.2 per cent between 1980 and 2009 (*see Thing 11*).

To sum up, the free-trade, free-market policies are policies that have rarely, if ever, worked. Most of the rich countries did not use such policies when they were developing countries themselves, while these policies have slowed down growth and increased income inequality in the developing countries in the last three decades. Few countries have become rich through free-trade, free-market policies and few ever will.

Thing 8
Capital has a nationality

What they tell you

The real hero of globalization has been the transnational corporation. Transnational corporations, as their name implies, are corporations that have gone beyond their original national boundaries. They may be still headquartered in the country where they were founded, but much of their production and research facilities are outside their home country, employing people, including many top decision-makers, from across the world. In this age of such nation-less capital, nationalistic policies towards foreign capital are at best ineffective and at worst counterproductive. If a country's government discriminates against them, transnational corporations will not invest in that country. The intention may be to help the national economy by promoting national firms, but such policies actually harm it by preventing the most efficient firms from establishing themselves in the country.

What they don't tell you

Despite the increasing 'transnationalization' of capital, most transnational companies in fact remain national companies with international operations, rather than genuinely nation-less companies. They conduct the bulk of their core activities, such as high-end research and strategizing, at home. Most of their top decision-makers are home-country nationals. When they have to shut down factories or cut jobs, they usually do it last at home for various political and, more importantly, economic reasons. This means that the home country appropriates the bulk of the benefits from a transnational corporation. Of course, their nationality is not the only thing that determines how corporations behave, but we ignore the nationality of capital at our peril.

Carlos Ghosn lives globalization

Carlos Ghosn was born in 1954 to Lebanese parents in the Brazilian city of Porto Velho. At the age of six, he moved with his mother to Beirut, Lebanon. After finishing secondary school there, he went to France and earned engineering degrees from two of the country's most prestigious educational institutions, École Polytechnique and École des Mines de Paris. During his eighteen years at the French tyre-maker Michelin, which he had joined in 1978, Ghosn acquired a reputation for effective management by turning the company's unprofitable South American operation around and by successfully managing the merger of its US subsidiary with Uniroyal Goodrich, which doubled the size of the company's US operation.

In 1996, Ghosn joined the state-owned French car-maker Renault and played a key role in reviving the company, affirming his reputation for ruthless cost-cutting and earning the sobriquet 'le cost killer', although his actual approach was more consensual than that name suggests. When Renault acquired Nissan, the loss-making Japanese car-maker, in 1999, Ghosn was sent to Japan to put Nissan back into shape. Initially, he faced stiff resistance to his un-Japanese way of management, such as sacking workers, but he turned the company completely around in a few years. After that, he has been so totally accepted by the Japanese that he has been made into a *manga* (comic book) character, the Japanese equivalent of beatification by the Catholic Church. In 2005, he stunned the world once again by going back to Renault as CEO and president, while staying on as a co-chairman of Nissan – a feat compared by some to a football coach managing two teams at the same time.

Carlos Ghosn's life story sums up the drama that is globalization. People migrate in search of a better life, sometimes literally to the other side of the world, as Ghosn's family did. Some of the migrants, like Ghosn's mother, go back home. This is a big contrast to the days when, for example, Italian immigrants to the US refused to teach their children Italian, as they were so determined not to go back to Italy and wanted their children totally assimilated. Many youngsters from poorer countries with ambition and brains now go to a richer country to study, as Ghosn did. These days, many managers work for a company based in a foreign country, which often means living and working in yet another foreign country (or two) because your company is transnational. Ghosn, a Lebanese Brazilian return-migrant, worked in Brazil, the US and Japan for two French companies.

In this globalized world, the argument goes, nationality of capital is meaningless. Corporations may have started and still be headquartered in a particular country, but they have broken out of their national borders. They now locate their activities wherever the return is the greatest. For example, Nestlé, the Swiss food giant, may be headquartered in the Swiss city of Vevey, but less than 5 per cent of its output is produced in Switzerland. Even if we consider Nestlé's 'home' to be Europe, rather than Switzerland, its home base accounts for only around 30 per cent of its earnings. It is not just the relatively low-grade activities such as production that transnational corporations are conducting outside their home countries. These days, even top-end activities such as R&D are often located outside the home country – increasingly in developing countries, such as China and India. Even their top managers are drawn, like Ghosn, from an international pool of talent, rather than from exclusively national pools.

The upshot is that a company has no national loyalty any more. A business will do what it has to do in order to increase its profit, even if it means hurting its home country by shutting plants down, slashing jobs, or even bringing in foreign workers. Given this, many people argue, it is unwise to put restrictions on foreign ownership of companies, as many governments used to. As long as the company generates wealth and jobs within its borders, the country should not care whether the company is owned by its citizens or foreigners. When all major companies are ready to move anywhere in search of profit opportunities, making investment by foreign companies difficult means that your country is not going to benefit from those foreign companies that have identified good investment prospects in your country. It all makes sense, doesn't it?

Chrysler – American, German, American (again) and (becoming) Italian

In 1998, Daimler-Benz, the German automobile company, and Chrysler, the US car-maker, were merged. It was really a take-over of Chrysler by Daimler-Benz. But when the merger was announced, it was depicted as a marriage of two equals. The new company, Daimler-Chrysler, even had equal numbers of Germans and Americans on the management board. That was, however, only for the first few years. Soon, the Germans vastly outnumbered the Americans on the board – usually ten to twelve to just one or two Americans, depending on the year.

Unfortunately, the takeover was not a great success, and in 2007 Daimler-Benz sold Chrysler off to Cerberus, an American private equity fund. Cerberus, being an American company, made up Chrysler's board of directors mostly with Americans (with some representation from Daimler, which still held a 19.9 per cent stake).

In the event, Cerberus failed to turn the company around and Chrysler went bankrupt in 2009. It was restructured with US federal government financial aid and a major equity investment by Fiat, the Italian car-maker. When Fiat became the leading shareholder, it made Sergio Marchionne, the CEO of Fiat, also the new CEO of Chrysler and appointed another Fiat manager to Chrysler's nine-member board of directors. Given that Fiat has only a 20 per cent stake at the moment but has the option to increase it to 35 per cent and eventually to 51 per cent, it is highly likely that the proportion of Italians on the board will increase over time, with the increase in Fiat's ownership share.

So Chrysler, once one of the quintessential American companies, has in the last decade come to be run by Germans, Americans (again) and (increasingly) Italians. There is no such thing as 'nationless' capital. When taken over by a foreign company, even mighty (former-)American firms end up being run by foreigners (but then that is what takeover means, when you think about it). In most companies, however transnational their operations may seem, the top decision-makers still remain the citizens of the home country – that is, the country where ownership resides – despite the fact that long-distance management (when the acquiring company does not dispatch top managers to the acquired firm) can reduce management efficiency, while dispatching top managers to a foreign country is expensive, especially when the physical and the cultural distances between the two countries are great. Carlos Ghosn is very much an exception that proves the rule.

It is not just in terms of the appointment of top decision-makers that corporations have a 'home bias'. Home bias is also very strong in research and development, which are at the core of a company's competitive strengths in most advanced industries. Most of a corporation's R&D activities stay at home. Insofar as they are relocated abroad, it is usually to other developed countries, and at that with a heavy 'regional' bias (the regions here meaning North America, Europe and Japan, which is a region unto itself in this respect). Recently an increasing number of R&D centres have been set up in developing countries, such as China and India, but the R&D they conduct tends to be at the lowest levels of sophistication.

Even in terms of production, arguably the easiest thing that a company does and therefore the most likely candidate for relocation abroad, most transnational corporations are still firmly based in their home countries. There are odd examples of firms, for instance Nestlé, which produce most of their outputs abroad, but they are very much the exception. Among US-based transnational corporations, less than one-third of the output of manufacturing firms is produced overseas. In the case of Japanese companies, the ratio is well below 10 per cent. In Europe, the ratio has risen fast recently, but most overseas production by European firms is within the European Union, so it should be understood more as a process of creating national firms for a new nation called Europe than as a process of European firms going truly transnational.

In short, few corporations are truly transnational. The vast majority of them still produce the bulk of their outputs in their home countries. Especially in terms of high-grade activities such as strategic decision-making and higher-end R&D, they remain firmly centred at their home countries. The talk of a borderless world is highly exaggerated.[1]

Why is there a home-country bias?

Why is there a home-country bias in this globalized world? The free-market view is that nationality of capital does not – and should not – matter, because companies have to maximize profit in order to survive and therefore that patriotism is a luxury they can ill afford. Interestingly, many Marxists would agree. They also believe that capital willingly destroys national borders for greater profits and for the expanded reproduction of itself. The language is radically different, but the message is the same – money is money, so why should a company do less profitable things simply because they are good for its home country?

However, there are good reasons why companies act with home-country biases. To begin with, like most of us, top business managers feel some personal obligations to the society they come from. They may frame such obligations in many different ways – patriotism, community spirit, *noblesse oblige*, or wanting to 'return something to the society that has made them what they are today' – and may feel them to different degrees. But the point is that they do feel them. And insofar as most top decision-makers in most companies are home-country nationals, there is bound to be some home-country bias in their decisions. Although free-market economists dismiss any motive other than pure self-seeking, 'moral' motives are real and are much more important than they lead us to believe (*see Thing 5*).

On top of those personal feelings of managers, a company often has real historical obligations to the country in which it has 'grown up'. Companies, especially (although not exclusively) in the early stages of their development, are often supported with public money, directly and indirectly (*see Thing 7*). Many of them receive direct subsidies for particular types of activities, such as equipment investment or worker training. They sometimes even get bailed out with public money, as Toyota was in 1949, Volkswagen in 1974 and GM in 2009. Or they may get indirect subsidies in the form of tariff protection or statutory monopoly rights.

Of course, companies often fail to mention, and even actively hide, such history, but there is an unspoken understanding among the relevant parties that companies do have some moral obligations to their home countries because of these historical debts. This is why national companies are much more open to moral suasion by the government and the public than foreign companies are, when they are expected, although cannot be legally obliged, to do something for the country against their (at least short-term) interests. For example, it was reported in October 2009 that South Korea's financial supervisory agency was finding it impossible to persuade foreign-owned banks to lend more to small and medium-sized companies, even though they, like the nationally owned banks, had already signed an MOU (memorandum of understanding) about that with the agency, when the global financial crisis broke out in the autumn of 2008.

Important though the moral and historical reasons are, by far the most important reason for home-country bias is economic – the fact that the core capabilities of a company cannot be easily taken across the border.

Usually, a company becomes transnational and sets up activities in foreign countries because it possesses some technological and/or organizational competences that the firms operating in the host countries do not possess. These competences are usually embodied in people (e.g., managers, engineers, skilled workers), organizations (e.g., internal company rules, organizational routines, 'institutional memory') and networks of related firms (e.g., suppliers, financiers, industrial associations or even old-boy networks that cut across company boundaries), all of which cannot be easily transported to another country.

Most machines may be moved abroad easily, but it is much more costly to move skilled workers or managers. It is even more difficult to transplant organizational routines or business networks on to another country. For example, when Japanese automobile companies started setting up subsidiaries in Southeast Asia in the 1980s, they asked their subcontractors also to set up their own subsidiaries, as they needed reliable subcontractors. Moreover, these intangible capabilities embodied in people, organizations and networks often need to have the right institutional environment (the legal system, informal rules, business culture) in order to function well. However powerful it may be, a company cannot transport its institutional surroundings to another country.

For all these reasons, the most sophisticated activities that require high levels of human and organizational competences and a conducive institutional environment tend to stay at home. Home biases do not exist simply because of emotional attachments or historical reasons. Their existence has good economic bases.

'Prince of darkness' changes his mind

Lord Peter Mandelson, the *de facto* deputy prime minister of the UK government at the time of writing (early 2010), has a bit of a reputation for his Machiavellian politics. A grandson of the highly respected Labour politician Herbert Morrison, and a TV producer by profession, Mandelson was the chief spin doctor behind the rise of the so-called New Labour under Tony Blair. His famous ability to sense and exploit shifts in political moods and accordingly organize an effective media campaign, combined with his ruthlessness, earned him the nickname 'prince of darkness'.

After a high-profile but turbulent cabinet career, marred by two resignations due to suspected corruption scandals, Mandelson quit British politics and moved to Brussels to become European Commissioner for Trade in 2004. Building on the image of a pro-business politician, gained during his brief spell as the UK's Secretary of State for Trade and Industry back in 1998, Mandelson established a firm reputation as one of the world's leading advocates of free trade and investment.

So it sent out a shockwave, when Mandelson, who had made

a surprise comeback to British politics and become Business Secretary in early 2009, said in an interview with the *Wall Street Journal* in September 2009 that, thanks to Britain's permissive attitude towards foreign ownership, 'UK manufacturing could be a loser', even though he added the proviso that this was 'over a lengthy period of time, certainly not overnight'.

Was it a typical Mandelson antic, with his instinct telling him that this was the time to play the nationalist card? Or did he finally cotton on to something that he and other British policy-makers should have realized a long time ago – that excessive foreign ownership of a national economy can be harmful?

Now, it may be argued, the fact that firms have a home-country bias does *not* necessarily mean that countries should put restrictions on foreign investment. True, given the home bias, investment by a foreign company may not be in the most desirable activities, but an investment is an investment and it will still increase output and create jobs. If you put restrictions on what foreign investors can do – for example, by telling them that they cannot invest in certain 'strategic' industries, by forbidding them from holding a majority share or demanding that they transfer technologies – foreign investors will simply go somewhere else and you will lose the jobs and the wealth that they would have created. Especially for developing countries, which do not have many national firms that can make similar investments, rejecting foreign investment because it is foreign many people believe is frankly irrational. Even if they get only lower-grade activities such as assembly operation, they are still better off with the investment than without it.

This reasoning is correct in its own terms, but there are more issues that need to be considered before we conclude that there should be no restriction on foreign investment (here, we put aside portfolio investment, which is investment in company shares for financial gains without involvement in direct management, and focus on foreign direct investment, which is usually defined as acquisition of more than 10 per cent of a company's shares with an intent to get involved in management).

First of all, we need to remember that a lot of foreign investment is what is known as 'brownfield investment,' that is, acquisition of existing firms by a foreign firm, rather than 'greenfield investment', which involves a foreign firm setting up new production facilities. Since the 1990s, brownfield investment has accounted for over half of total world foreign direct investment (FDI), even reaching 80 per cent in 2001, at the height of the international mergers and acquisitions (M&A) boom. This means that the majority of FDI involves taking control of existing firms, rather than the creation of new output and jobs. Of course, the new owners may inject better managerial and technological capabilities and revive an ailing company – as seen in the case of Nissan under Carlos Ghosn – but very often such an acquisition is made with a view to utilizing capabilities that already exist in the acquired company rather than creating new ones. And, more importantly, once your national firm is acquired by a foreign firm, the home bias of the acquiring company will in the long run impose a ceiling on how far it progresses in the internal pecking order of the acquiring company.

Even in the case of greenfield investment, home-country bias is a factor to consider. Yes, greenfield investment creates new productive capabilities, so it is by definition better than the alternative, that is, no investment. However, the question that policy-makers need to consider before accepting it is how it is going to affect the future trajectory of their national economy. Different activities have different potentials for technological innovation and productivity growth, and therefore what you do today influences what you will be doing in the future and what you will get out of it. As a popular saying among American industrial policy experts in the 1980s went, we cannot pretend that it does not matter whether you produce potato chips, wood chips or microchips. And the chance is that a foreign company is more likely to produce potato chips or wood chips than microchips in your country.

Given this, especially for a developing country, whose national firms are still underdeveloped, it may be better to restrict FDI at least in some industries and try to raise national firms so that they become credible alternative investors to foreign companies. This will make the country lose some investment in the short run, but it may enable it to have more higher-end activities within its borders in the long run. Or, even better, the developing country government can allow foreign investment under conditions that will help the country upgrade the capabilities of national firms faster – for example, by requiring joint ventures (which will promote the transfer of managerial techniques), demanding more active technology transfer, or mandating worker training.

Now, saying that foreign capital is likely to be less good for your country than your own national capital is not to say that we should always prefer national capital to foreign capital. This is because its nationality is not the only thing that determines the behaviour of capital. The intention and the capability of the capital in question also matter.

Suppose that you are thinking of selling a struggling nationally owned car company. Ideally, you want the new owner to have the willingness and the ability to upgrade the company in the long run. The prospective buyer is more likely to have the technological capabilities to do so when it is an already established automobile producer, whether national or foreign, rather than when it is finance capital, such as a private equity fund.

In recent years, private equity funds have played an increasingly important role in corporate acquisitions. Even though they have no in-house expertise in particular industries, they may, in theory, acquire a company for the long term and hire industry experts as managers and ask them to upgrade its capabilities. However, in practice, these funds usually have no intention to upgrade the acquired company for the long term. They acquire firms with a view to selling them on in three to five years after restructuring them into profitability. Such restructuring, given the time horizon, usually involves cutting costs (especially sacking workers and refraining from long-term investments), rather than raising capabilities. Such restructuring is likely to hurt the long-term prospects of the company by weakening its ability to generate productivity growth. In the worst cases, private equity funds may acquire companies with the explicit intention to engage in asset-stripping, selling the valuable assets of a company without regard to its long-term future. What the now-notorious Phoenix Venture Holdings did to the British car-maker Rover, which they had bought from BMW, is a classic example of this (the so-called 'Phoenix Four' became particularly notorious for paying themselves huge salaries and their friends exorbitant consultancy fees).

Of course, this is not to say that firms that are already operating in the industry will always have the intention to upgrade the acquired company for the long term either. When GM acquired a series of smaller foreign car companies – such as Sweden's Saab and Korea's Daewoo – during the decade before its bankruptcy in 2009, the intention was to live off the technologies accumulated by these companies, rather than to upgrade them (*see Thing 18*). Moreover, recently the distinction between industrial capital and finance capital has come to be blurred, with industrial companies such as GM and GE making more profits in finance than in industry (*see Thing 22*), so the fact that the acquiring firm operates in a particular industry is not a guarantee of a long-term commitment to that industry.

So, if a foreign company operating in the same industry is buying up your national company with a serious long-term commitment, selling it to that company may be better than selling it to your own national private equity fund. However, other things being equal, the chance is that your national company is going to act in a way that is more favourable to your national economy.

Thus, despite the globalization rhetoric, the nationality of a firm is still a key to deciding where its high-grade activities, such as R&D and strategizing, are going to be located. Nationality is not the only determinant of firm behaviour, so we need to take into account other factors, such as whether the investor has a track record in the industry concerned and how strong its long-term commitment to the acquired company really is. While a blind rejection of foreign capital is wrong, it would be very naïve to design economic policies on the myth that capital does not have national roots any more. After all, Lord Mandelson's belatedly found reservations turn out to have a serious basis in reality.

Thing 9
We do not live in a post-industrial age

What they tell you

Our economy has been fundamentally transformed during the last few decades. Especially in the rich countries, manufacturing industry, once the driving force of capitalism, is not important any more. With the natural tendency for the (relative) demand for services to rise with prosperity and with the rise of high-productivity knowledge-based services (such as banking and management consulting), manufacturing industries have gone into decline in all rich countries. These countries have entered the 'post-industrial' age, where most people work in services and most outputs arc services. The decline of manufacturing is not only something natural that we needn't worry about but something that we should really celebrate. With the rise of knowledge-based services, it may be better even for some developing countries to skip those doomed manufacturing activities altogether and leapfrog straight to a service-based post-industrial economy.

What they don't tell you

We may be living in a post-industrial society in the sense that most of us work in shops and offices rather than in factories. But we have not entered a post-industrial stage of development in the sense that industry has become unimportant. Most (although not all) of the shrinkage in the share of manufacturing in total output is not due to the fall in the absolute quantity of manufactured goods produced but due to the fall in their prices relative to those for services, which is caused by their faster growth in productivity (output per unit of input). Now, even though de-industrialization is mainly due to this differential productivity growth across sectors, and thus may not be something negative in itself, it has negative consequences for economy-wide productivity growth and for the balance of payments, which cannot be ignored. As for the idea that developing countries can largely skip industrialization and enter the post-industrial phase directly, it is a fantasy. Their limited scope for productivity growth makes services a poor engine of growth. The low tradability of services means that a more service-based economy will have a lower ability to export. Lower export earnings means a weaker ability to buy advanced technologies from abroad, which in turn leads to a slower growth.

Is there anything that is not made in China?

One day, Jin-Gyu, my nine-year-old son (yes, that's the one who appeared as 'my six-year-old son' in my earlier book *Bad Samaritans* – really quite a versatile actor, he is) came and asked me: 'Daddy, is there anything that is not made in China?' I told him that, yes, it may not look that way, but other countries still make things. I then struggled to come up with an example. I was about to mention his 'Japanese' Nintendo DSi game console, but then I remembered seeing 'Made in China' on it. I managed to tell him that some mobile phones and flat-screen TVs are made in Korea, but I could not think of many other things that a nine-year-old would recognize (he is still too young for things like BMW). No wonder China is now called the 'workshop of the world'.

It is hard to believe, but the phrase 'workshop of the world' was originally coined for Britain, which today, according to Nicolas Sarkozy, the French president, has 'no industry'. Having successfully launched the Industrial Revolution before other countries, Britain became such a dominant industrial power by the mid nineteenth century that it felt confident enough to completely liberalize its trade (*see Thing 7*). In 1860, it produced 20 per cent of world manufacturing output. In 1870, it accounted for 46 per cent of world trade in manufactured goods. The current Chinese share in world exports is only around 17 per cent (as of 2007), even though 'everything' seems to be made in China, so you can imagine the extent of British dominance then.

However, Britain's pole position was shortlived. Having liberalized its trade completely around 1860, its relative position started declining from the 1880s, with countries such as the US and Germany rapidly catching up. It lost its leading position in the world's industrial hierarchy by the time of the First World War, but the dominance of manufacturing in the British economy itself continued for a long time afterwards. Until the early 1970s, together with Germany, Britain had one of the world's highest shares of manufacturing employment in total employment, at around 35 per cent. At the time, Britain was the quintessential manufacturing economy, exporting manufactured goods and importing food, fuel and raw materials. Its manufacturing trade surplus (manufacturing exports minus manufacturing imports) stayed consistently between 4 per cent and 6 per cent of GDP during the 1960s and 70s.

Since the 1970s, however, the British manufacturing sector has shrunk rapidly in importance. Manufacturing output as a share of Britain's GDP used to be 37 per cent in 1950. Today, it accounts for only around 13 per cent. Manufacturing's share in total employment fell from around 35 per cent in the early 1970s to just over 10 per cent.[1] Its position in international trade has also dramatically changed. These days, Britain runs manufacturing trade deficits in the region of 2–4 per cent of GDP per year. What has happened? Should Britain be worried?

The predominant opinion is that there is nothing to worry about. To begin with, it is not as if Britain is the only country in which these things have happened. The declining shares of manufacturing in total output and employment – a phenomenon known as de-industrialization – is a natural occurrence, many commentators argue, common to all rich countries (accelerated in the British case by the finding of North Sea oil). This is widely believed to be because, as they become richer, people begin to demand more services than manufactured goods. With falling demand, it is natural that the manufacturing sector shrinks and the country enters the post-industrial stage. Many people actually celebrate the rise of services. According to them, the recent expansion of knowledge-based services with rapid productivity growth – such as finance, consulting, design, computing and information services, R&D – means that services have replaced manufacturing as the engine of growth, at least in the rich countries. Manufacturing is now a low-grade activity that developing countries such as China perform.

Computers and haircuts: why de-industrialization happens

Have we really entered the post-industrial age? Is manufacturing irrelevant now? The answers are: 'only in some ways', and 'no'.

It is indisputable that much lower proportions of people in the rich countries work in factories than used to be the case. There was a time in the late nineteenth and early twentieth centuries when in some countries (notably Britain and Belgium) around 40 per cent of those employed worked in the manufacturing industry. Today, the ratio is at most 25 per cent, and in some countries (especially the US, Canada and Britain) barely 15 per cent.

With so much fewer people (in proportional terms) working in factories, the nature of society has changed. We are partly formed by our work experiences (a point which most economists fail to recognize), so where and how we work influences who we are. Compared to factory workers, office workers and shop assistants do much less physical work and, not having to work with conveyor belts and other machines, have more control over their labour process. Factory workers cooperate more closely with their colleagues during work and outside work, especially through trade union activities. In contrast, people working in shops and offices tend to work on more individual bases and are not very unionized. Shop assistants and some office workers interact directly with customers, whereas factory workers never see their customers. I am not enough of a sociologist or a psychologist to say anything profound in this regard, but all this means that people in today's rich countries not only work differently from but are different from their parents and grandparents. In this way, today's rich countries have become post-industrial societies in the social sense.

However, they have *not* become post-industrial in the economic sense. Manufacturing still plays the leading role in their economies. In order to see this point, we first need to understand why de-industrialization has happened in the rich countries.

A small, but not negligible, part of de-industrialization is due to optical illusions, in the sense that it reflects changes in statistical classification rather than changes in real activities. One such illusion is due to the outsourcing of some activities that are really services in their physical nature but used to be provided in-house by manufacturing firms and thus classified as manufacturing output (e.g., catering, cleaning, technical supports). When they are outsourced, recorded service outputs increase without a real increase in service activities. Even though there is no reliable estimate of its magnitude, experts agree that outsourcing has been a significant source of de-industrialization in the US and Britain, especially during the 1980s. In addition to the outsourcing effect, the extent of manufacturing contraction is exaggerated by what is called the 'reclassification effect'.[2] A UK government report estimates that up to 10 per cent of the fall in manufacturing employment between 1998 and 2006 in the UK may be accounted for by some manufacturing firms, seeing their service activities becoming predominant, applying to the government statistical agency to be reclassified as service firms, even when they are still engaged in some manufacturing activities.

One cause of genuine de-industrialization has recently attracted a lot of attention. It is the rise of manufacturing imports from low-cost developing countries, especially China. However dramatic it may look, it is not the main explanation for de-industrialization in the rich countries. China's exports did not make a real impact until the late 1990s, but the de-industrialization process had already started in the 1970s in most rich countries. Most estimates show that the rise of China as the new workshop of the world can explain only around 20 per cent of de-industrialization in the rich countries that has happened so far.

Many people think that the remaining 80 per cent or so can be largely explained by the natural tendency of the (relative) demand for manufactured goods to fall with rising prosperity. However, a closer look reveals that this demand effect is actually very small. It looks as if we are spending ever higher shares of our income on services not because we are consuming ever more services in absolute terms but mainly because services are becoming ever more expensive in relative terms.

With the (inflation-adjusted) amount of money you paid to get a PC ten years ago, today you can probably buy three, if not four, computers of equal or even greater computing power (and certainly smaller size). As a result, you probably have two, rather than just one, computers. But, even with two computers, the portion of your income that you spend on computers has gone down quite a lot (for the sake of argument, I am assuming that your income, after adjusting for inflation, is the same). In contrast, you are probably getting the same number of haircuts as you did ten years ago (if you haven't gone thin on top, that is). The price of haircuts has probably gone up somewhat, so the proportion of your income that goes to your haircuts is greater than it was ten years ago. The result is that it looks as if you are spending a greater (smaller) portion of your income on haircuts (computers) than before, but the reality is that you are actually consuming more computers than before, while your consumption of haircuts is the same.

Indeed, if you adjust for the changes in relative prices (or, to use technical jargon, if you measure things in *constant* prices), the decline of manufacturing in the rich countries has been far less steep than it appears to be. For example, in the case of Britain, the share of manufacturing in total output, without counting the relative price effects (to use the jargon, in *current* prices), fell by over 40 per cent between 1955 and 1990 (from 37 per cent to 21 per cent). However, when taking the relative price effects into account, the fall was only by just over 10 per cent (from 27 per cent to 24 per cent).[3] In other words, the *real* demand effect – that is the demand effect after taking relative price changes into account – is small.

Then why are the relative prices of manufactured goods falling? It is because manufacturing industries tend to have faster productivity growth than services. As the output of the manufacturing sector increases faster than the output of the service sector, the prices of the manufactured goods relative to those of services fall. In manufacturing, where mechanization and the use of chemical processes are much easier, it is easier to raise productivity than in services. In contrast, by their very nature, many service activities are inherently impervious to productivity increase *without diluting the quality of the product*.

In some cases, the very attempt to increase productivity will destroy the product itself. If a string quartet trots through a twenty-seven-minute piece in nine minutes, would you say that its productivity has trebled?

For some other services, the apparent higher productivity is due to the debasement of the product. A teacher can raise her apparent productivity by four times by having four times as many pupils in her classroom, but the quality of her 'product' has been diluted by the fact that she cannot pay as much individual attention as before. A lot of the increases in retail service productivity in countries such as the US and Britain has been bought by lowering the quality of the retail service itself while ostensibly offering cheaper shoes, sofas and apples: there are fewer sales assistants at shoe stores, so you wait twenty minutes instead of five; you have to wait four weeks, rather than two, for the delivery of your new sofa and probably also have to take a day off work because they will only deliver 'sometime between 8 a.m. and 6 p.m.'; you spend much more time than before driving to the new supermarket and walking through the now longer aisles when you get there, because those apples are cheaper than in the old supermarket only because the new supermarket is in the middle of nowhere and thus can have more floor space.

There are some service activities, such as banking, which have greater scope for productivity increase than other services. However, as revealed by the 2008 financial crisis, much of the productivity growth in those activities was due not to a real rise in their productivity (e.g., reduction in trading costs due to better computers) but to financial innovations that obscured (rather than genuinely reduced) the riskiness of financial assets, thereby allowing the financial sector to grow at an unsustainably rapid rate (*see Thing 22*).

To sum up, the fall in the share of manufacturing in total output in the rich countries is *not* largely due to the fall in (relative) demand for manufactured goods, as many people think.

Nor is it due mainly to the rise of manufactured exports from China and other developing countries, although that has had big impacts on some sectors. It is instead the falling relative prices of the manufactured goods due to faster growth in productivity in the manufacturing sector that is the main driver of the de-industrialization process. Thus, while the citizens of the rich countries may be living in post-industrial societies in terms of their *employment*, the importance of manufacturing in terms of *production* in those economies has not been diminished to the extent that we can declare a post-industrial age.

Should we worry about de-industrialization?

But if de-industrialization is due to the very dynamism of a country's manufacturing sector, isn't it a good thing?

Not necessarily. The fact that de-industrialization is mainly caused by the *comparative* dynamism of the manufacturing sector *vis-à-vis* the service sector does not tell us anything about how well it is doing compared to its counterparts in other countries. If a country's manufacturing sector has slower productivity growth than its counterparts in other countries, it will become internationally uncompetitive, leading to balance of payments problems in the short run and falling standards of living in the long term. In other words, de-industrialization may be accompanied by either economic success or failure. Countries should not be lulled into a false sense of security by the fact that de-industrialization is due to *comparative* dynamism of the manufacturing sector, as even a manufacturing sector that is very undynamic by international standards can be (and usually is) more dynamic than the service sector of the same country.

Whether or not a country's manufacturing sector is dynamic by international standards, the shrinkage of the relative weight of the manufacturing sector has a negative impact on productivity growth. As the economy becomes dominated by the service sector, where productivity growth is slower, productivity growth for the whole economy will slow down. Unless we believe (as some do) that the countries experiencing de-industrialization are now rich enough not to need more productivity growth, productivity slowdown is something that countries should get worried about – or at least reconcile themselves to.

De-industrialization also has a negative effect on a country's balance of payments because services are inherently more difficult to export than manufactured goods. A balance of payments deficit means that the country cannot 'pay its way' in the world. Of course, a country can plug the hole through foreign borrowing for a while, but eventually it will have to lower the value of its currency, thereby reducing its ability to import and thus its living standard.

At the root of the low 'tradability' of services lies the fact that, unlike manufactured goods that can be shipped anywhere in the world, most services require their providers and consumers to be in the same location. No one has yet invented ways to provide a haircut or house-cleaning long-distance. Obviously, this problem will be solved if the service provider (the hairdresser or the cleaner in the above examples) can move to the customer's country, but that in most cases means immigration, which most countries restrict heavily (*see Thing 3*). Given this, a rising share of services in the economy means that the country, other things being equal, will have lower export earnings. Unless the exports of manufactured goods rise disproportionately, the country won't be able to pay for the same amount of imports as before. If its de-industrialization is of a negative kind accompanied by weakening international competitiveness, the balance of payments problem could be even more serious, as the manufacturing sector then won't be able to increase its exports.

Not all services are equally non-tradable. The knowledge-based services that I mentioned earlier – banking, consulting, engineering, and so on – are highly tradable. For example, in Britain since the 1990s, exports of knowledge-based services have played a crucial role in plugging the balance of payments gap left behind by de-industrialization (and the fall in North Sea oil exports, which had enabled the country – just – to survive the negative balance of payments consequences of de-industrialization during the 1980s).

However, even in Britain, which is most advanced in the exports of these knowledge-based services, the balance of payments surplus generated by those services is well below 4 per cent of GDP, just enough to cover the country's manufacturing trade deficits. With the likely strengthening of global financial regulation as a consequence of the 2008 world financial crisis, it is unlikely that Britain can maintain this level of trade surplus in finance and other knowledge-based services in the future. In the case of the US, supposedly another model post-industrial economy, the trade surplus in knowledge-based services is actually less than 1 per cent of GDP – nowhere near enough to make up for its manufacturing trade deficits, which are around 4 per cent of GDP.[4] The US has been able to maintain such a large manufacturing trade deficit only because it could borrow heavily from abroad – an ability that can only shrink in the coming years, given the changes in the world economy – and not because the service sector stepped in to fill the gap, as in the British case. Moreover, it is questionable whether the strengths of the US and Britain in the knowledge-based services can be maintained over time. In services such as engineering and design, where insights gained from the production process are crucial, a continuous shrinkage of the industrial base will lead to a decline in the quality of their (service) products and a consequent loss in export earnings.

If Britain and the US – two countries that are supposed to be the most developed in the knowledge-based services – are unlikely to meet their balance of payments needs in the long run through the exports of these services, it is highly unlikely that other countries can.

Post-industrial fantasies

Believing de-industrialization to be the result of the change of our engine of growth from manufacturing to services, some have argued that developing countries can largely skip industrialization and move directly to the service economy. Especially with the rise of service offshoring, this view has become very popular among some observers of India. Forget all those polluting industries, they say, why not go from agriculture to services directly? If China is the workshop of the world, the argument goes, India should try to become the 'office of the world'.

However, it is a fantasy to think that a poor country can develop mainly on the basis of the service sector. As pointed out earlier, the manufacturing sector has an inherently faster productivity growth than the service sector. To be sure, there are some service industries that have rapid productivity growth potential, notably the knowledge-based services that I mentioned above. However, these are service activities that mainly serve manufacturing firms, so it is very difficult to develop those industries without first developing a strong manufacturing base. If you base your development largely on services from early on, your long-term productivity growth rate is going to be much slower than when you base it on manufacturing.

Moreover, we have already seen that, given that services are much less tradable, countries specializing in services are likely to face much more serious balance of payments problems than countries that specialize in manufacturing. This is bad enough for a developed country, where balance of payments problems will lower standards of living in the long run. However, it is seriously detrimental for a developing country. The point is that, in order to develop, a developing country has to import superior technologies from abroad (either in the form of machines or in the form of technology licensing). Therefore, when it has a balance of payments problem, its very ability to upgrade and thus develop its economy by deploying superior technologies is hampered.

As I say these negative things about economic development strategies based on services, some of you may say: what about countries like Switzerland and Singapore? Haven't they developed on the basis of services?

However, these economies are not what they are reported to be either. They are in fact manufacturing success stories. For example, many people think that Switzerland lives off the stolen money deposited in its banks by Third World dictators or by selling cowbells and cuckoo clocks to Japanese and American tourists, but it is actually one of the most industrialized economies in the world. We don't see many Swiss manufactured products around because the country is small (around 7 million people), which makes the total amount of Swiss manufactured goods rather small, and because its producers specialize in producer goods, such as machinery and industrial chemicals, rather than consumer goods that are more visible. But in per capita terms, Switzerland has the highest industrial output in the world (it could come second after Japan, depending on the year and the data you look at). Singapore is also one of the five most industrialized economies in the world (once again, measured in terms of manufacturing value-added per head). Finland and Sweden make up the rest of the top five. Indeed, except for a few places such as the Seychelles that has a very small population and exceptional resources for tourism (85,000 people with around $9,000 per capita income), no country has so far achieved even a decent (not to speak of high) living standard by relying on services and none will do so in the future.

To sum up, even the rich countries have not become unequivocally post-industrial. While most people in those countries do not work in factories any more, the manufacturing sector's importance in their production systems has not fallen very much, once we take into account the relative price effects. But even if de-industrialization is not necessarily a symptom of industrial decline (although it often is), it has negative effects for long-term productivity growth and the balance of payments, both of which need reckoning. The myth that we now live in a post-industrial age has made many governments ignore the negative consequences of de-industrialization.

As for the developing countries, it is a fantasy to think that they can skip industrialization and build prosperity on the basis of service industries. Most services have slow productivity growth and most of those services that have high productivity growth are services that cannot be developed without a strong manufacturing sector. Low tradability of services means that a developing country specializing in services will face a bigger balance of payments problem, which for a developing country means a reduction in its ability to upgrade its economy. Post-industrial fantasies are bad enough for the rich countries, but they are positively dangerous for developing countries.

Thing 10
The US does not have the highest living standard in the world

What they tell you

Despite its recent economic problems, the US still enjoys the highest standard of living in the world. At market exchange rates, there are several countries that have a higher per capita income than the US. However, if we consider the fact that the same dollar (or whatever common currency we choose) can buy more goods and services in the US than in other rich countries, the US turns out to have the highest living standard in the world, barring the mini-city-state of Luxemburg. This is why other countries seek to emulate the US, illustrating the superiority of the free-market system, which the US most closely (if not perfectly) represents.

What they don't tell you

The average US citizen does have greater command over goods and services than his counterpart in any other country in the world except Luxemburg. However, given the country's high inequality, this average is less accurate in representing how people live than the averages for other countries with a more equal income distribution. Higher inequality is also behind the poorer health indicators and worse crime statistics of the US. Moreover, the same dollar buys more things in the US than in most other rich countries mainly because it has cheaper services than in other comparable countries, thanks to higher immigration and poorer employment conditions. Furthermore, Americans work considerably longer than Europeans. Per hour worked, their command over goods and services is smaller than that of several European countries. While we can debate which is a better lifestyle – more material goods with less leisure time (as in the US) or fewer material goods with more leisure time (as in Europe) – this suggests that the US does not have an unambiguously higher living standard than comparable countries.

The roads are not paved with gold

Between 1880 and 1914, nearly 3 million Italians migrated to the US. When they arrived, many of them were bitterly disappointed. Their new home was not the paradise they had thought it would be. It is said that many of them wrote back home, saying 'not only are the roads not paved with gold, they are not paved at all; in fact, we are the ones who are supposed to pave them'.

Those Italian immigrants were not alone in thinking that the US is where dreams come true. The US became the richest country in the world only around 1900, but even in the early days of its existence, it had a strong hold on the imagination of poor people elsewhere. In the early nineteenth century, US per capita income was still only around the European average and something like 50 per cent lower than that of Britain and the Netherlands. But poor Europeans still wanted to move there because the country had an almost unlimited supply of land (well, if you were willing to push out a few native Americans) and an acute labour shortage, which meant wages three or four times higher than those in Europe (*see Thing 7*). Most importantly, the lack of feudal legacy meant that the country had much higher social mobility than the Old World countries, as celebrated in the idea of the American dream.

It is not just prospective immigrants who are attracted to the US. Especially in the last few decades, businessmen and policy-makers around the world have wanted, and often tried, to emulate the US economic model. Its free enterprise system, according to admirers of the US model, lets people compete without limits and rewards the winners without restrictions imposed by the government or by misguided egalitarian culture. The system therefore creates exceptionally strong incentives for entrepreneurship and innovation. Its free labour market, with easy hiring and firing, allows its enterprises to be agile and thus more competitive, as they can redeploy their workers more quickly than their competitors, in response to changing market conditions. With entrepreneurs richly rewarded and workers having to adapt quickly, the system does create high inequality. However, its proponents argue, even the 'losers' in this game willingly accept such outcomes because, given the country's high social mobility, their own children could be the next Thomas Edison, J. P. Morgan or Bill Gates. With such incentives to work hard and exercise ingenuity, no wonder the country has been the richest in the world for the last century.

Americans just live better . . .

Actually, this is not quite true. The US is not the richest country in the world any more. Now several European countries have higher per capita incomes. The World Bank data tell us that the per capita income of the US in 2007 was $46,040. There were seven countries with higher per capita income in US dollar terms – starting with Norway ($76,450) at the top, through Luxemburg, Switzerland, Denmark, Iceland, Ireland and ending with Sweden ($46,060). Discounting the two mini-states of Iceland (311,000 people) and Luxemburg (480,000 people), this makes the US only the sixth richest country in the world.

But, some of you may say, that cannot be right. When you go to the US, you just see that people there live better than the Norwegians or the Swiss do.

One reason why we get that impression is that the US is much more unequal than the European countries and therefore looks more prosperous to foreign visitors than it really is – foreign visitors to any country rarely get to see the deprived parts, of which the US has many more than Europe. But even ignoring this inequality factor, there is a good reason why most people think that the US has a higher living standard than European countries.

You may have paid 35 Swiss francs, or $35, for a 5-mile (or 8-km) taxi ride in Geneva, when a similar ride in Boston would have cost you around $15. In Oslo, you may have paid 550 kroner, or $100, for a dinner that could not possibly have been more than $50, or 275 kroner, in St Louis. The reverse would have been the case if you had changed your dollars into Thai baht or Mexican pesos on your holidays. Having your sixth back massage of the week or ordering the third margarita before dinner, you would have felt as if your $100 had been stretched into $200, or even $300 (or was that the alcohol?). If market exchange rates accurately reflected differences in living standards between countries, these kinds of things should not happen.

Why are there such huge differences between the things that you can buy in different countries with what should be the same sums of money? Such differences exist basically because market exchange rates are largely determined by the supply and demand for internationally traded goods and services (although in the short run currency speculation can influence market exchange rates), while what a sum of money can buy in a particular country is determined by the prices of all goods and services, and not just those that are internationally traded.

The most important among the non-traded things are person-to-person labour services, such as driving taxis and serving meals in restaurants. Trade in such services requires international migration, but that is severely limited by immigration control, so the prices of such labour services end up being hugely different across countries (*see Things 3 and 9*). In other words, things such as taxi rides and meals are expensive in countries such as Switzerland and Norway because they have expensive workers. They are cheap in countries with cheap workers, such as Mexico and Thailand. When it comes to internationally traded things such as TVs or mobile phones, their prices are basically the same in all countries, rich and poor.

In order to take into account the differential prices of non-traded goods and services across countries, economists have come up with the idea of an 'international dollar'. Based on the notion of purchasing power parity (PPP) – that is, measuring the value of a currency according to how much of a common consumption basket it can buy in different countries – this fictitious currency allows us to convert incomes of different countries into a common measure of living standards.

The result of converting the incomes of different countries into the international dollar is that the incomes of rich countries tend to become lower than their incomes at market exchange rates, while those of poor countries tend to become higher. This is because a lot of what we consume is services, which are much more expensive in the rich countries. In some cases, the difference between market exchange rate income and PPP income is not great. According to the World Bank data, the market exchange rate income of the US was $46,040 in 2007, while its PPP income was more or less the same at $45,850. In the case of Germany, the difference between the two was greater, at $38,860 vs. $33,820 (a 15 per cent difference, so to speak, although we cannot really compare the two numbers this directly). In the case of Denmark, the difference was nearly 50 per cent ($54,910 vs. $36,740). In contrast, China's 2007 income more than doubles from $2,360 to $5,370 and India's by nearly three times from $950 to $2,740, when calculated in PPP terms.

Now, the calculation of each currency's exchange rate with the (fictitious) international dollar is not a straightforward affair, not least because we have to assume that all countries consume the same basket of goods and services, which is patently not the case. This makes the PPP incomes extremely sensitive to the methodologies and the data used. For example, when the World Bank changed its method of estimating PPP incomes in 2007, China's PPP income per capita fell by 44 per cent (from $7,740 to $5,370), while Singapore's rose by 53 per cent (from $31,710 to $48,520) overnight.

Despite these limits, a country's income in international dollars probably gives us a better idea of its living standard than does its dollar income at the market exchange rate. And if we calculate incomes of different countries in international dollars, the US (almost) comes back to the top of the world. It depends on the estimate, but Luxemburg is the only country that has a higher PPP income per capita than that of the US in all estimates. So, as long as we set aside the tiny city-state of Luxemburg, with less than half a million people, the average US citizen can buy the largest amount of goods and services in the world with her income.

Does this allow us to say that the US has the highest living standard in the world? Perhaps. But there are quite a few things we have to consider before we jump to that conclusion.

. . . or do they?

To begin with, having a higher *average* income than other countries does not necessarily mean that all US citizens live better than their foreign counterparts. Whether this is the case depends on the distribution of income. Of course, in no country does the average income give the right picture of how people live, but in a country with higher inequality it is likely to be particularly misleading. Given that the US has by far the most unequal distribution of income among the rich countries, we can safely guess that the US per capita income overstates the actual living standards of more of its citizens than in other countries. And this conjecture is indirectly supported by other indicators of living standards. For example, despite having the highest average PPP income, the US ranks only around thirtieth in the world in health statistics such as life expectancy and infant mortality (OK, the inefficiency of the US healthcare system contributes to it, but let's not get into that). The much higher crime rate than in Europe or Japan – in per capita terms, the US has eight times more people in prison than Europe and twelve times more than Japan – shows that there is a far bigger underclass in the US.

Second, the very fact that its PPP income is more or less the same as its market exchange rate income is proof that the higher average living standard in the US is built on the poverty of many. What do I mean by this? As I have pointed out earlier, it is normal for a rich country's PPP income to be lower, sometimes significantly, than its market exchange rate income, because it has expensive service workers. However, this does not happen to the US, because, unlike other rich countries, it has cheap service workers. To begin with, there is a large inflow of low-wage immigrants from poor countries, many of them illegal, which makes them even cheaper. Moreover, even the native workers have much weaker fallback positions in the US than in European countries of comparable income level. Because they have much less job security and weaker welfare supports, US workers, especially the non-unionized ones in the service industries, work for lower wages and under inferior conditions than do their European counterparts. This is why things like taxi rides and meals at restaurants are so much cheaper in the US than in other rich countries. This is great when you are the customer, but not if you are the taxi driver or the waitress. In other words, the higher purchasing power of average US income is bought at the price of lower income and inferior working conditions for many US citizens.

Last but not least, in comparing living standards across countries, we should not ignore the differences in working hours. Even if someone is earning 50 per cent more money than I earn, you wouldn't say that he has a higher living standard than I do, if that person has to work double the number of hours that I do. The same applies to the US. The Americans, befitting their reputation for workaholism, work longer hours than the citizens of any other country that has a per capita income of more than $30,000 at market exchange rate in 2007 (Greece being the poorest of the lot, at just under $30,000 per capita income). Americans work 10 per cent longer than most Europeans and around 30 per cent longer than the Dutch and the Norwegians. According to a calculation by the Icelandic economist Thorvaldur Gylfason, in terms of income (in PPP terms) per hour worked in 2005, the US ranked only eighth – after Luxemburg, Norway, France (yes, France, that nation of loungers), Ireland, Belgium, Austria, and the Netherlands – and was very closely followed by Germany.[1] In other words, per unit of effort, the Americans are not getting as high a living standard as their counterparts in competitor nations. They make up for this lower productivity through much longer hours.

Now, it is perfectly reasonable for someone to argue that she wants to work longer hours if that is necessary to have a higher income – she would rather have another TV than one more week of holiday. And who am I, or anyone else, to say that the person got her priority wrong?

However, it is still legitimate to ask whether people who work longer hours even at very high levels of income are doing the right thing. Most people would agree that, at a low level of income, an increase in income is likely to improve your quality of life, even if it means longer working hours. At this level, even if you have to work longer in your factory, higher income is likely to bring a higher overall quality of life, by improving your health (through better food, heating, hygiene and healthcare) and by reducing the physical demands of household work (through more household appliances, piped water, gas and electricity – *see Thing 4*). However, above a certain level of income, the relative value of material consumption *vis-à-vis* leisure time is diminished, so earning a higher income at the cost of working longer hours may reduce the quality of your life.

More importantly, the fact that the citizens of a country work longer than others in comparable countries does not necessarily mean that they *like* working longer hours. They may be compelled to work long hours, even if they actually want to take longer holidays. As I pointed out above, how long a person works is affected not only by his own preference regarding work – leisure balance but also by things such as welfare provision, protection of worker rights and union power. Individuals have to take these things as given, but nations have a choice over them. They can rewrite the labour laws, beef up the welfare state and effect other policy changes to make it less necessary for individuals to work long hours.

Much of the support for the American model has been based on the 'fact' that the US has the highest living standard in the world. While there is no question that the US has one of the highest living standards in the world, its alleged superiority looks much weaker once we have a broader conception of living standards than what the average income of a country will buy. Higher inequality in the US means that its average income is less indicative of the living standards of its citizens than in other countries.

This is reflected in indicators such as health and crime, where the US performs much worse than comparable countries. The higher purchasing power of US citizens (compared to the citizens of other rich countries) is owed in large part to the poverty and insecurity of many of their fellow citizens, especially in service industries. The Americans also work considerably longer than their counterparts in competitor nations. Per hour worked, US income is lower than that of several European countries, even in purchasing power terms. It is debatable that that can be described as having a higher living standard.

There is no simple way to compare living standards across countries. Per capita income, especially in purchasing power terms, is arguably the most reliable indicator. However, by focusing just on how many goods and services our income can buy, we miss out a lot of other things that constitute elements of the 'good life', such as the amount of quality leisure time, job security, freedom from crime, access to healthcare, social welfare provisions, and so on. While different individuals and countries will definitely have different views on how to weigh these indicators against each other and against income figures, non-income dimensions should not be ignored, if we are to build societies where people genuinely 'live well'.

Thing 11
Africa is not destined for underdevelopment

What they tell you

Africa is destined for underdevelopment. It has a poor climate, which leads to serious tropical disease problems. It has lousy geography, with many of its countries landlocked and surrounded by countries whose small markets offer limited export opportunities and whose violent conflicts spill into neighbouring countries. It has too many natural resources, which make its people lazy, corrupt and conflict-prone. African nations are ethnically divided, which renders them difficult to manage and more likely to experience violent conflicts. They have poor-quality institutions that do not protect investors well. Their culture is bad – people do not work hard, they do not save and they cannot cooperate with each other. All these structural handicaps explain why, unlike other regions of the world, the continent has failed to grow even after it has implemented significant market liberalization since the 1980s. There is no other way forward for Africa than being propped up by foreign aid.

What they don't tell you

Africa has *not* always been stagnant. In the 1960s and 70s, when all the supposed structural impediments to growth were present and often more binding, it actually posted a decent growth performance. Moreover, all the structural handicaps that are supposed to hold back Africa have been present in most of today's rich countries – poor climate (arctic and tropical), landlockedness, abundant natural resources, ethnic divisions, poor institutions and bad culture. These structural conditions seem to act as impediments to development in Africa only because its countries do not yet have the necessary technologies, institutions and organizational skills to deal with their adverse consequences. The real cause of African stagnation in the last three decades is free-market policies that the continent has been compelled to implement during the period. Unlike history or geography, policies can be changed. Africa is not destined for underdevelopment.

The world according to Sarah Palin . . . or *was it* The Rescuers?

Sarah Palin, the Republican vice-presidential candidate in the 2008 US election, is reported to have thought that Africa was a country, rather than a continent. A lot of people wondered where she got that idea, but I think I know the answer. It was from the 1977 Disney animation *The Rescuers*.

The Rescuers is about a group of mice called the Rescue Aid Society going around the world, helping animals in trouble. In one scene, there is an international congress of the society, with mouse delegates from all sorts of countries in their traditional costumes and appropriate accents (if they happen to speak). There is the French mouse in his beret, the German mouse in her sombre blue dress and the Turkish mouse in his fez. And then there is the mouse in his fur hat and beard representing Latvia and the female mouse representing, well, Africa.

Perhaps Disney didn't literally think that Africa was a country, but allocating one delegate each to a country with 2.2 million people and to a continent of more than 900 million people and nearly sixty countries (the exact number depends on whether you recognize entities such as Somaliland and Western Sahara as countries) tells you something about its view of Africa. Like Disney, many people see Africa as an amorphous mass of countries suffering from the same hot weather, tropical diseases, grinding poverty, civil war and corruption.

While we should be careful not to lump all African countries together, there is no denying that most African countries are very poor – especially if we confine our interest to Sub-Saharan Africa (or 'black' Africa), which is really what most people mean when they say Africa. According to the World Bank, the average per capita income of Sub-Saharan Africa was estimated to be $952 in 2007. This is somewhat higher than the $880 of South Asia (Afghanistan, Bangladesh, Bhutan, India, Maldives, Nepal, Pakistan and Sri Lanka), but lower than that of any other region of the world.

What is more, many people talk of Africa's 'growth tragedy'. Unlike South Asia, whose growth rates have picked up since the 1980s, Africa seems to be suffering from 'a chronic failure of economic growth'.[1] Sub-Saharan Africa's per capita income today is more or less the same as what it was in 1980. Even more worrying is the fact that this lack of growth seems to be due not mainly to poor policy choices (after all, like many other developing countries, countries in the region have implemented free-market reforms since the 1980s) but mainly to the handicaps handed down to them by nature and history and thus extremely difficult, if not impossible, to change.

The list of supposed 'structural' handicaps that are holding Africa back is impressive.

First, there are all those conditions defined by nature – climate, geography and natural resources. Being too close to the equator, it has rampant tropical diseases, such as malaria, which reduce worker productivity and raise healthcare costs. Being landlocked, many African countries find it difficult to integrate into the global economy. They are in 'bad neighbourhoods' in the sense that they are surrounded by other poor countries that have small markets (which restrict their trading opportunities) and, frequently, violent conflicts (which often spill over into neighbouring countries). African countries are also supposed to be 'cursed' by their abundant natural resources. It is said that resource abundance makes Africans lazy – because they 'can lie beneath a coconut tree and wait for the coconut to fall', as a popular expression of this idea goes (although those who say that obviously have not tried it; you risk having your head smashed). 'Unearned' resource wealth is also supposed to encourage corruption and violent conflicts over the spoils. The economic successes of resource-poor East Asian countries, such as Japan and Korea, are often cited as cases of 'reverse resource curse'.

Not just nature but Africa's history is also supposed to be holding it back. African nations are ethnically too diverse, which causes people to be distrustful of each other and thus makes market transactions costly. It is argued that ethnic diversity may encourage violent conflicts, especially if there are a few equally strong groups (rather than many small groups, which are more difficult to organize). The history of colonialism is thought to have produced low-quality institutions in most African countries, as the colonizers did not want to settle in countries with too many tropical diseases (so there is an interaction between climate and institutions) and thus installed only the minimal institutions needed for resource extraction, rather than for the development of the local economy. Some even venture that African culture is bad for economic development – Africans do not work hard, do not plan for the future and cannot cooperate with each other.[2]

Given all this, Africa's future prospects seem bleak. For some of these structural handicaps, any solution seems unachievable or unacceptable. If being landlocked, being too close to the equator and sitting in a bad neighbourhood are holding Uganda back, what should it do? Physically moving a country is not an option, so the only feasible answer is colonialism – that is, Uganda should invade, say, Norway, and move all the Norwegians to Uganda. If having too many ethnic groups is bad for development, should Tanzania, which has one of the greatest ethnic diversities in the world, indulge in a spot of ethnic cleansing? If having too many natural resources hampers growth, should the Democratic Republic of Congo try to sell the portions of its land with mineral deposits to, say, Taiwan so that it can pass on the natural resource curse to someone else? What should Mozambique do if its colonial history has left it with bad institutions? Should it invent a time machine and fix that history? If Cameroon has a culture that is bad for economic development, should it start some mass brain-washing programme or put people in some re-education camp, as the Khmer Rouge did in Cambodia?

All of these policy conclusions are either physically impossible (moving a country, inventing a time machine) or politically and morally unacceptable (invasion of another country, ethnic cleansing, re-education camps). Therefore, those who believe in the power of these structural handicaps but find these extreme solutions unacceptable argue that African countries should be put on some kind of permanent 'disability benefit' through foreign aid and extra help with international trade (e.g., rich countries lowering their agricultural protection only for African – and other similarly poor and structurally disadvantaged – countries).

But is there any other way for Africa's future development beyond accepting its fate or relying on outside help? Do African countries have no hope of standing on their own feet?

An African growth tragedy?

One question that we need to ask before we try to explain Africa's growth tragedy and explore possible ways to overcome it is whether there is indeed such a tragedy. And the answer is 'no'. The lack of growth in the region has *not* been chronic.

During the 1960s and 70s, per capita income in Sub-Saharan Africa grew at a respectable rate. At around 1.6 per cent, it was nowhere near the 'miracle' growth rate of East Asia (5–6 per cent) or even that of Latin America (around 3 per cent) during the period. However, this is not a growth rate to be sniffed at. It compares favourably with the rates of 1–1.5 per cent achieved by today's rich countries during their Industrial 'Revolution' (roughly 1820–1913).

The fact that Africa grew at a respectable rate before the 1980s suggests that the 'structural' factors cannot be the main explanation of the region's (what in fact is recent) growth failure. If they were, African growth should always have been non-existent. It is not as if the African countries suddenly moved to the tropics or some seismic activity suddenly made some of them landlocked. If the structural factors were so crucial, African economic growth should have accelerated over time, as at least some of those factors would have been weakened or eliminated. For example, poor-quality institutions left behind by the colonists could have been abandoned or improved. Even ethnic diversity could have been reduced through compulsory education, military service and mass media, in the same way in which France managed to turn 'peasants into Frenchmen', as the title of a classic 1976 book by the American historian Eugen Weber goes.[3] However, this is not what has happened – African growth suddenly collapsed since the 1980s.

So, if the structural factors have always been there and if their influences would have, if anything, diminished over time, those factors cannot explain why Africa used to grow at a decent rate in the 1960s and 70s and then suddenly failed to grow. The sudden collapse in growth must be explained by something that happened around 1980. The prime suspect is the dramatic change in policy direction around the time.

Since the late 1970s (starting with Senegal in 1979), Sub-Saharan African countries were forced to adopt free-market, free-trade policies through the conditions imposed by the so-called Structural Adjustment Programs (SAPs) of the World Bank and the IMF (and the rich countries that ultimately control them). Contrary to conventional wisdom, these policies are *not* good for economic development (*see Thing 7*). By suddenly exposing immature producers to international competition, these policies led to the collapse of what little industrial sectors these countries had managed to build up during the 1960s and 70s. Thus, having been forced back into relying on exports of primary commodities, such as cocoa, coffee and copper, African countries have continued to suffer from the wild price fluctuations and stagnant production technologies that characterize most such commodities. Furthermore, when the SAPs demanded a rapid increase in exports, African countries, with technological capabilities only in a limited range of activities, ended up trying to export similar things – be they traditional products such as coffee and cocoa or new products such as cut flowers. The result was often a collapse of prices in those commodities due to a large increase in their supplies, which sometimes meant that these countries were exporting more in quantity but earning less in revenue. The pressure on governments to balance their budgets led to cuts in expenditures whose impacts are slow to show, such as infrastructure. Over time, however, the deteriorating quality of infrastructure disadvantaged African producers even more, making their 'geographical disadvantages' loom even larger.

The result of the SAPs – and their various later incarnations, including today's PRSPs (Poverty Reduction Strategy Papers) – was a stagnant economy that has failed to grow (in per capita terms) for three decades. During the 1980s and 90s, per capita income in Sub-Saharan Africa *fell* at the rate of 0.7 per cent per year. The region finally started to grow in the 2000s, but the contraction of the preceding two decades meant that the average annual growth rate of per capita income in Sub-Saharan Africa between 1980 and 2009 was 0.2 per cent. So, after nearly thirty years of using 'better' (that is, free-market) policies, its per capita income is basically at the same level as it was in 1980.

So, the so-called structural factors are really scapegoats wheeled out by free-market economists. Seeing their favoured policies failing to produce good outcomes, they had to find other explanations for Africa's stagnation (or retrogression, if you don't count the last few years of growth spike due to commodity boom, which has come to an end). It was unthinkable for them that such 'correct' policies could fail. It is no coincidence that structural factors came to be cited as the main explanations of poor African economic performance *only after* growth evaporated in the early 1980s.

Can Africa change its geography and history?

Pointing out that the above-mentioned structural variables were invoked in an attempt to save free-market economics from embarrassment does not mean that they are irrelevant. Many of the theories offered as to how a particular structural variable affects economic outcome do make sense. Poor climate can hamper development. Being surrounded by poor and conflict-ridden countries limits export opportunities and makes cross-border spill-over of conflicts more likely. Ethnic diversity or resource bonanzas can generate perverse political dynamics. However, these outcomes are not inevitable.

To begin with, there are many different ways in which those structural factors can play out. For example, abundant natural resources can create perverse outcomes, but can also promote development. If that weren't the case, we wouldn't consider the poor performances of resource-rich countries to be perverse in the first place. Natural resources allow poor countries to earn the foreign exchanges with which they can buy advanced technologies. Saying that those resources are a curse is like saying that all children born into a rich family will fail in life because they will get spoilt by their inherited wealth. Some do so exactly for this reason, but there are many others who take advantage of their inheritance and become even more successful than their parents. The fact that a factor is structural (that is, it is given by nature or history) does not mean that the outcome of its influence is predetermined.

Indeed, the fact that all those structural handicaps are not insurmountable is proven by the fact that most of today's rich countries have developed despite suffering from similar handicaps.[4]

Let us first take the case of the climate. Tropical climate is supposed to cripple economic growth by creating health burdens due to tropical diseases, especially malaria. This is a terrible problem, but surmountable. Many of today's rich countries used to have malaria and other tropical diseases, at least during the summer – not just Singapore, which is bang in the middle of the tropics, but also Southern Italy, the Southern US, South Korea and Japan. These diseases do not matter very much any more only because these countries have better sanitation (which has vastly reduced their incidence) and better medical facilities, thanks to economic development. A more serious criticism of the climate argument is that frigid and arctic climates, which affect a number of rich countries, such as Finland, Sweden, Norway, Canada and parts of the US, impose burdens as economically costly as tropical ones – machines seize up, fuel costs skyrocket, and transportation is blocked by snow and ice. There is no *a priori* reason to believe that cold weather is better than hot weather for economic development. The cold climate does not hold those countries back because they have the money and the technologies to deal with them (the same can be said of Singapore's tropical climate). So blaming Africa's underdevelopment on climate is confusing the cause of underdevelopment with its symptoms – poor climate does not cause underdevelopment; a country's inability to overcome its poor climate is merely a symptom of underdevelopment.

In terms of geography, the landlocked status of many African countries has been much emphasized. But then what about Switzerland and Austria? These are two of the richest economies in the world, and they are landlocked. The reader may respond by saying that these countries could develop because they had good river transport, but many landlocked African countries are potentially in the same position: e.g., Burkina Faso (the Volta), Mali and Niger (the Niger), Zimbabwe (the Limpopo) and Zambia (the Zambezi). So it is the lack of investment in the river transport system, rather than the geography itself, that is the problem. Moreover, due to freezing seas in winter, Scandinavian countries used to be effectively landlocked for half of the year, until they developed the ice-breaking ship in the late nineteenth century. A bad neighbourhood effect may exist, but it need not be binding – look at the recent rapid growth of India, which is located in the poorest region in the world (poorer than Sub-Saharan Africa, as mentioned above), which also has its share of conflicts (the long history of military conflicts between India and Pakistan, the Maoist Naxalite guerrillas in India, the Tamil–Sinhalese civil war in Sri Lanka).

Many people talk of the resource curse, but the development of countries such as the US, Canada and Australia, which are much better endowed with natural resources than all African countries, with the possible exceptions of South Africa and the DRC (Democratic Republic of Congo), show that abundant resources can be a blessing. In fact, most African countries are not that well endowed with natural resources – fewer than a dozen African countries have so far discovered any significant mineral deposits.[5] Most African countries may be abundantly endowed with natural resources in relative terms, but that is only because they have so few man-made resources, such as machines, infrastructure, and skilled labour. Moreover, in the late nineteenth and early twentieth centuries, the fastest-growing regions of the world were resource-rich areas such as North America, Latin America and Scandinavia, suggesting that the resource curse has not always existed.

Ethnic divisions can hamper growth in various ways, but their influence should not be exaggerated. Ethnic diversity is the norm elsewhere too. Even ignoring ethnic diversities in immigration-based societies such as the US, Canada and Australia, many of today's rich countries in Europe have suffered from linguistic, religious and ideological divides – especially of the 'medium-degree' (a few, rather than numerous, groups) that is supposed to be most conducive to violent conflicts. Belgium has two (and a bit, if you count the tiny German-speaking minority) ethnic groups. Switzerland has four languages and two religions, and has experienced a number of mainly religion-based civil wars. Spain has serious minority problems with the Catalans and the Basques, which have even involved terrorism. Due to its 560-year rule over Finland (1249 to 1809, when it was ceded to Russia), Sweden has a significant Finnish minority (around 5 per cent of the population) and Finland a Swedish one of similar scale. And so on.

Even East Asian countries that are supposed to have particularly benefited from their ethnic homogeneity have serious problems with internal divisions. You may think Taiwan is ethnically homogeneous as its citizens are all 'Chinese', but the population consists of two (or four, if you divide them up more finely) linguistic groups (the 'mainlanders' vs. the Taiwanese) that are hostile to each other. Japan has serious minority problems with the Koreans, the Okinawans, the Ainus and the Burakumins. South Korea may be one of the most ethno-linguistically homogeneous countries in the world, but that has not prevented my fellow countrymen from hating each other. For example, there are two regions in South Korea that particularly hate each other (Southeast and Southwest), so much so that some people from those regions would not allow their children to get married to someone from 'the other place'. Very interestingly, Rwanda is nearly as homogeneous in ethno-linguistic terms as Korea, but that did not prevent the ethnic cleansing of the formerly dominant minority Tutsis by the majority Hutus – an example that proves that 'ethnicity' is a political, rather than a natural, construction. In other words, rich countries do not suffer from ethnic heterogeneity not because they do not have it but because they have succeeded in nation-building (which, we should note, was often an unpleasant and even violent process).

People say that bad institutions are holding back Africa (and they are), but when the rich countries were at similar levels of material development to those we find in Africa currently, their institutions were in a far worse state.[6] Despite that, they grew continuously and have reached high levels of development. They built the good institutions largely after, or at least in tandem with, their economic development. This shows that institutional quality is as much an outcome as the causal factor of economic development. Given this, bad institutions cannot be the explanation of growth failure in Africa.

People talk about 'bad' cultures in Africa, but most of today's rich countries had once been argued to have comparably bad cultures, as I documented in the chapter 'Lazy Japanese and thieving Germans' in my earlier book *Bad Samaritans*. Until the early twentieth century, Australians and Americans would go to Japan and say the Japanese were lazy. Until the mid nineteenth century, the British would go to Germany and say that the Germans were too stupid, too individualistic and too emotional to develop their economies (Germany was not unified then) – the exact opposite of the stereotypical image that they have of the Germans today and exactly the sort of things that people now say about Africans. The Japanese and German cultures were transformed with economic development, as the demands of a highly organized industrial society made people behave in more disciplined, calculating and cooperative ways. In that sense, culture is more of an outcome, rather than a cause, of economic development. It is wrong to blame Africa's (or any region's or any country's) under-development on its culture.

Thus seen, what appear to be unalterable structural impediments to economic development in Africa (and indeed elsewhere) are usually things that can be, and have been, overcome with better technologies, superior organizational skills and improved political institutions. The fact that most of today's rich countries themselves used to suffer (and still suffer to an extent) from these conditions is an indirect proof of this point. Moreover, despite having these impediments (often in more severe forms), African countries themselves did not have a problem growing in the 1960s and 70s. The main reason for Africa's recent growth failure lies in policy – namely, the free-trade, free-market policy that has been imposed on the continent through the SAP. Nature and history do not condemn a country to a particular future. If it is policy that is causing the problem, the future can be changed even more easily. The fact that we have failed to see this, and not its allegedly chronic growth failure, is the real tragedy of Africa.

Thing 12
Governments can pick winners

What they tell you

Governments do not have the necessary information and expertise to make informed business decisions and 'pick winners' through industrial policy. If anything, government decision-makers are likely to pick some spectacular losers, given that they are motivated by power rather than profit and that they do not have to bear the financial consequences of their decisions. Especially if government tries to go against market logic and promote industries that go beyond a country's given resources and competences, the results are disastrous, as proven by the 'white elephant' projects that litter developing countries.

What they don't tell you

Governments can pick winners, sometimes spectacularly well. When we look around with an open mind, there are many examples of successful winner-picking by governments from all over the world. The argument that government decisions affecting business firms are bound to be inferior to the decisions made by the firms themselves is unwarranted. Having more detailed information does not guarantee better decisions – it may actually be more difficult to make the right decision, if one is 'in the thick of it'. Also, there are ways for the government to acquire better information and improve the quality of its decisions. Moreover, decisions that are good for individual firms may not be good for the national economy as a whole. Therefore, the government picking winners against market signals can improve national economic performance, especially if it is done in close (but not too close) collaboration with the private sector.

The worst business proposition in human history

Eugene Black, the longest-serving president in the history of the World Bank (1949–63), is reported to have criticized developing countries for being fixated on three totems – the highway, the integrated steel mill and the monument to the head of the state.

Mr Black's remark on the monument may have been unfair (many political leaders in developing countries at the time were not self-aggrandizing), but he was right to be worried about the then widespread tendency to go for prestige projects, such as highways and steel mills, regardless of their economic viability. At the time, too many developing countries built highways that remained empty and steel mills that survived only because of massive government subsidies and tariff protection. Expressions like 'white elephant' or 'castle in the desert' were invented during this period to describe such projects.

But of all the then potential castles in the desert, South Korea's plan to build an integrated steel mill, hatched in 1965, was one of the most outlandish.

At the time, Korea was one of the poorest countries in the world, relying on natural resource-based exports (e.g., fish, tungsten ore) or labour-intensive manufactured exports (e.g., wigs made with human hair, cheap garments). According to the received theory of international trade, known as the 'theory of comparative advantage', a country like Korea, with a lot of labour and very little capital, should *not* be making capital-intensive products, like steel.[1]

Worse, Korea did not even produce the necessary raw materials. Sweden developed an iron and steel industry quite naturally because it has a lot of iron ore deposits. Korea produced virtually no iron ore or coking coal, the two key ingredients of modern steel-making. Today, these could have been imported from China, but this was the time of the Cold War when there was no trade between China and South Korea. So the raw materials had to be imported from countries such as Australia, Canada and the US – all of them five or six thousand miles away – thereby significantly adding to the cost of production.

No wonder the Korean government was finding it difficult to convince potential foreign donors and lenders of its plan, even though it proposed to subsidize the steel mill left, right and centre – free infrastructure (ports, roads, railroads), tax breaks, accelerated depreciation of its capital equipment (so that tax liabilities would be minimized in the early years), reduced utility rates, and what not.

While the negotiations with potential donors – such as the World Bank and the governments of the US, UK, West Germany, France and Italy – were going on, the Korean government did things to make the project look even less appealing. When the company to run the steel mill – the Pohang Iron and Steel Company (POSCO) – was set up in 1968, it was as a state-owned enterprise (SOE), despite widespread concerns about the inefficiencies of SOEs in developing countries. And to cap it all, the company was to be led by Mr Park Tae-Joon, a former army general with minimal business experience as the head of a state-owned tungsten-mining company for a few years. Even for a military dictatorship, this was going too far. The country was about to start the biggest business venture in its history, and the man put in charge was not even a professional businessman!

Thus, the potential donors faced arguably the worst business proposal in human history – a state-owned company, run by a politically appointed soldier, making a product that all received economic theories said was not suitable to the country. Naturally, the World Bank advised the other potential donors not to support the project, and every one of them officially pulled out of the negotiations in April 1969.

Undeterred, the Korean government managed to persuade the Japanese government to channel a large chunk of the reparation payments it was paying for its colonial rule (1910–45) into the steel-mill project and to provide the machines and the technical advice necessary for the mill.

The company started production in 1973 and established its presence remarkably quickly. By the mid 1980s, it was considered one of the most cost-efficient producers of low-grade steel in the world. By the 1990s, it was one of the world's leading steel companies. It was privatized in 2001, not for poor performance but for political reasons, and today is the fourth-largest steel producer in the world (by quantity of output).

So we have a great puzzle on our hands. How did one of the worst business proposals in history produce one of the most successful businesses in history? Actually, the puzzle is even greater, because POSCO is not the only successful Korean company that was set up through government initiative.

Throughout the 1960s and 70s, the Korean government pushed many private sector firms into industries that they would not have entered of their own accord. This was often done through carrots, such as subsidies or tariff protection from imports (although the carrots were also sticks in the sense that they would be denied to under-performers). However, even when all those carrots were not enough to convince the businessmen concerned, sticks – big sticks – were pulled out, such as threats to cut off loans from the then wholly state-owned banks or even a 'quiet chat' with the secret police.

Interestingly, many of the businesses thus promoted by the government turned out to be great successes. In the 1960s, the LG Group, the electronics giant, was banned by the government from entering its desired textile industry and was forced to enter the electric cable industry. Ironically, the cable company became the foundation of its electronics business, for which LG is currently world-famous (you would know, if you have ever wanted the latest Chocolate mobile phone). In the 1970s, the Korean government put enormous pressure on Mr Chung Ju-Yung, the legendary founder of the Hyundai Group, famous for his risk appetite, to start a shipbuilding company. Even Chung is said to have initially baulked at the idea but relented when General Park Chung-Hee, the country's then dictator and the architect of Korea's economic miracle, personally threatened his business group with bankruptcy. Today, the Hyundai shipbuilding company is one of the biggest shipbuilders in the world.

Picking losers?

Now, according to the dominant free-market economic theory, things like the successes of POSCO, LG and Hyundai described above simply shouldn't happen. The theory tells us that capitalism works best when people are allowed to take care of their own businesses without any government interference. Government decisions are bound to be inferior to the decisions made by those who are directly concerned with the matter in question, it is argued. This is because the government does not possess as much information about the business at hand as the firm directly concerned with it. So, for example, if a company prefers to enter Industry A over Industry B, it must be because it knows that A would be more profitable than B, given its competences and market conditions. It would be totally presumptuous of some government official, however clever she may be by some absolute standard, to tell the company's managers that they should invest in Industry B, when she simply does not have those managers' business acumen and experiences. In other words, they argue, the government cannot pick winners.

The situation is actually more extreme than that, free-market economists say. Not only are government decision-makers unable to pick winners, they are likely to pick losers. Most importantly, government decision-makers – politicians and bureaucrats – are driven by the desire to maximize power, rather than profits. Therefore, they are bound to go for white elephant projects that have high visibility and political symbolism, regardless of their economic feasibility. Moreover, since government officials play with 'other people's money', they do not really have to worry about the economic viability of the project that they are promoting (on the subject of 'other people's money', *see Thing 2*). Between the wrong goals (prestige over profit) and the wrong incentives (not personally bearing the consequences of their decisions), these officials are almost certain to pick losers, were they to intervene in business affairs. Business should *not* be the business of government, it is said.

The best-known example of government picking a loser because of the wrong goals and incentives is the Concorde project, jointly financed by the British and the French governments in the 1960s. Concorde certainly remains one of the most impressive feats of engineering in human history. I still remember seeing one of the most memorable advertising slogans I've ever encountered, on a British Airways billboard in New York – it urged people to 'arrive before you leave' by flying Concorde (it took around three hours to cross the Atlantic on a Concorde, while the time difference between New York and London is five hours). However, considering all the money spent on its development and the subsidies that the two governments had to give to

British Airways and Air France even to buy the aircrafts, Concorde was a resounding business failure.

An even more outrageous example of a government picking a loser because it is divorced from market logic is the case of the Indonesian aircraft industry. The industry was started in the 1970s, when the country was one of the poorest in the world. This decision was made only because Dr Bacharuddin Habibie, number two to President Mohammed Suharto for over twenty years (and the country's president for just over a year, after his fall), happened to be an aerospace engineer who had trained and worked in Germany.

But if all received economic theories and the evidence from other countries suggest that governments are likely to pick losers rather than winners, how could the Korean government succeed in picking so many winners?

One possible explanation is that Korea is an exception. For whatever reasons, Korean government officials were so exceptionally capable, the argument might run, that they could pick winners in a way that no one else could. But that must mean that we Koreans are the smartest people in history. As a good Korean, I would not mind an explanation that portrays us in such glorious light, but I doubt whether non-Koreans would be convinced by it (and they are right – *see Thing 23*).

Indeed, as I discuss in some detail elsewhere in the book (most notably, *see Things 7 and 19*), Korea is not the only country in which the government has had success in picking winners.[2] Other East Asian miracle economies did the same. The Korean strategy of picking winners, while involving more aggressive means, was copied from the one practised by the Japanese government. And the Taiwanese and Singaporean governments were no worse at the job than their Korean counterpart, although the policy tools they used were somewhat different.

More importantly, it isn't just East Asian governments that

have successfully picked winners. In the second half of the twentieth century, the governments of countries such as France, Finland, Norway and Austria shaped and directed industrial development with great success through protection, subsidies and investments by SOEs. Even while it pretends that it does not, the US government has picked most of the country's industrial winners since the Second World War through massive support for research and development (R&D). The computer, semiconductors, aircraft, internet and biotechnology industries have all been developed thanks to subsidized R&D from the US government. Even in the nineteenth and early twentieth centuries, when government industrial policies were much less organized and effective than in the late twentieth century, virtually all of today's rich countries used tariffs, subsidies, licensing, regulation and other policy measures to promote particular industries over others, with considerable degrees of success (*see Thing 7*).

If governments can and do pick winners with such regularity, sometimes with spectacular results, you may wonder whether there is something wrong with the dominant economic theory that says that it cannot be done. Yes, I would say that there are many things wrong with the theory.

First of all, the theory implicitly assumes that those who are closest to the situation will have the best information and thus make the best decision. This may sound plausible but, if proximity to the situation guaranteed a better decision, no business would ever make a wrong decision. Sometimes being too close to the situation can actually make it more, rather than less, difficult to see the situation objectively. This is why there are so many business decisions that the decision-makers themselves believe to be works of genius that others view with scepticism, if not downright contempt. For example, in 2000, AOL, the internet company, acquired Time Warner media group. Despite the deep scepticism of many outsiders, Steve Case, AOL's then chairman, called it a 'historic merger' that would transform 'the landscape of media and the internet'. Subsequently the merger turned out to be a spectacular failure, prompting Jerry Levin, the Time Warner chief at the time of the merger, to admit in January 2010 that it was 'the worst deal of the century'.

Of course, by saying that we cannot necessarily assume a government's decision concerning a firm will be worse than a decision by the firm itself, I am not denying the importance of having good information. However, insofar as such information is needed for its industrial policy, the government can make sure that it has such information. And indeed, the governments that have been more successful at picking winners tend to have more effective channels of information exchange with the business sector.

One obvious way for a government to ensure that it has good business information is to set up an SOE and run the business itself. Countries such as Singapore, France, Austria, Norway and Finland relied heavily on this solution. Second, a government can legally require that firms in industries that receive state support regularly report on some key aspects of their businesses. The Korean government did this very thoroughly in the 1970s, when it was providing a lot of financial support for several new industries, such as shipbuilding, steel and electronics. Yet another method is to rely on informal networks between government officials and business elites so that the officials develop a good understanding of business situations, although an exclusive reliance on this channel can lead to excessive 'clubbiness' or downright corruption. The French policy network, built around the graduates of ENA (École Nationale d'Administration), is the most famous example of this, showing both its positive and negative sides. Somewhere in between the two extremes of legal requirement and personal networks, the Japanese have developed the 'deliberation councils', where government officials and business leaders regularly exchange information through formal channels, in the presence of third-party observers from academia and the media.

Moreover, dominant economic theory fails to recognize that there could be a clash between business interests and national interests. Even though businessmen may generally (but not necessarily, as I argued above) know their own affairs better than government officials and therefore be able to make decisions that best serve their companies' interests, there is no guarantee that their decisions are going to be good for the national economy. So, for example, when it wanted to enter the textile industry in the 1960s, the managers of LG were doing the right thing for their company, but in pushing them to enter the electric cable industry, which enabled LG to become an electronics company, the Korean government was serving Korea's national interest – and LG's interest in the long run – better. In other words, the government picking winners may hurt some business interests but it may produce a better outcome from a social point of view (*see Thing 18*).

Winners are being picked all the time

So far, I have listed many successful examples of government picking winners and explained why the free-market theory that denies the very possibility of government picking winners is full of holes.

By doing this, I am not trying to blind you to cases of government failure. I have already mentioned the series of castles in the desert built in many developing countries in the 1960s and 70s, including Indonesia's aircraft industry. However, it is more than that. Government attempts to pick winners have failed even in countries that are famous for being good at it, such as Japan, France or Korea. I've already mentioned the French government's ill-fated foray into Concorde. In the 1960s, the Japanese government tried in vain to arrange a takeover of Honda, which it considered to be too small and weak, by Nissan, but it later turned out that Honda was a much more successful firm than Nissan. The Korean government tried to promote the aluminium-smelting industry in the late 1970s, only to see the industry whacked by a massive increase in energy prices, which account for a particularly high proportion of aluminium production costs. And they are just the most prominent examples.

However, in the same way that the success stories do not allow us to support governments picking winners under all circumstances, the failures, however many there are, do not invalidate all government attempts to pick winners.

When you think about it, it is natural that governments fail in picking winners. It is in the very nature of risk-taking entrepreneurial decisions in this uncertain world that they often fail. After all, private sector firms try to pick winners all the time, by betting on uncertain technologies and entering activities that others think are hopeless, and often fail. Indeed, in exactly the same way that even those governments that have the best track records at picking winners do not pick winners all the time, even the most successful firms do not make the right decisions all the time – just think about Microsoft's disastrous Windows Vista operating system (with which I am very unhappily writing this book) and Nokia's embarrassing failure with the N-Gage phone/game console.

The question is not then whether governments can pick winners, as they obviously can, but how to improve their 'batting average'. And contrary to popular perception, governmental batting averages can be quite dramatically improved, if there is sufficient political will. The countries that are frequently associated with success in picking winners prove the point. The Taiwanese miracle was engineered by the Nationalist Party government, which had been a byword for corruption and incompetence until it was forced to move to Taiwan after losing the Chinese mainland to the Communists in 1949. The Korean government in the 1950s was famously inept at economic management, so much so that the country was described as a bottomless pit by USAID, the US government aid agency. In the late nineteenth and early twentieth centuries, the French government was famous for its unwillingness and inability to pick winners, but it became the champion of picking winners in Europe after the Second World War.

The reality is that winners are being picked all the time both by the government and by the private sector, but the most successful ones tend to be done in joint efforts between the two. In all types of winner-picking – private, public, joint – there are successes and failures, sometimes spectacular ones. If we remain blinded by the free-market ideology that tells us only winner-picking by the private sector can succeed, we will end up ignoring a huge range of possibilities for economic development through public leadership or public–private joint efforts.

Thing 13
Making rich people richer doesn't
make the rest of us richer

What they tell you

We have to create wealth before we can share it out. Like it or not, it is the rich people who are going to invest and create jobs. The rich are vital to both spotting market opportunities and exploiting them. In many countries, the politics of envy and populist policies of the past have put restrictions on wealth creation by imposing high taxes on the rich. This has to stop. It may sound harsh, but in the long run poor people can become richer only by making the rich even richer. When you give the rich a bigger slice of the pie, the slices of the others may become smaller in the short run, but the poor will enjoy bigger slices in absolute terms in the long run, because the pie will get bigger.

What they don't tell you

The above idea, known as 'trickle-down economics', stumbles on its first hurdle. Despite the usual dichotomy of 'growth-enhancing pro-rich policy' and 'growth-reducing pro-poor policy', pro-rich policies have failed to accelerate growth in the last three decades. So the first step in this argument – that is, the view that giving a bigger slice of pie to the rich will make the pie bigger – does not hold. The second part of the argument – the view that greater wealth created at the top will eventually trickle down to the poor

– does not work either. Trickle down does happen, but usually its impact is meagre if we leave it to the market.

The ghost of Stalin – or is it Preobrazhensky?

With the devastation of the First World War, the Soviet economy was in dire straits in 1919. Realizing that the new regime had no chance of surviving without reviving food production, Lenin launched the New Economic Policy (NEP), allowing market transactions in agriculture and letting the peasants keep the profits from those transactions.

The Bolshevik party was split. On the left of the party, arguing that the NEP was no more than a regression to capitalism, was Leon Trotsky. He was supported by the brilliant self-taught economist Yevgeni Preobrazhensky. Preobrazhensky argued that if the Soviet economy was to develop it needed to increase investment in industries. However, Preobrazhensky argued, it was very difficult to increase such investment because virtually all the surplus the economy generated (that is, over and above what was absolutely necessary for the physical survival of its population) was controlled by the farmers, as the economy was mostly agricultural. Therefore, he reasoned, private property and the market should be abolished in the countryside, so that all investible surplus could be squeezed out of it by the government suppressing agricultural prices. Such surplus was then to be shifted to the industrial sector, where the planning authority could make sure that all of it was invested. In the short run, this would suppress living standards, especially for the peasantry, but in the long run it would make everyone better off, because it would maximize investment and therefore the growth potential of the economy.

Those on the right of the party, such as Josef Stalin and Nikolai

Bukharin, Preobrazhensky's erstwhile friend and intellectual rival, called for realism. They argued that, even if it was not very 'communist' to allow private property in land and livestock in the countryside, they could not afford to alienate the peasantry, given its predominance. According to Bukharin, there was no other choice than 'riding into socialism on a peasant nag'. Throughout most of the 1920s, the right had the upper hand. Preobrazhensky was increasingly marginalized and forced into exile in 1927.

However, in 1928, it all changed. Upon becoming the sole dictator, Stalin filched his rivals' ideas and implemented the strategy advocated by Preobrazhensky. He confiscated land from the kulaks, the rich farmers, and brought the entire countryside under state control through collectivization of agriculture. The lands confiscated from the kulaks were turned into state farms (*sovkhoz*), while small farmers were forced to join cooperatives or collective farms (*kolkhoz*), with a nominal share ownership.

Stalin did not follow Preobrazhensky's recommendation exactly. Actually, he went rather soft on the countryside and did not squeeze the peasants to the maximum. Instead, he imposed lower-than-subsistence wages on industrial workers, which in turn forced urban women to join the industrial workforce in order to enable their families to survive.

Stalin's strategy had huge costs. Millions of people resisting, or being accused of resisisting, agricultural collectivization ended up in labour camps. There was a collapse in agricultural output, following the dramatic fall in the number of traction animals, partly due to the slaughtering by their owners in anticipation of confiscation and partly due to the shortage of grains to feed them thanks to forced grain shipments to the cities. This agricultural breakdown resulted in the severe famine of 1932–3 in which millions of people perished.

The irony is that, without Stalin adopting Preobrazhensky's strategy, the Soviet Union would not have been able to build the industrial base at such a speed that it was able to repel the Nazi invasion on the Eastern Front in the Second World War. Without the Nazi defeat on the Eastern Front, Western Europe would not have been able to beat the Nazis. Thus, ironically, Western Europeans owe their freedom today to an ultra-left-wing Soviet economist called Preobrazhensky.

Why am I nattering on about some forgotten Russian Marxist economist from nearly a century ago? It is because there is a striking parallel between Stalin's (or rather Preobrazhensky's) strategy and today's pro-rich policies advocated by free-market economists.

Capitalists vs. workers

From the eighteenth century, the feudal order, whereby people were born into certain 'stations' and remained there for the rest of their lives, came under attack from liberals throughout Europe. They argued that people should be rewarded according to their achievements rather than their births (*see Thing 20*).

Of course, these were liberals of nineteenth-century vintage, so they had views that today's liberals (least of all American liberals, who would be called 'left of centre', rather than liberal, in Europe) would find objectionable. Above all, they were against democracy. They believed that giving votes to poor men – women were not even considered, as they were believed to lack full mental faculty – would destroy capitalism. Why was that?

The nineteenth-century liberals believed that abstinence was the key to wealth accumulation and thus economic development. Having acquired the fruits of their labour, people need to abstain

from instant gratification and invest it, if they were to accumu-
late wealth. In this world view, the poor were poor because
they did not have the character to exercise such abstinence.
Therefore, if you gave the poor voting rights, they would want
to maximize their current consumption, rather than investment,
by imposing taxes on the rich and spending them. This might
make the poor better off in the short run, but it would make
them worse off in the long run by reducing investment and thus
growth.

In their anti-poor politics, the liberals were intellectually
supported by the Classical economists, with David Ricardo, the
nineteenth-century British economist, as the most brilliant of
them all. Unlike today's liberal economists, the Classical economists did not see the capitalist economy as being made up of
individuals. They believed that people belonged to different
classes – capitalists, workers and landlords – and behaved differently according to their classes. The most important inter-class
behavioural difference was considered to be the fact that capitalists invested (virtually) all of their incomes while the other classes
– the working class and the landlord class – consumed them. On
the landlord class, opinion was split. Some, like Ricardo, saw it
as a consuming class that hampered capital accumulation, while
others, such as Thomas Malthus, thought that its consumption
helped the capitalist class by offering extra demands for their
products. However, on the workers, there was a consensus. They
spent all of their income, so if the workers got a higher share of
the national income, investment and thus economic growth
would fall.

This is where ardent free-marketeers like Ricardo meet ultra-
left wing communists like Preobrazhensky. Despite their apparent
differences, both of them believed that the investible surplus
should be concentrated in the hands of the investor, the capitalist
class in the case of the former and the planning authority in the

case of the latter, in order to maximize economic growth in the long run. This is ultimately what people today have in mind when they say that 'you first have to create wealth before you can redistribute it'.

The fall and rise of pro-rich policies

Between the late nineteenth and early twentieth centuries, the worst fears of liberals were realized, and most countries in Europe and the so-called 'Western offshoots' (the US, Canada, Australia and New Zealand) extended suffrage to the poor (naturally only to the males). However, the dreaded over-taxation of the rich and the resulting destruction of capitalism did not happen. In the decades that followed the introduction of universal male suffrage, taxation on the rich and social spending did not increase by much. So, the poor were not that impatient after all.

Moreover, when the dreaded over-taxation of the rich started in earnest, it did not destroy capitalism. In fact, it made it even stronger. Following the Second World War, there was a rapid growth in progressive taxation and social welfare spending in most of the rich capitalist countries. Despite this (or rather partly because of this – *see Thing 21*), the period between 1950 and 1973 saw the highest-ever growth rates in these countries – known as the 'Golden Age of Capitalism'. Before the Golden Age, per capita income in the rich capitalist economies used to grow at 1–1.5 per cent per year. During the Golden Age, it grew at 2–3 per cent in the US and Britain, 4–5 per cent in Western Europe, and 8 per cent in Japan. Since then, these countries have never managed to grow faster than that.

When growth slowed down in the rich capitalist economies from the mid 1970s, however, the free-marketeers dusted off their nineteenth-century rhetoric and managed to convince others

that the reduction in the share of the income going to the investing class was the reason for the slowdown.

Since the 1980s, in many (although not all) of these countries,
governments that espouse upward income redistribution have
ruled most of the time. Even some so-called left-wing parties,
such as Britain's New Labour under Tony Blair and the American
Democratic Party under Bill Clinton, openly advocated such a
strategy – the high point being Bill Clinton introducing his
welfare reform in 1996, declaring that he wanted to 'end welfare
as we know it'.

In the event, trimming the welfare state down proved more
difficult than initially thought (*see Thing 21*). However, its growth
has been moderated, despite the structural pressure for greater
welfare spending due to the ageing of the population, which
increases the need for pensions, disability allowances, healthcare
and other spending directed to the elderly.

More importantly, in most countries there were also many
policies that ended up redistributing income from the poor to
the rich. There have been tax cuts for the rich – top income-tax
rates were brought down. Financial deregulation has created huge
opportunities for speculative gains as well as astronomical
paycheques for top managers and financiers (*see Things 2 and 22*).
Deregulation in other areas has also allowed companies to make
bigger profits, not least because they were more able to exploit
their monopoly powers, more freely pollute the environment
and more readily sack workers. Increased trade liberalization and
increased foreign investment – or at least the threat of them –
have also put downward pressure on wages.

As a result, income inequality has increased in most rich countries. For example, according to the ILO (International Labour
Organization) report *The World of Work 2008*, of the twenty
advanced economies for which data was available, between 1990
and 2000 income inequality rose in sixteen countries, with only

Switzerland among the remaining four experiencing a significant fall.[1] During this period, income inequality in the US,
already by far the highest in the rich world, rose to a level comparable to that of some Latin American countries such as Uruguay
and Venezuela. The relative increase in income inequality was
also high in countries such as Finland, Sweden and Belgium, but
these were countries that previously had very low levels of
inequality – perhaps too low in the case of Finland, which had
an even more equal income distribution than many of the former
socialist countries.

According to the Economic Policy Institute (EPI), the centre-
left think-tank in Washington, DC, between 1979 and 2006 (the
latest year of available data), the top 1 per cent of earners in the
US more than doubled their share of national income, from
10 per cent to 22.9 per cent. The top 0.1 per cent did even better,
increasing their share by more than three times, from 3.5 per cent
in 1979 to 11.6 per cent in 2006.[2] This was mainly because of the
astronomical increase in executive pay in the country, whose lack
of justification is increasingly becoming obvious in the aftermath
of the 2008 financial crisis (*see Thing 14*).

Of the sixty-five developing and former socialist countries
covered in the above-mentioned ILO study, income inequality
rose in forty-one countries during the same period. While the
proportion of countries experiencing rising inequality among
them was smaller than for the rich countries, many of these countries already had very high inequality, so the impacts of rising
inequality were even worse than in the rich countries.

Water that does not trickle down

All this upward redistribution of income might have been justified, had it led to accelerated growth. But the fact is that economic

growth has actually slowed down since the start of the neo-liberal pro-rich reform in the 1980s. According to World Bank data, the world economy used to grow in per capita terms at over 3 per cent during the 1960s and 70s, while since the 1980s it has been growing at the rate of 1.4 per cent per year (1980–2009).

In short, since the 1980s, we have given the rich a bigger slice of our pie in the belief that they would create more wealth, making the pie bigger than otherwise possible in the long run. The rich got the bigger slice of the pie all right, but they have actually *reduced* the pace at which the pie is growing.

The problem is that concentrating income in the hands of the supposed investor, be it the capitalist class or Stalin's central planning authority, does not lead to higher growth if the investor fails to invest more. When Stalin concentrated income in Gosplan, the planning authority, there was at least a guarantee that the concentrated income would be turned into investment (even though the productivity of the investment may have been adversely affected by factors such as the difficulty of planning and work incentive problems – *see Thing 19*). Capitalist economies do not have such a mechanism. Indeed, despite rising inequality since the 1980s, investment as a ratio of national output has fallen in all G7 economies (the US, Japan, Germany, the UK, Italy, France and Canada) and in most developing countries (*see Things 2 and 6*).

Even when upward income redistribution creates more wealth than otherwise possible (which has *not* happened, I repeat), there is no guarantee that the poor will benefit from those extra incomes. Increasing prosperity at the top might eventually trickle down and benefit the poor, but this is not a foregone conclusion.

Of course, trickle down is not a completely stupid idea. We cannot judge the impact of income redistribution only by its immediate effects, however good or bad they may look. When rich people have more money, they may use it to increase investment and growth, in which case the long-run effect of upward income redistribution may be the growth in the absolute size, although not necessarily the relative share, of income that everyone gets.

However, the trouble is that trickle down usually does not happen very much if left to the market. For example, once again according to the EPI, the top 10 per cent of the US population appropriated 91 per cent of income growth between 1989 and 2006, while the top 1 per cent took 59 per cent. In contrast, in countries with a strong welfare state it is a lot easier to spread the benefits of extra growth that follows upward income redistribution (if it happens) through taxes and transfers. Indeed, before taxes and transfers, income distribution is actually more unequal in Belgium and Germany than in the US, while in Sweden and the Netherlands it is more or less the same as in the US.[3] In other words, we need the electric pump of the welfare state to make the water at the top trickle down in any significant quantity.

Last but not least, there are many reasons to believe that downward income redistribution can help growth, if done in the right way at the right time. For example, in an economic downturn like today's, the best way to boost the economy is to redistribute wealth downward, as poorer people tend to spend a higher proportion of their incomes. The economy-boosting effect of the extra billion dollar given to the lower-income households through increased welfare spending will be bigger than the same amount given to the rich through tax cuts. Moreover, if wages are not stuck at or below subsistence levels, additional income may encourage workers' investment in education and health, which may raise their productivity and thus economic growth. In addition, greater income equality may promote social peace by reducing industrial strikes and crime, which may in turn encourage investment, as it reduces the danger of disruption to the production process and thus to the process of generating wealth. Many scholars believe that such a mechanism was at work during the Golden Age of Capitalism, when low income inequality coexisted with rapid growth.

Thus seen, there is no reason to presume that upward income redistribution will accelerate investment and growth. This has not happened in general. Even when there is more growth, the trickle down that occurs through the market mechanism is very limited, as seen in the above comparison of the US with other rich countries with a good welfare state.

Simply making the rich richer does not make the rest of us richer. If giving more to the rich is going to benefit the rest of the society, the rich have to be *made* to deliver higher investment and thus higher growth through policy measures (e.g., tax cuts for the rich individuals and corporations, conditional on investment), and then share the fruits of such growth through a mechanism such as the welfare state.

Thing 14
US managers are over-priced

What they tell you

Some people are paid a lot more than others. Especially in the US, companies pay their top managers what some people consider to be obscene amounts. However, this is what market forces demand. Given that the pool of talent is limited, you simply have to pay large sums of money if you are to attract the best talents. From the point of view of a giant corporation with billions of dollars of turnover, it is definitely worth paying extra millions, or even tens of millions, of dollars to get the best talent, as her ability to make better decisions than her counterparts in competitor companies can bring in extra hundreds of millions of dollars in revenue. However unjust these levels of compensation may appear, we should not engage in acts of envy and spite and try to artificially suppress them. Such attempts would be simply counterproductive.

What they don't tell you

US managers are over-priced in more than one sense. First, they are over-priced compared to their predecessors. In relative terms (that is, as a proportion of average worker compensation), American CEOs today are paid around ten times more than their predecessors of the 1960s, despite the fact that the latter ran companies that were much more successful, in relative terms, than today's American companies. US managers are also over-priced compared to their counterparts in other rich countries. In absolute terms, they are paid, depending on the measure we use and the country we compare with, up to twenty times more than their competitors running similarly large and successful companies. American managers are not only over-priced but also overly protected in the sense that they do not get punished for poor performance. And all this is not, unlike what many people argue, purely dictated by market forces. The managerial class in the US has gained such economic, political and ideological power that it has been able to manipulate the forces that determine its pay.

Executive pay and the politics of class envy

The average CEO compensation (salaries, bonuses, pensions and stock options) in the US is 300–400 times the average worker compensation (wages and benefits). Some people are terribly upset about this. For example, Mr Barack Obama, the US president, is frequently quoted criticizing what he sees as excessive executive pay.

Free-market economists see no problem in this pay disparity. If the CEOs are paid 300 times more than the average worker, they say, it must be because they add 300 times more value to the company. If someone does not have the productivity to justify her high pay, market forces will soon ensure that she is sacked (*see Thing 3*). Those who raise issues with executive pay, like Mr Obama, are populists who engage in the politics of class envy. Unless those who are less productive accept, they argue, that people need to be paid according to their productivity, capitalism cannot function properly.

One could almost believe in the above arguments, if one made a small concession – ignoring the facts.

I am not disputing that some people are more productive than others and that they need to be paid more – sometimes a lot more (although they should not be too smug about it – *see Thing 3*). The real question is whether the current degree of difference is justified.

Now, accurately totting up executive pay is very difficult. To begin with, the disclosure of executive pay is not very good in many countries. When we look at compensation as a whole, rather than just salaries, we need to include stock options. Stock options give the recipient the right to buy a certain number of the company's stocks in the future, so they do not have an exact value in the present and their value needs to be estimated. Depending on the methodology used for the estimation, the valuation can vary a lot.

As mentioned earlier, bearing these caveats in mind, the ratio of CEO compensation to average worker compensation in the US used to be in the region of 30 to 40 to 1 in the 1960s and 70s. This ratio has grown at a rapid rate since the early 1980s, reaching around 100 to 1 in the early 1990s and rising to 300–400 to 1 by the 2000s.

Contrast this to the changes in what the American workers get. According to the Economic Policy Institute (EPI), the Washington-based centre-left think-tank, the average hourly wage for the US workers in 2007 dollars (that is, adjusted for inflation) rose from $18.90 in 1973 to $21.34 in 2006. That is a 13 per cent increase in thirty-three years, which is around 0.4 per cent growth per year.[1] The picture is even bleaker when we look at overall compensation (wages plus benefits) and not just wages. Even if we look at only the recovery periods (given that worker compensation falls during recessions), median worker compensation rose at the rate of 0.2 per cent per year during 1983–9, at the rate of 0.1 per cent per year between 1992 and 2000 and did not grow at all during 2002–7.[2]

In other words, worker pay in the US has been virtually stagnant since the mid 1970s. Of course, this is not to say that Americans have not seen any rise in living standards since the

1970s. Family income, as opposed to individual worker compensation, has risen, but that is only because more and more families have both partners working.

Now, if we believed in the free-market logic that people are paid according to their contribution, the increase in the relative compensation of the CEOs from 30–40 times that of average worker compensation (which has not changed very much) to 300–400 times must mean that the American CEOs have become ten times more productive (in relative terms) than they were in the 1960s and 70s. Is this true?

The average quality of US managers may have been rising due to better education and training, but is it really plausible that they are ten times better than their equivalents were one generation ago? Even looking back at only the last twenty years, during which time I have been teaching in Cambridge, I sincerely doubt whether the American students we get (who are potential CEO material) are three to four times better today than when I started teaching in the early 1990s. But that should be the case, if American CEO pay had risen in relative terms purely because of the rising quality of the CEOs: during this period, the average CEO compensation in the US rose from 100 times the average worker compensation to 300–400 times.

A common explanation of this recent steep rise in relative pay is that companies have become bigger and therefore the difference that the CEO can make has become bigger. According to a popular example used by Professor Robert H. Frank of Cornell University in his widely cited *New York Times* column, if a company has $10 billion earnings, a few better decisions made by a better CEO can easily increase the company's earnings by $30 million.[3] So, the implicit message goes, what is an extra $5 million for the CEO, when she has given an extra $30 million to the company?

There is some logic to this argument, but if the growing size of the company is the main explanation for CEO pay inflation, why did it suddenly take off in the 1980s, when US company size has been growing all the time?

Also, the same argument should apply to the workers as well, at least to some extent. Modern corporations work on the basis of complex divisions of labour and cooperation, so the view that what the CEO does is the only thing that matters for company performance is highly misleading (*see Things 3 and 15*). As companies grow bigger, the potential for workers benefiting or damaging the company grows bigger as well and therefore it becomes more and more important to hire better workers. If that were not the case, why do companies bother with human resources departments?

Moreover, if the increasing importance of top managerial decisions is the main reason for CEO salary inflation, why are CEOs in Japan and Europe running similarly large companies paid only a fraction of what the American CEOs are paid? According to the EPI, as of 2005, Swiss and German CEOs were paid respectively 64 per cent and 55 per cent of what their American counterparts received. The Swedish and the Dutch were paid only around 44 per cent and 40 per cent of the American CEOs' pay; Japanese CEOs only a paltry 25 per cent. The average CEO pay for thirteen rich countries other than the US was only 44 per cent of the US level.[4]

The above figures actually vastly understate the international differences in CEO remuneration as they do not include stock options, which tend to be much higher in the US than in other countries. Other data from the EPI suggest that, in the US, CEO pay including stock options could be easily three to four times, and possibly five to six times, that of their pay excluding stock options, although it is difficult to know exactly the magnitude involved. This means that, if we include stock options, the Japanese CEO compensation (with only a small stock option component, if at all) could be as low as 5 per cent, instead of 25 per cent, that of US CEO compensation.

Now, if the American CEOs are worth anything between

twice (compared to the Swiss CEOs, excluding stock options) and twenty times (compared to the Japanese CEOs, including stock options), their counterparts abroad, how come the companies they run have been losing out to their Japanese and European rivals in many industries?

You may suggest that the Japanese and European CEOs can work at much lower absolute pay than the American CEOs because their countries' general wage levels are lower. However, wages in Japan and the European countries are basically at the same level as those in the US. The average worker pay in the thirteen countries studied by the EPI was 85 per cent of the US worker pay in 2005. The Japanese workers get paid 91 per cent the American wages, but their CEOs get paid only 25 per cent of what the American CEOs get (excluding stock options). The Swiss workers and the German workers get *higher* wages than the US workers (130 per cent and 106 per cent of the US wage, respectively), while their CEOs get paid only 55 per cent and 64 per cent of the US salaries (once again, excluding share options, which are much higher in the US).[5]

Thus seen, US managers are over-priced. The American workers get paid only 15 per cent or so more than their counterparts in competitor nations, while the American CEOs are paid at least twice (compared to the Swiss managers, excluding stock options) and possibly up to twenty times (compared to the Japanese managers, including stock options) that of what their counterparts in comparable countries are paid. Despite this, the American CEOs are running companies that are no better, and frequently worse, than their Japanese or European competitors.

Heads I win, tails you lose

In the US (and the UK, which has the second highest CEO–worker pay ratio after the US), the compensation packages for top managers are loaded in one way. Apart from being paid excessive amounts, these managers do not get punished for bad management. The most that will happen to them is to be kicked out of their current job, but that will almost always be accompanied by a fat severance payment cheque. Sometimes the expelled CEO will get even more than what is required in the contract. According to two economists, Bebchuk and Fried, 'when Mattel CEO Jill Barad resigned under fire [in 2000], the board forgave a $4.2 million loan, gave her an additional $3.3 million in cash to cover the taxes for forgiveness of another loan and allowed her unvested options to vest automatically. These gratuitous benefits were in addition to the considerable benefits that she received under her employment agreement, which included a termination payment of $26.4 million and a stream of retirement benefits exceeding $700,000 per year.'[6]

Should we care? Not really, free-market economists would argue. If some companies are stupid enough to pay gratuitous benefits to failed CEOs, they would say, let them do it. They will be outcompeted by more hard-nosed competitors that do not engage in such nonsense. So, even though there may be some poorly designed compensation schemes around, they will eventually be eliminated through competitive pressures of the market.

This seems plausible. The competitive process works to eliminate inefficient practices, be they obsolete textile technologies or biased executive pay schemes. And the fact that American and British companies have been losing to foreign companies, which on the whole have better managerial incentives, is a proof of it.

However, it will take a long time for this process to eliminate wrong managerial compensation practices (after all, this has been going on for decades). Before its recent bankruptcy, people had known for at least three decades that GM was on a decline, but no one did anything to stop the top managers from receiving compensation packages more fitting to their predecessors in the mid twentieth century, when the company had absolute dominance worldwide (*see Thing 18*).

Despite this, little is done to check excessive and biased (in that failures are hardly punished) executive pay packages because the managerial classes in the US and Britain have become so powerful, not least because of the fat paycheques they have been getting over the last few decades. They have come to control the boardrooms, through interlocking directorship and manipulation of information that they provide to independent directors, and as a result few boards of directors question the level and the structure of executive pay set by the CEO. High and rising dividend payments also keep the shareholders happy (*see Thing 2*). By flexing their economic muscle, the managerial classes have gained enormous influence over the political sphere, including the supposedly centre-left parties such as Britain's New Labour and America's Democratic Party. Especially in the US, many private sector CEOs end up running government departments. Most importantly, they have used their economic and political influence to spread the free-market ideology that says that whatever exists must be there because it is the most efficient.

The power of this managerial class has been most vividly demonstrated by the aftermath of the 2008 financial crisis. When the American and the British governments injected astronomical sums of taxpayers' money into troubled financial institutions in the autumn of 2008, few of the managers who were responsible for their institution's failure were punished. Yes, a small number of CEOs have lost their jobs, but few of those who have remained in their jobs have taken a serious pay cut and there has been an enormous, and effective, resistance to the attempt by the US Congress to put a cap on pay of the managers of financial firms receiving taxpayers' money. The British government refused to do anything about the £15–20 million pensions payout (which gives him around £700,000 yearly income) to the disgraced former boss of the RBS (Royal Bank of Scotland), Sir Fred Goodwin, although the intense negative publicity forced him subsequently to return £4 million. The fact that the British and the American taxpayers, who have become the shareholders of the bailed-out financial institutions, cannot even punish their now-employees for poor performance and force them to accept a more efficient compensation scheme shows the extent of power that the managerial class now possesses in these countries.

Markets weed out inefficient practices, but only when no one has sufficient power to manipulate them. Moreover, even if they are eventually weeded out, one-sided managerial compensation packages impose huge costs on the rest of the economy while they last. The workers have to be constantly squeezed through downward pressure on wages, casualization of employment and permanent downsizing, so that the managers can generate enough extra profits to distribute to the shareholders and keep them from raising issues with high executive pay (for more on this, *see Thing 2*). Having to maximize dividends to keep the shareholders quiet, investment is minimized, weakening the company's long-term productive capabilities. When combined with excessive managerial pay, this puts the American and British firms at a disadvantage in international competition, eventually costing the workers their jobs. Finally, when things go wrong on a large scale, as in the 2008 financial crisis, taxpayers are forced to bail out the failed companies, while the managers who created the failure get off almost scot-free.

When the managerial classes in the US and, to a lesser extent Britain, possess such economic, political and ideological power that they can manipulate the market and pass on the negative consequences of their actions to other people, it is an illusion to think that executive pay is something whose optimal levels and structures are going to be, and should be, determined by the market.

Thing 15
People in poor countries are more entrepreneurial than people in rich countries

What they tell you

Entrepreneurship is at the heart of economic dynamism. Unless there are entrepreneurs who seek out new money-making opportunities by generating new products and meeting unmet demands, the economy cannot develop. Indeed, one of the reasons behind the lack of economic dynamism in a range of countries, from France to all those states in the developing world, is the lack of entrepreneurship. Unless all those people who aimlessly loiter around in poor countries change their attitudes and actively seek out profit-making opportunities, their countries are not going to develop.

What they don't tell you

People who live in poor countries have to be very entrepreneurial even just to survive. For every loiterer in a developing country, you have two or three children shining shoes and four or five people hawking things. What makes the poor countries poor is not the absence of entrepreneurial energy at the personal level, but the absence of productive technologies and developed social organizations, especially modern firms. The increasingly apparent problems with microcredit – very small loans given to poor people in developing countries with the pronounced aim of helping them set up businesses – shows the limitations of individual entrepreneurship. Especially in the last century, entrepreneurship has become a collective activity, so the poverty of collective organization has become an even bigger obstacle to economic development rather than the deficient entrepreneurial spirits of individuals.

The problem with the French . . .

George W. Bush, the former US president, is reputed to have complained that the problem with the French is that they do not have a word for entrepreneurship in their language. His French may not have been up to scratch, but Mr Bush was articulating a fairly common Anglo-American prejudice against France as an un-dynamic and backward-looking country full of lazy workers, sheep-burning farmers, pretentious left-wing intellectuals, meddling bureaucrats and, last but not least, pompous waiters.

Whether or not Mr Bush's conception of France is right (more on this later, and *see Thing 10*), the perspective behind his statement is widely accepted – you need entrepreneurial people to have a successful economy. In this view, the poverty of the developing countries is also attributed to the lack of entrepreneurship in those countries. Look at all those men sitting around having their eleventh cup of mint tea of the day, observers from the rich countries say, these countries really need more go-getters and movers-and-shakers in order to pull themselves out of poverty.

However, anyone who is from or has lived for a period in a developing country will know that it is teeming with entrepreneurs. On the streets of poor countries, you will meet men, women and children of all ages selling everything you can think of, and things that you did not even know could be bought. In many poor countries, you can buy a place in the queue for the visa section of the American embassy (sold to you by professional queuers), the service to 'watch your car' (meaning 'refrain from damaging your car') in street-parking slots, the right to set up a food stall on a particular corner (perhaps sold by the corrupt local police boss) or even a patch of land to beg from (sold to you by the local thugs). These are all products of human ingenuity and entrepreneurship.

In contrast, most citizens of rich countries have not even come near to becoming entrepreneurs. They mostly work for a company, some of them employing tens of thousands, doing highly specialized and narrowly specified jobs. Even though some of them dream of, or at least idly talk about, setting up their own businesses and 'becoming my own boss', few put it into practice because it is a difficult and risky thing to do. As a result, most people from rich countries spend their working lives implementing someone else's entrepreneurial vision, and not their own.

The upshot is that people are far more entrepreneurial in the developing countries than in the developed countries. According to an OECD study, in most developing countries 30–50 per cent of the non-agricultural workforce is self-employed (the ratio tends to be even higher in agriculture). In some of the poorest countries the ratio of people working as one-person entrepreneurs can be way above that: 66.9 per cent in Ghana, 75.4 per cent in Bangladesh and a staggering 88.7 per cent in Benin.[1] In contrast, only 12.8 per cent of the non-agricultural workforce in developed countries is self-employed. In some countries the ratio does not even reach one in ten: 6.7 per cent in Norway, 7.5 per cent in the US and 8.6 per cent in France (it turns out that Mr Bush's complaint about the French was a classic case of the pot calling the kettle black). So, even excluding the farmers (which would make the ratio even higher), the chance of an average developing-country person being an entrepreneur is more than twice that for a developed-country person (30 per cent vs. 12.8 per cent). The difference is ten times, if we compare

Bangladesh with the US (7.5 per cent vs. 75.4 per cent). And in the most extreme case, the chance of someone from Benin being an entrepreneur is a whopping thirteen times higher than the equivalent chance for a Norwegian (88.7 per cent vs. 6.7 per cent).

Moreover, even those people who are running businesses in the rich countries need not be as entrepreneurial as their counterparts in the poor countries. For developing-country entrepreneurs, things go wrong all the time. There are power cuts that screw up the production schedule. Customs won't clear the spare parts needed to fix a machine, which has been delayed anyway due to problems with the permit to buy US dollars. Inputs are not delivered at the right time, as the delivery truck broke down – yet again – due to potholes on the road. And the petty local officials are bending, and even inventing, rules all the time in order to extract bribes. Coping with all these obstacles requires agile thinking and the ability to improvise. An average American businessman would not last a week in the face of these problems, if he were made to manage a small company in Maputo or Phnom Penh.

So we are faced with an apparent puzzle. Compared to the rich countries, we have far more people in developing countries (in proportional terms) engaged in entrepreneurial activities. On top of that, their entrepreneurial skills are much more frequently and severely tested than those of their counterparts in the rich countries. Then how is it that these more entrepreneurial countries are the poorer ones?

Great expectations – microfinance enters the scene

The seemingly boundless entrepreneurial energy of poor people in poor countries has, of course, not gone unnoticed. There is an increasingly influential view that the engine of development for poor countries should be the so-called 'informal sector', made up of small businesses that are not registered with the government.

The entrepreneurs in the informal sector, it is argued, are struggling not because they lack the necessary vision and skills but because they cannot get the money to realize their visions. The regular banks discriminate against them, while the local money-lenders charge prohibitive rates of interest. If they are given a small amount of credit (known as a 'microcredit') at a reasonable interest rate to set up a food stall, buy a mobile phone to rent out, or get some chickens to sell their eggs, they will be able to pull themselves out of poverty. With these small enterprises making up the bulk of the developing country's economy, their successes would translate into overall economic development.

The invention of microcredit is commonly attributed to Muhammad Yunus, the economics professor who has been the public face of the microcredit industry since he set up the pioneering Grameen Bank in his native Bangladesh in 1983, although there were similar attempts before. Despite lending to poor people, especially poor women, who were traditionally considered to be high-risk cases, the Grameen Bank boasted a very high repayment ratio (95 per cent or more), showing that the poor are highly bankable. By the early 1990s, the success of the Grameen Bank, and of some similar banks in countries such as Bolivia, was noticed, and the idea of microcredit – or more broadly microfinance, which includes savings and insurance, and not just credit – spread fast.

The recipe sounds perfect. Microcredit allows the poor to get out of poverty through their own efforts, by providing them with the financial means to realize their entrepreneurial potential. In the process, they gain independence and self-respect, as they are no longer relying on handouts from the government and foreign aid agencies for their survival. Poor women are particularly empowered by microcredit, as it gives them the ability to earn an income and thus improve their bargaining positions *vis-à-vis* their male partners. Not having to subsidize the poor, the government feels less pressure on its budget. The wealth created in the process, naturally, makes the overall economy, and not just the informal sector entrepreneurs, richer. Given all this, it is not a surprise that Professor Yunus believes that, with the help of microfinance, we can create 'a poverty-free world [where the] only place you can see poverty is in the museum'.

By the mid 2000s, the popularity of microfinance reached fever pitch. The year 2005 was designated the International Year of Microcredit by the United Nations, with endorsements from royalty, like Queen Rania of Jordan, and celebrities, like the actresses Natalie Portman and Aishwarya Rai. The ascendancy of microfinance reached its peak in 2006, when the Nobel Peace Prize was awarded jointly to Professor Yunus and his Grameen Bank.

The grand illusion

Unfortunately, the hype about microfinance is, well, just that – hype. There are growing criticisms of microfinance, even by some of its early 'priests'. For example, in a recent paper with David Roodman, Jonathan Morduch, a long-time advocate of microfinance, confesses that '[s]trikingly, 30 years into the microfinance movement we have little solid evidence that it improves the lives of clients in measurable ways'.[2] The problems are too numerous even to list here; anyone who is interested can read the fascinating recent book by Milford Bateman, *Why Doesn't Microfinance Work?*[3] But those most relevant to our discussion are as follows.

The microfinance industry has always boasted that its operations remain profitable without government subsidies or contributions from international donors, except perhaps in the initial teething phase. Some have used this as evidence that the poor are as good at playing the market as anyone else, if you will just let them. However, it turns out that, without subsidies from governments or international donors, microfinance institutions have to charge, and have been charging, near-usurious rates. It has been revealed that the Grameen Bank could initially charge reasonable interest rates only because of the (hushed-up) subsidies it was getting from the Bangladeshi government and international donors. If they are not subsidized, microfinance institutions have to charge interest rates of typically 40–50 per cent for their loans, with rates as high as 80–100 per cent in countries such as Mexico. When, in the late 1990s, it came under pressure to give up the subsidies, the Grameen Bank had to relaunch itself (in 2001) and start charging interest rates of 40–50 per cent.

With interest rates running up to 100 per cent, few businesses can make the necessary profits to repay the loans, so most of the loans made by microfinance institutions (in some cases as high as 90 per cent) have been used for the purpose of 'consumption smoothing' – people taking out loans to pay for their daughter's wedding or to make up for a temporary fall in income due to the illness of a working family member. In other words, the vast bulk of microcredit is *not* used to fuel entrepreneurship by the poor, the alleged goal of the exercise, but to finance consumption.

More importantly, even the small portion of microcredit that goes into business activities is not pulling people out of poverty. At first, this sounds inexplicable. Those poor people who take out microcredit know what they are doing. Unlike their counterparts in rich countries, most of them have run businesses of one kind or another. Their business wits are sharpened to the limit by their desperation to survive and sheer desire to get out of poverty. They have to generate very high profits because they have to pay the market rate of interest. So what is going wrong? Why are all these people – highly motivated, in possession of relevant skills and strongly pressured by the market – making huge efforts with their business ventures, producing such meagre results?

When a microfinance institution first starts its operation in a locality, the first posse of its clients may see their income rising – sometimes quite dramatically. For example, when in 1997 the Grameen Bank teamed up with Telenor, the Norwegian phone company, and gave out microloans to women to buy a mobile phone and rent it out to their villagers, these 'telephone ladies' made handsome profits – $750–$1,200 in a country whose annual average per capita income was around $300. However, over time, the businesses financed by microcredit become crowded and their earnings fall. To go back to the Grameen phone case, by 2005 there were so many telephone ladies that their income was estimated to be around only $70 per year, even though the national average income had gone up to over $450. This problem is known as the 'fallacy of composition' – the fact that some people can succeed with a particular business does not mean that everyone can succeed with it.

Of course, this problem would not exist if new business lines could be constantly developed – if one line of activity becomes unprofitable due to overcrowding, you simply open up another. So, for example, if phone renting becomes less profitable, you could maintain your level of income by manufacturing mobile phones or writing the software for mobile phone games. You will obviously have noticed the absurdity of these suggestions – the telephone ladies of Bangladesh simply do not have the wherewithal to move into phone manufacturing or software design. The problem is that there is only a limited range of (simple) businesses that the poor in developing countries can take on, given their limited skills, the narrow range of technologies available, and the limited amount of finance that they can mobilize through microfinance. So, you, a Croatian farmer who bought one more milk cow with a microcredit, stick to selling milk even as you watch the bottom falling out of your local milk market thanks to the 300 other farmers like you selling more milk, because turning yourself into an exporter of butter to Germany or cheese to Britain simply isn't possible with the technologies, the organizational skills and the capital you have.

No more heroes any more

Our discussion so far shows that what makes the poor countries poor is not the lack of raw individual entrepreneurial energy, which they in fact have in abundance. The point is that what really makes the rich countries rich is their ability to channel the individual entrepreneurial energy into collective entrepreneurship.

Very much influenced by capitalist folklore, with characters such as Thomas Edison and Bill Gates, and by the pioneering work of Joseph Schumpeter, the Austrian-born Harvard economics professor, our view of entrepreneurship is too much tinged by the individualistic perspective – entrepreneurship is what those heroic individuals with exceptional vision and determination do. By extension, we believe that any individual, if they try hard enough, can become successful in business. However, if it ever was true, this individualistic view of entrepreneurship is becoming increasingly obsolete. In the course of capitalist development, entrepreneurship has become an increasingly collective endeavour.

To begin with, even exceptional individuals like Edison and Gates have become what they have only because they were supported by a whole host of collective institutions (*see Thing 3*): the whole scientific infrastructure that enabled them to acquire their knowledge and also experiment with it; the company law and other commercial laws that made it possible for them subsequently to build companies with large and complex organizations; the educational system that supplied highly trained scientists, engineers, managers and workers that manned those companies; the financial system that enabled them to raise a huge amount of capital when they wanted to expand; the patent and copyright laws that protected their inventions; the easily accessible market for their products; and so on.

Furthermore, in the rich countries, enterprises cooperate with each other a lot more than do their counterparts in poor countries, even if they operate in similar industries. For example, the dairy sectors in countries such as Denmark, the Netherlands and Germany have become what they are today only because their farmers organized themselves, with state help, into cooperatives and jointly invested in processing facilities (e.g., creaming machines) and overseas marketing. In contrast, the dairy sectors in the Balkan countries have failed to develop despite quite a large amount of microcredit channelled into them, because all their dairy farmers tried to make it on their own. For another example, many small firms in Italy and Germany jointly invest in R&D and export marketing, which are beyond their individual means, through industry associations (helped by government subsidies), whereas typical developing country firms do not invest in these areas because they do not have such a collective mechanism.

Even at the firm level, entrepreneurship has become highly collective in the rich countries. Today, few companies are managed by charismatic visionaries like Edison and Gates, but by professional managers. Writing in the mid twentieth century, Schumpeter was already aware of this trend, although he was none too happy about it. He observed that the increasing scale of modern technologies was making it increasingly impossible for a large company to be established and run by a visionary individual entrepreneur. Schumpeter predicted that the displacement of heroic entrepreneurs with what he called 'executive types' would sap the dynamism from capitalism and eventually lead to its demise (*see Thing 2*).

Schumpeter has been proven wrong in this regard. Over the last century, the heroic entrepreneur has increasingly become a rarity and the process of innovation in products, processes and marketing – the key elements of Schumpeter's entrepreneurship – has become increasingly 'collectivist' in its nature. Yet, despite this, the world economy has grown much faster since the Second World War, compared to the period before it. In the case of Japan, the firms have even developed institutional mechanisms to exploit the creativity of even the lowliest production-line workers. Many attribute the success of the Japanese firms, at least partly, to this characteristic (*see Thing 5*).

If effective entrepreneurship ever was a purely individual thing, it has stopped being so at least for the last century. The collective ability to build and manage effective organizations and institutions is now far more important than the drives or even the talents of a nation's individual members in determining its prosperity (*see Thing 17*). Unless we reject the myth of heroic individual entrepreneurs and help them build institutions and organizations of collective entrepreneurship, we will never see the poor countries grow out of poverty on a sustainable basis.

Thing 16
We are not smart enough to leave things to the market

We should leave markets alone, because, essentially, market participants know what they are doing – that is, they are rational. Since individuals (and firms as collections of individuals who share the same interests) have their own best interests in mind and since they know their own circumstances best, attempts by outsiders, especially the government, to restrict the freedom of their actions can only produce inferior results. It is presumptuous of any government to prevent market agents from doing things they find profitable or to force them to do things they do not want to do, when it possesses inferior information.

What they don't tell you

People do not necessarily know what they are doing, because our ability to comprehend even matters that concern us directly is limited – or, in the jargon, we have 'bounded rationality'. The world is very complex and our ability to deal with it is severely limited. Therefore, we need to, and usually do, deliberately restrict our freedom of choice in order to reduce the complexity of problems we have to face. Often, government regulation works, especially in complex areas like the modern financial market, not because the government has superior knowledge but because it restricts choices and thus the complexity of the problems at hand, thereby reducing the possibility that things may go wrong.

Markets may fail, but . . .

As expressed by Adam Smith in the idea of the invisible hand, free-market economists argue that the beauty of the free market is that the decisions of isolated individuals (and firms) get reconciled without anybody consciously trying to do so. What makes this possible is that economic actors are rational, in the sense that they know best their own situations and the ways to improve them. It is possible, it is admitted, that certain individuals are irrational or even that a generally rational individual behaves irrationally on occasion. However, in the long run, the market will weed out irrational behaviours by punishing them – for example, investors who 'irrationally' invest in over-priced assets will reap low returns, which forces them either to adjust their behaviour or be wiped out. Given this, free-market economists argue, leaving it up to the individuals to decide what to do is the best way to manage the market economy.

Of course, few people would argue that markets are perfect. Even Milton Friedman admitted that there are instances in which markets fail. Pollution is a classic example. People 'over-produce' pollution because they are not paying for the costs of dealing with it. So what are optimal levels of pollution for individuals (or individual firms) add up to a sub-optimal level from the social point of view. However, free-market economists are quick to point out that market failures, while theoretically possible, are rare in reality. Moreover, they argue, often the best solution to market failures is to introduce more market forces. For example, they argue that the way to reduce pollution is to create a market for it – by creating 'tradable emission rights', which allow people to sell and buy the rights to pollute according to their needs within a socially optimal maximum. On top of that, free-market economists add, governments also fail (*see Thing 12*). Governments may lack the necessary information to correct market failures. Or they may be run by politicians and bureaucrats who promote their own interests rather than national interests (*see Thing 5*). All this means that usually the costs of government failure are greater than the costs of market failure that it is (allegedly) trying to fix. Therefore, free-market economists point out, the presence of market failure does not justify government intervention.

The debate on the relative importance of market failures and government failures still rages on, and I am not going to be able to conclude that debate here. However, in this *Thing*, I can at least point out that the problem with the free market does not end with the fact that individually rational actions can lead to a collective irrational outcome (that is, market failure). The problem is that we are not even rational to begin with. And when the rationality assumption does not hold, we need to think about the role of the market and of the government in a very different way even from the market failure framework, which after all also assumes that we *are* rational. Let me explain.

If you're so smart . . .

In 1997, Robert Merton and Myron Scholes were awarded the Nobel Prize in economics for their 'new method to determine the value of derivatives'. Incidentally, the prize is not a *real* Nobel prize but a prize given by the Swedish central bank 'in memory of Alfred Nobel'. As a matter of fact, several years ago the Nobel family even threatened to deny the prize the use of their ancestor's name, as it had been mostly given to free-market economists of whom Alfred Nobel would not have approved, but that is another story.

In 1998, a huge hedge fund called Long-Term Capital Management (LTCM) was on the verge of bankruptcy, following the

Russian financial crisis. The fund was so large that its bankruptcy was expected to bring everyone else down with it. The US financial system avoided a collapse only because the Federal Reserve Board, the US central bank, twisted the arms of the dozen or so creditor banks to inject money into the company and become reluctant shareholders, gaining control over 90 per cent of the shares. LTCM was eventually folded in 2000.

LTCM, founded in 1994 by the famous (now infamous) financier John Merriwether, had on its board of directors – would you believe it? – Merton and Scholes. Merton and Scholes were not just lending their names to the company for a fat cheque: they were working partners and the company was actively using their asset-pricing model.

Undeterred by the LTCM débâcle, Scholes went on to set up another hedge fund in 1999, Platinum Grove Asset Management (PGAM). The new backers, one can only surmise, thought that the Merton–Scholes model must have failed back in 1998 due to a totally unpredictable *sui generis* event – the Russian crisis. After all, wasn't it still the best asset-pricing model available in the history of humanity, approved by the Nobel committee?

The investors in PGAM were, unfortunately, proven wrong. In November 2008, it practically went bust, temporarily freezing investor withdrawal. The only comfort they could take was probably that they were not alone in being failed by a Nobel laureate. The Trinsum Group, for which Scholes's former partner, Merton, was the chief science officer, also went bankrupt in January 2009.

There is a saying in Korea that even a monkey can fall from a tree. Yes, we all make mistakes, and one failure – even if it is a gigantic one like LTCM – we can accept as a mistake. But the same mistake twice? Then you know that the first mistake was not really a mistake. Merton and Scholes did not know what they were doing.

When Nobel Prize-winners in economics, especially those who got the prize for their work on asset pricing, cannot read the financial market, how can we run the world according to an economic principle that assumes people always know what they are doing and therefore should be left alone? As Alan Greenspan, former chairman of the Federal Reserve Board, had to admit in a Congressional hearing, it was a 'mistake' to 'presume that the self-interest of organisations, specifically banks, is such that they were best capable of protecting shareholders and equity in the firms'. Self-interest will protect people only when they know what is going on and how to deal with it.

There are many stories coming out of the 2008 financial crisis that show how the supposedly smartest people did not truly understand what they were doing. We are not talking about the Hollywood big shots, such as Steven Spielberg and John Malkovich, or the legendary baseball pitcher Sandy Koufax, depositing their money with the fraudster Bernie Madoff. While these people are among the world's best in what they do, they may not necessarily understand finance. We are talking about the expert fund managers, top bankers (including some of the world's largest banks, such as the British HSBC and the Spanish Santander), and world-class colleges (New York University and Bard College, which had access to some of the world's most reputed economics faculty members) falling for the same trick by Madoff.

Worse, it isn't just a matter of being deceived by fraudsters like Madoff or Alan Stanford. The failure by the bankers and other supposed experts in the field to understand what was going on has been pervasive, even when it comes to legitimate finance. One of them apparently shocked Alistair Darling, then British Chancellor of the Exchequer, by telling him in the summer of 2008 that 'from now on we will only lend when we understand the risks involved'.[1] For another, even more astonishing, example, only six months before the collapse of AIG, the American insurance company bailed out by the US government in the autumn of 2008, its chief financial officer, Joe Cassano, is reported to have said that '[i]t is hard for us, without being flippant, to even see a scenario within any kind of realm of reason that would see us losing one dollar in any of the [credit default swap, or CDS] transactions'. Most of you – especially if you are an American taxpayer cleaning up Mr Cassano's mess – might find that supposed lack of flippancy less than amusing, given that AIG went bust because of its failure in its $441 billion portfolio of CDS, rather than its core insurance business.

When the Nobel Prize-winners in financial economics, top bankers, high-flying fund managers, prestigious colleges and the smartest celebrities have shown that they do not understand what they are doing, how can we accept economic theories that work only because they assume that people are fully rational? The upshot is that we are simply not smart enough to leave the market alone.

But where do we go from there? Is it possible to think about regulating the market when we are not even smart enough to leave it alone? The answer is yes. Actually it is more than that. Very often, we need regulation exactly because we are not smart enough. Let me show why.

The last Renaissance Man

Herbert Simon, the winner of the 1978 Nobel Prize in economics, was arguably the last Renaissance Man on earth. He started out as a political scientist and moved on to the study of public administration, writing the classic book in the field, *Administrative Behaviour*. Throwing in a couple of papers in physics along the way, he moved into the study of organizational behaviour, business administration, economics, cognitive psychology and artificial intelligence (AI). If anyone understood how people think and organize themselves, it was Simon.

Simon argued that our rationality is 'bounded'. He did not believe that we are entirely irrational, although he himself and many other economists of the behaviouralist school (as well as many cognitive psychologists) have convincingly documented how much of our behaviour is irrational.[2] According to Simon, we try to be rational, but our ability to be so is severely limited. The world is too complex, Simon argued, for our limited intelligence to understand fully. This means that very often the main problem we face in making a good decision is not the lack of information but our limited capability to process that information – a point nicely illustrated by the fact that the celebrated advent of the internet age does not seem to have improved the quality of our decisions, judging by the mess we are in today.

To put it another way, the world is full of uncertainty. Uncertainty here is not just not knowing exactly what is going to happen in the future. For certain things, we can reasonably calculate the probability of each possible contingency, even though we cannot predict the exact outcome – economists call this 'risk'. Indeed, our ability to calculate the risk involved in many aspects of human life – the likelihoods of death, disease, fire, injury, crop failure, and so on – is the very foundation of the insurance industry. However, for many other aspects of our life, we do not even know all the possible contingencies, not to speak of their respective likelihoods, as emphasized, among others, by the insightful American economist Frank Knight and the great British economist John Maynard Keynes in the early twentieth century. Knight and Keynes argued that the kind of rational behaviour that forms the foundation of much of modern economics is impossible under this kind of uncertainty.

The best explanation of the concept of uncertainty – or the complexity of the world, to put it another way – was given by, perhaps surprisingly, Donald Rumsfeld, the Defense Secretary in the first government of George W. Bush. In a press briefing regarding the situation in Afghanistan in 2002, Rumsfeld opined: 'There are known knowns. There are things we know that we know. There are known unknowns. That is to say, there are things that we now know we don't know. But there are also unknown unknowns.

There are things we do not know we don't know.' I don't think those at the Plain English Campaign that awarded the 2003 Foot in Mouth award to the statement quite understood the significance of this statement for our understanding of human rationality.

So what do we do, when the world is so complex and our ability to understand it so limited? Simon's answer was that we deliberately restrict our freedom of choice in order to reduce the range and the complexity of the problems that we have to deal with.

This sounds esoteric, but when you think about it, this is exactly what we do all the time. Most of us create routines in our life so that we don't have to make too many decisions too often. The optimal amount of sleep and the optimal breakfast menu differ every day, depending on our physical conditions and the tasks ahead. Yet most of us go to bed at the same time, wake up at the same time and eat similar things for breakfast, at least during the weekdays.

Simon's favourite example of how we need some rules in order to cope with our bounded rationality was chess. With only thirty-two pieces and sixty-four squares, chess may seem to be a relatively simple affair, but in fact involves a huge amount of calculation. If you were one of those 'hyper-rational' beings (as Simon calls them) that populate standard economics textbooks, you would, of course, figure out all the possible moves and calculate their likelihoods before you make a move. But, Simon points out, there being around 10^{120} (yes, that is 120 zeroes) possibilities in an average game of chess, this 'rational' approach requires mental capacity that no human being possesses. Indeed, studying chess masters, Simon realized that they use rules of thumb (heuristics) to focus on a small number of possible moves, in order to reduce the number of scenarios that need to be analysed, even though the excluded moves may have brought better results.

If chess is this complicated, you can imagine how complicated things are in our economy, which involves billions of people and millions of products. Therefore, in the same way in which individuals create routines in their daily lives or chess games, companies operate with 'productive routines', which simplify their options and search paths. They build certain decision-making structures, formal rules and conventions that automatically restrict the range of possible avenues that they explore, even when the avenues thus excluded outright may have been more profitable. But they still do it because otherwise they may drown in a sea of information and never make a decision. Similarly, societies create informal rules that deliberately restrict people's freedom of choice so that they don't have to make fresh choices constantly. So, they develop a convention for queuing so that people do not have to, for example, constantly calculate and recalculate their positions at a crowded bus stop in order to ensure that they get on the next bus.

The government need not *know better*

So far so good, you may think, but what does Simon's theory of bounded rationality really have to say about regulation?

Free-market economists have argued against government regulation on the (apparently reasonable) ground that the government does not know better than those whose actions are regulated by it. By definition, the government cannot know someone's situation as well as the individual or firm concerned. Given this, they argue, it is impossible that government officials can improve upon the decisions made by the economic agents.

However, Simon's theory shows that many regulations work *not* because the government necessarily knows better than the regulated (although it may sometimes do – *see Thing 12*) but because they limit the complexity of the activities, which enables the regulated to make better decisions. The 2008 world financial crisis illustrates this point very nicely.

In the run-up to the crisis, our ability to make good decisions was simply overwhelmed because things were allowed to evolve in too complex a manner through financial innovation. So many complex financial instruments were created that even financial experts themselves did not fully understand them, unless they specialized in them – and sometimes not even then (*see Thing 22*). The top decision-makers of the financial firms certainly did not grasp much of what their businesses were doing. Nor could the regulatory authorities fully figure out what was going on. As discussed above, now we are seeing a flood of confessions – some voluntary, others forced – from the key decision-makers.

If we are going to avoid similar financial crises in the future, we need to restrict severely freedom of action in the financial market. Financial instruments need to be banned unless we fully understand their workings and their effects on the rest of the financial sector and, moreover, the rest of the economy. This will mean banning many of the complex financial derivatives whose workings and impacts have been shown to be beyond the comprehension of even the supposed experts.

You may think I am too extreme. However, this is what we do all the time with other products – drugs, cars, electrical products, and many others. When a company invents a new drug, for example, it cannot be sold immediately. The effects of a drug, and the human body's reaction to it, are complex. So the drug needs to be tested rigorously before we can be sure that it has enough beneficial effects that clearly overwhelm the side-effects and allow it to be sold. There is nothing exceptional about proposing to ascertain the safety of financial products before they can be sold.

Unless we deliberately restrict our choices by creating restrictive rules, thereby simplifying the environment that we have to deal with, our bounded rationality cannot cope with the complexity of the world. It is not because the government necessarily knows better that we need regulations. It is in the humble recognition of our limited mental capability that we do.

Thing 17
More education in itself is not going to make a country richer

What they tell you

A well-educated workforce is absolutely necessary for economic development. The best proof of this is the contrast between the economic successes of the East Asian countries, with their famously high educational achievements, and the economic stagnation of Sub-Saharan African countries, which have some of the lowest educational records in the world. Moreover, with the rise of the so-called 'knowledge economy', in which knowledge has become the main source of wealth, education, especially higher education, has become the absolute key to prosperity.

What they don't tell you

There is remarkably little evidence showing that more education leads to greater national prosperity. Much of the knowledge gained in education is actually not relevant for productivity enhancement, even though it enables people to lead a more fulfilling and independent life. Also, the view that the rise of the knowledge economy has critically increased the importance of education is misleading. To begin with, the idea of the knowledge economy itself is problematic, as knowledge has always been the main source of wealth. Moreover, with increasing de-industrialization and mechanization, the knowledge requirements may even have fallen for most jobs in the rich countries. Even when it comes to higher education, which is supposed to matter more in the knowledge economy, there is no simple relationship between it and economic growth. What really matters in the determination of national prosperity is not the educational levels of individuals but the nation's ability to organize individuals into enterprises with high productivity.

Education, education, education

'Education, education, education' – this is how the former British Prime Minister Tony Blair summed up his prospective government's top three policy priorities during the 1997 election campaign, which brought his 'New' Labour party to power after nearly two decades in the wilderness.

The subsequent success or otherwise of New Labour's education policy may be disputed, but what is indisputable is that the comment perfectly captured Mr Blair's exceptional ability to say the right thing at the right time (that is, before he lost his head over Iraq). Many a politician before Mr Blair had talked about and pushed for better education, but he was speaking at a time when, having witnessed the rise of the knowledge economy since the 1980s, the whole world was becoming convinced that education was the key to economic prosperity. If education had been important for economic success in the days of smoke-stack industries, more and more people were becoming convinced, it would be the be-all and end-all in the information age, when brains, and not brawn, are the main source of wealth.

The argument seems straightforward. More educated people are more productive – as evidenced by the higher salaries they get. So it is a matter of mathematical logic that an economy with more educated people will be more productive. The fact that poorer countries have a lower stock of educated people – or 'human capital' in some economists' jargon – also proves the point. The average duration of schooling is around nine years in OECD countries, while it is not even three in Sub-Saharan African countries. Also well known are the exceptionally high educational achievements of the 'miracle' economies in East Asia – such as Japan, South Korea, Taiwan, Hong Kong and Singapore. Their educational achievements are manifested not just in quantitative terms such as high literacy rates or enrolment rates at various levels of education. The quality of their education is very high as well. They rank right at the top of the league in internationally standardized tests such as the Trends in International Mathematics and Science Study (TIMSS) for fourth and eighth graders, and the Program for International Student Assessment (PISA), which measures fifteen-year-olds' ability to apply maths knowledge to real-world problems. Need we say more?

We don't need no education . . .

Self-evident though the importance of education in raising an economy's productivity may seem, there is actually a lot of evidence that questions this piece of conventional wisdom.

Let's first take the case of the East Asian miracle economies, in whose development education is supposed to have played a critical role. In 1960, Taiwan had a literacy rate of only 54 per cent, while the Philippines' was 72 per cent. Despite its lower education level, Taiwan has since then notched up one of the best economic growth performances in human history, while the Philippines has done rather poorly. In 1960, the Philippines had almost double the per capita income of Taiwan ($200 vs. $122), but today Taiwan's per capita income is around ten times that of the Philippines ($18,000 vs. $1,800). In the same year,

Korea had a 71 per cent literacy rate – comparable to that of the Philippines but still well below Argentina's 91 per cent. Despite the significantly lower literacy rate, Korea has since grown much faster than Argentina. Korea's per capita income was just over one-fifth that of Argentina's in 1960 ($82 vs. $378). Today it is three times higher (around $21,000 vs. around $7,000).

Obviously, there are many more things than education that determine a country's economic growth performance. But these examples undermine the common myth that education was the key to the East Asian miracle. The East Asian economies did *not* have unusually high educational achievement at the start of their economic miracles, while countries like the Philippines and Argentina did very poorly despite having significantly better-educated populations.

At the other end of the spectrum, the experience of Sub-Saharan Africa also shows that investing more in education is no guarantee of better economic performance. Between 1980 and 2004, literacy rates in Sub-Saharan African countries rose quite substantially from 40 per cent to 61 per cent.[1] Despite such rises, per capita income in the region actually *fell* by 0.3 per cent per year during this period. If education is so important for economic development, as most of us believe, something like this should not happen.

The apparent lack of positive effects of education on growth is not found only in the extreme cases that I have chosen – East Asia at one end and Sub-Saharan Africa at the other. It is a more general phenomenon. In a widely cited 2004 article, 'Where has all the education gone?', Lant Pritchett, a Harvard economist who worked at the World Bank for a long time, analysed the data from dozens of rich and developing countries during the 1960–87 period and conducted an extensive review of similar studies, in order to establish whether education positively influences growth.[2] His conclusion is that there is very little evidence to support the view that increased education leads to higher economic growth.

Don't know much about history, don't know much biology

Why is there so little evidence to support what seems to be such an obvious proposition that more education should make a country richer? It is because, to put it simply, education is not as important in raising the productivity of an economy as we believe.

To begin with, not all education is even *meant* to raise productivity. There are many subjects that have no impact, even indirectly, on most workers' productivity – literature, history, philosophy and music, for example (*see Thing 3*). From a strictly economic point of view, teaching these subjects is a waste of time. We teach our children those subjects because we believe that they will eventually enrich their lives and also make them good citizens. Even though this justification for educational spending is increasingly under attack in an age in which everything is supposed to justify its existence in terms of its contribution to productivity growth, it remains a very important – in my view, the most important – reason to invest in education.

Moreover, even subjects like mathematics or sciences, which are supposed to be important for raising productivity, are not relevant for most workers – investment bankers do not need biology or fashion designers mathematics in order to be good at what they do. Even for those jobs for which these subjects are relevant, much of what you learn at school or even university is often not directly relevant for practical work. For example, the link between what a production line worker in a car factory learned in school physics and his productivity is rather tenuous. The importance of apprenticeship and on-the-job training in many professions testifies to the limited relevance of school education for worker productivity. So, even the supposedly productivity-oriented parts of education are not as relevant for raising productivity as we think.

Cross-country statistical analyses have failed to find any

relationship between a country's maths scores and its economic performance.[3] But let me give you more concrete examples. In the mathematical part of the 2007 TIMSS, US fourth-graders were behind not only the famously mathematical children of the East Asian countries but also their counterparts from countries such as Kazakhstan, Latvia, Russia and Lithuania.[4] Children in all other rich European economies included in the test, except England and the Netherlands, scored lower than the US children.[5] Eighth-graders from Norway, the richest country in the world (in terms of per capita income at market exchange rate – *see Thing 10*), were behind their counterparts not only in all other rich countries but also in much poorer countries, including Lithuania, Czech Republic, Slovenia, Armenia and Serbia (it is interesting to note that all these countries are former socialist countries).[6] Eighth-graders from Israel, a country famous for its educational zeal and exceptional performance in high-end research, scored behind Norway, falling behind Bulgaria as well. Similar stories were observed in science tests.

How about the knowledge economy?

Even if education's impact on growth has been meagre so far, you may wonder whether the recent rise of the knowledge economy may have changed all that. With ideas becoming the main source of wealth, it may be argued, education will from now on become much more important in determining a country's prosperity.

Against this, I must first of all point out that the knowledge economy is nothing new. We have always lived in one in the sense that it has always been a country's command over knowledge (or lack of it) that made it rich (or poor). China was the richest country in the world during the first millennium because it possessed technical knowledge that others did not – paper, movable type, gunpowder and the compass being the most famous, but by no means the only, examples. Britain became the world's economic hegemon in the nineteenth century because it came to lead the world in technological innovation. When Germany became as poor as Peru and Mexico right after the Second World War, no one suggested that it should be reclassified as a developing country, because people knew that it still had command over technological, organizational and institutional knowledge that had made it one of the most formidable industrial powers before the war. In that sense, the importance (or otherwise) of education has not changed in the recent period.

Of course, the knowledge stock that the humanity collectively commands today is much bigger than in the past, but that does not mean that everyone, or even the majority of the people, has to be better educated than in the past. If anything, the amount of productivity-related knowledge that an average worker needs to possess has fallen for many jobs, especially in rich countries. This may sound absurd, but let me explain.

To begin with, with the continuous rise in manufacturing productivity, a greater proportion of the workforce in rich countries now works in low-skilled service jobs that do not require much education – stacking shelves in supermarkets, frying burgers in fast food restaurants and cleaning offices (*see Things 3 and 9*). Insofar as the proportion of people in such professions increases, we may actually do with an increasingly less, not more, educated labour force, if we are only interested in the productivity effects of education.

Moreover, with economic development, a higher proportion of knowledge becomes embodied in machines. This means that the economy-wide productivity increases despite individual workers having less understanding of what they do than their counterparts in the past. For the most striking example, these days most shop assistants in rich countries do not even need to know how to add – a skill that their counterparts in earlier times definitely needed – as bar-code machines do that for them. For another example, blacksmiths in poor countries probably know more about the nature of metals in relation to tool-making than do most employees of Bosch or Black & Decker. For yet another example, those who work at the small electronics shops littering the streets of poor countries can fix many more things than can individual workers at Samsung or Sony.

A large part of this is due to the simple fact that mechanization is the most important way to increase productivity. But an influential Marxist school of thought argues that capitalists deliberately 'de-skill' their workers by using the most mechanized production technologies possible, even if they are not the most economical, in order to make the workers more easily replaceable and thus easier to control.[7] Whatever the exact cause of the mechanization process, the upshot is that more technologically developed economies may actually need fewer educated people.

The Swiss paradox

Now, it may be argued that, even though economic development may not necessarily require the average worker to be more educated, it needs more educated people at the higher end. After all, as I have pointed out above, the ability to generate more productive knowledge than others is what makes a country richer than others. Thus seen, it may be argued, it is the quality of universities, rather than that of primary schools, that determines a nation's prosperity.

However, even in this supposedly knowledge-driven era, the relationship between higher education and prosperity is not straightforward. Let us take the striking example of Switzerland. The country is one of the top few richest and most industrialized countries in the world (*see Things 9 and 10*), but it has, surprisingly, the lowest – actually by far the lowest – university enrolment rate in the rich world; until the early 1990s, only around one-third of the average for other rich countries. Until as late as 1996, the Swiss university enrolment rate was still less than half the OECD average (16 per cent vs. 34 per cent).[8] Since then, Switzerland increased its rate considerably, bringing it up to 47 per cent by 2007, according to UNESCO data. However, the Swiss rate still remains the lowest in the rich world and is way below what we find in the most university-heavy countries, such as Finland (94 per cent), the US (82 per cent) and Denmark (80 per cent). It is, interestingly, also far lower than that of many considerably poorer economies, such as Korea (96 per cent), Greece (91 per cent), Lithuania (76 per cent) and Argentina (68 per cent).

How is it possible that Switzerland has stayed at the very top of the international productivity league despite providing much less higher education than not just its main competitors but also many economies that are much poorer?

One possible explanation is that universities in different countries have different qualities. So, if Korean or Lithuanian universities are not as good as Swiss universities, it may be possible for Switzerland to be richer than Korea or Lithuania, even if a much lower proportion of the Swiss have university education than do the Koreans or the Lithuanians. However, this argument loses much of its force when we compare Switzerland with Finland or the US. We cannot in all seriousness suggest that Swiss universities are so much better than Finnish or American ones that Switzerland can get away with university enrolment rates half theirs.

The main explanation for the 'Swiss paradox' should be found, once again, in the low productivity content of education. However, in the case of higher education, the non-productivity component is not so much about teaching people subjects that will help them with things such as personal fulfilment, good citizenship and national identity, as in the case of primary and secondary education. It is about what economists call the 'sorting' function.

Higher education, of course, imparts certain productivity-related knowledge to its recipients, but another important function of it is to establish each individual's ranking in the hierarchy of employability.[9] In many lines of work, what counts is general intelligence, discipline and the ability to organize oneself, rather than specialist knowledge, much of which you can, and have to, actually pick up on-the-job. So, even if what you learn in a university as a history major or a chemist may not be relevant to your work as a prospective manager in an insurance company or as a government official in the Department of Transport, the fact that you have graduated from a university tells your potential employers that you are likely to be smarter, more self-disciplined and better organized than those who have not. By hiring you as a university graduate, your employer is then hiring you for those general qualities, not for your specialist knowledge, which is often irrelevant to the job you will be performing.

Now, with the increasing emphasis on higher education in the recent period, an unhealthy dynamic has been established for higher education in many high-income and upper-middle-income countries that can afford to expand universities (Switzerland has not been immune to this, as figures above suggest). Once the proportion of people going to university goes over a critical threshold, people *have to* go to university in order to get a decent job. When, say, 50 per cent of the population goes to university, not going to university is implicitly declaring that you are in the bottom half of the ability distribution, which is not the greatest way to start your job search. So, people go to university, fully knowing that they will 'waste time' studying things that they will never need for their work. With everyone wanting to go to university, the demand for higher education increases, which then leads to the supply of more university places, which raises university enrolment rate further, increasing the pressure to go to university even more. Over time, this leads to a process of degree inflation. Now that 'everyone' has a university degree, you have to do a master's, or even a PhD, in order to stand out, even if the productivity content of those further degrees may be minimal for your future jobs.

Given that Switzerland was until the mid 1990s able to maintain one of the highest national productivities in the world with a university enrolment of 10–15 per cent, we could say that enrolment rates much higher than that are really unnecessary. Even if we accept that skills requirement has risen so much with the rise of the knowledge economy that the 40-plus per cent enrolment rate that Switzerland now has is the minimum (which I seriously doubt), this still means that at least half of university education in countries such as the US, Korea and Finland is 'wasted' in the essentially zero-sum game of sorting. The higher education system in these countries has become like a theatre in which some people decided to stand to get a better view, prompting others behind them to stand. Once enough people stand, everyone has to stand, which means that no one is getting a better view, while everyone has become more uncomfortable.

Education vs. enterprise

If not just basic education but also higher education does not matter so much in determining a nation's prosperity, we must seriously rethink the role of education in our economy.

In the case of rich countries, their obsession with higher education has to be tamed. This obsession has led to unhealthy degree inflation and the consequent over-investment of huge scale in higher education in many countries. I am not against countries having a very high – or even 100 per cent – university enrolment rate for other reasons, but they should not delude themselves into believing that it would have a significant productivity effect.

In the case of developing countries, an even more radical change of perspective is needed. While they should expand education in order to prepare their youngsters for a more meaningful life, when it comes to the question of productivity increase, these countries need to look beyond the education of individuals and pay more attention to building the right institutions and organizations for productivity growth.

What really distinguishes the rich countries from the poorer ones is much less how well educated their individual citizens are than how well their citizens are organized into collective entities with high productivity – be that giant firms such as Boeing or Volkswagen or the smaller world-class firms of Switzerland and Italy (*see Thing 15*). Development of such firms needs to be supported by a range of institutions that encourage investment and risk-taking – a trade regime that protects and nurtures firms in 'infant industries' (*see Things 7 and 12*), a financial system that provides 'patient capital' necessary for long-term productivity-enhancing investments (*see Thing 2*), institutions that provide second chances for both the capitalists (a good bankruptcy law) and for the workers (a good welfare state) (*see Thing 21*), public subsidies and regulation regarding R&D and training (*see Things 18 and 19*), and so on.

Education is valuable, but its main value is not in raising productivity. It lies in its ability to help us develop our potentials and live a more fulfilling and independent life. If we expanded education in the belief that it will make our economies richer, we will be sorely disappointed, for the link between education and national productivity is rather tenuous and complicated. Our overenthusiasm with education should be tamed, and, especially in developing countries, far greater attention needs to be paid to the issue of establishing and upgrading productive enterprises and institutions that support them.

Thing 18
What is good for General Motors is not necessarily good for the United States

What they tell you

At the heart of the capitalist system is the corporate sector. This is where things are produced, jobs created and new technologies invented. Without a vibrant corporate sector, there is no economic dynamism. What is good for business, therefore, is good for the national economy. Especially given the increasing international competition in a globalizing world, countries that make opening and running businesses difficult or make firms do unwanted things will lose investment and jobs, eventually falling behind. Government needs to give the maximum degree of freedom to business.

What they don't tell you

Despite the importance of the corporate sector, allowing firms the maximum degree of freedom may not even be good for the firms themselves, let alone the national economy. In fact, not all regulations are bad for business. Sometimes, it is in the long-run interest of the business sector to restrict the freedom of individual firms so that they do not destroy the common pool of resources that all of them need, such as natural resources or the labour force. Regulations can also help businesses by making them do things that may be costly to them individually in the short run but raise their collective productivity in the long run

– such as the provision of worker training. In the end, what matters is not the quantity but the quality of business regulation.

How Detroit won the war

They say that Detroit won the Second World War. Yes, the Soviet Union sacrificed the most people – the estimated death toll in the Great Patriotic War (as it is known in Russia) was upward of 25 million, nearly half of all deaths worldwide. But it – and, of course, the UK – would not have survived the Nazi offensive without the arms sent over from what Franklin Roosevelt called 'the arsenal of democracy', that is, the United States. And most of those arms were made in the converted factories of the Detroit car-makers – General Motors (GM), Ford and Chrysler. So, without the industrial might of the US, represented by Detroit, the Nazis would have taken over Europe and at least the western part of the Soviet Union.

Of course, history is never straightforward. What made the early success of Nazi Germany in the war possible was the ability of its army to move quickly – its famous *Blitzkrieg*, or Lightning War. And what made that high mobility of the German army possible was its high degree of motorization, many technologies for which were supplied by none other than GM (through its Opel subsidiary, acquired in 1929). Moreover, evidence is emerging that, in defiance of the law, throughout the war GM secretly maintained its link with Opel, which built not only military cars but aircraft, landmines and torpedoes. So it seems that GM was arming both sides and profiting from it.

Even among the Detroit car-makers – collectively known as the Big Three – GM by then stood pre-eminent. Under the leadership of Alfred Sloan Jr, who ran it for thirty-five years (1923–58), GM had overtaken Ford as the largest US car-maker by the late 1920s and gone on to become the all-American automobile company, producing, in Sloan's words, 'a car for every purse and purpose', arranged along a 'ladder of success', starting with Chevrolet, moving up through Pontiac, Oldsmobile, Buick and finally culminating in Cadillac.

By the end of the Second World War, GM was not just the biggest car-maker in the US, it had become the biggest company in the country (in terms of revenue). It was so important that, when asked in the Congressional hearing for his appointment as US Defense Secretary in 1953 whether he saw any potential conflict between his corporate background and his public duties, Mr Charlie Wilson, who used to be the CEO of General Motors, famously replied that what is good for the United States is good for General Motors and vice versa.

The logic behind this argument seems difficult to dispute. In a capitalist economy, private sector companies play the central role in creating wealth, jobs and tax revenue. If they do well, the whole economy does well by extension. Especially when the enterprise in question is one of the largest and technologically most dynamic enterprises, like GM in the 1950s, its success or otherwise has significant effects on the rest of the economy – the supplier firms, the employees of those firms, the producers of goods that the giant firm's employees, who can number in the hundreds of thousands, may buy, and so on. Therefore, how these giant firms do is particularly important for the prosperity of the national economy.

Unfortunately, proponents of this logic say, this obvious argument was not widely accepted during much of the twentieth century. One can understand why communist regimes were against the private sector – after all, they believed that private property was the source of all the evils of capitalism. However, between the Great Depression and the 1970s, private business was viewed with suspicion even in most capitalist economies.

Businesses were, so the story goes, seen as anti-social agents whose profit-seeking needed to be restrained for other, supposedly loftier, goals, such as justice, social harmony, protection of the weak and even national glory. As a result, complicated and cumbersome systems of licensing were introduced in the belief that governments need to regulate which firms do what in the interest of wider society. In some countries, governments even pushed firms into unwanted businesses in the name of national development (*see Things 7 and 12*). Large firms were banned from entering those segments of the market populated by small farms, factories and retail shops, in order to preserve the traditional way of life and protect 'small men' against big business. Onerous labour regulations were introduced in the name of protecting worker rights. In many countries, consumer rights were extended to such a degree that it hurt business.

These regulations, pro-business commentators argue, not only harmed the large firms but made everyone else worse off by reducing the overall size of the pie to be shared out. By limiting the ability of firms to experiment with new ways of doing business and enter new areas, these regulations slowed down the growth of overall productivity. In the end, however, the folly of this anti-business logic became too obvious, the argument goes. As a result, since the 1970s, countries from all around the world have come to accept that what is good for business is good for the national economy and have adopted a pro-business policy stance. Even communist countries have given up their attempts to stifle the private sector since the 1990s. Need we ponder upon this issue any more?

How the mighty has fallen

Five decades after Mr Wilson's remark, in the summer of 2009, GM went bankrupt. Notwithstanding its well-known aversion to state ownership, the US government took over the company and, after an extensive restructuring, launched it as a new entity. In the process, it spent a staggering $57.6 billion of taxpayers' money.

It may be argued that the rescue was in the American national interest. Letting a company of GM's size and inter-linkages collapse suddenly would have had huge negative ripple effects on jobs and demand (e.g., fall in consumer demand from unemployed GM workers, evaporation of GM's demand for products from its supplier firms), aggravating the financial crisis that was unfolding in the country at the time. The US government chose the lesser of the two evils, on behalf of the taxpayers. What was good for GM was still good for the United States, it may be argued, even though it was not a very good thing in absolute terms.

However, that does not mean that we should not question how GM got into that situation in the first place. When faced with stiff competition from imports from Germany, Japan and then Korea from the 1960s, GM did not respond in the most natural, if difficult, way it should have – producing better cars than those of its competitors. Instead, it tried to take the easy way out.

First, it blamed 'dumping' and other unfair trade practices by its competitors and got the US government to impose import quotas on foreign, especially Japanese, cars and force open competitors' home markets. In the 1990s, when these measures proved insufficient to halt its decline, it had tried to make up for its failings in car-making by developing its financial arm, GMAC (General Motors Acceptance Corporation). GMAC moved beyond its traditional function of financing car purchases and started conducting financial transactions for their own sake. GMAC itself proved quite successful – in 2004, for example, 80 per cent of GM's profit came from GMAC (*see Thing 22*).[1] But that could not really hide the fundamental problem – that the company could not make good cars at competitive prices. Around the same time, the company tried to shortcut the need for investing in the development of better technologies by buying up smaller foreign competitors (such as Saab of Sweden and Daewoo of Korea), but these were nowhere near enough to revive the company's former technological superiority. In other words, in the last four decades, GM has tried everything to halt its decline except making better cars because trying to make better cars itself was, well, too much trouble.

Obviously, all these decisions may have been best from GM's point of view at the time when they were made – after all, they allowed the company to survive for a few more decades with the least effort – but they have *not* been good for the rest of the United States. The huge bill that American taxpayers have been landed with through the rescue package is the ultimate proof of that, but along the way, the rest of the US could have done better, had GM been forced to invest in the technologies and machines needed to build better cars, instead of lobbying for protection, buying up smaller competitors and turning itself into a financial company.

More importantly, all those actions that have enabled GM to get out of difficulties with the least effort have ultimately not been good even for GM itself – unless you equate GM with its managers and a constantly changing group of shareholders. These managers drew absurdly high salaries by delivering higher profits by not investing for productivity growth while squeezing other weaker 'stakeholders' – their workers, supplier firms and the employees of those firms. They bought the acquiescence of shareholders by offering them dividends and share buybacks to such an extent that the company's future was jeopardized. The shareholders did not mind, and indeed many of them encouraged such practices, because most of them were floating shareholders who were not really concerned with the long-term future of the company because they could leave at a moment's notice (*see Thing 2*).

The story of GM teaches us some salutary lessons about the potential conflicts between corporate and national interests – what is good for a company, however important it may be, may not be good for the country. Moreover, it highlights the conflicts between different stakeholders that make up the firm – what is good for some stakeholders of a company, such as managers and short-term shareholders, may not be good for others, such as workers and suppliers. Ultimately, it also tells us that what is good for a company in the short run may not even be good for it in the long run – what is good for GM today may not be good for GM tomorrow.

Now, some readers, even ones who were already persuaded by this argument, may still wonder whether the US is just an exception that proves the rule. Under-regulation may be a problem for the US, but in most other countries, isn't the problem over-regulation?

299 permits

In the early 1990s, the Hong Kong-based English-language business magazine, *Far Eastern Economic Review*, ran a special issue on South Korea. In one article the magazine expressed puzzlement at the fact that, even though it needed up to 299 permits from up to 199 agencies to open a factory in the country, South Korea had grown at over 6 per cent in per capita terms for the previous three decades. How was this possible? How can a country with such an oppressive regulatory regime grow so fast?

Before trying to make sense of this puzzle, I must point out that it was not just Korea before the 1990s in which seemingly onerous regulations coexisted with a vibrant economy. The situation was similar in Japan and Taiwan throughout their 'miracle' years between the 1950s and the 1980s. The Chinese economy has been heavily regulated in a similar manner during the last three decades of rapid growth. In contrast, over the last three decades, many developing countries in Latin America and Sub-Saharan

Africa have de-regulated their economies in the hope that it would stimulate business activities and accelerate their growth. However, puzzlingly, since the 1980s, they have grown far more slowly than in the 1960s and 70s, when they were supposedly held back by excessive regulations (*see Things 7 and 11*).

The first explanation for the puzzle is that, strange as it may seem to most people without business experience, businesspeople will get 299 permits (with some circumvented along the way with bribes, if they can get away with it), if there is enough money to be made at the end of the process. So, in a country that is growing fast and where good business opportunities are cropping up all the time, even the hassle of acquiring 299 permits would not deter business people from opening a new line of business. In contrast, if there is little money to be made at the end of the process, even twenty-nine permits may look too onerous.

More importantly, the reason why some countries that have heavily regulated business have done economically well is that many regulations are actually good for business.

Sometimes regulations help business by limiting the ability of firms to engage in activities that bring them greater profits in the short run but ultimately destroy the common resource that all business firms need. For example, regulating the intensity of fish farming may reduce the profits of individual fish farms but help the fish-farming industry as a whole by preserving the quality of water that all the fish farms have to use. For another example, it may be in the interest of individual firms to employ children and lower their wage bills. However, a widespread use of child labour will lower the quality of the labour force in the longer run by stunting the physical and mental development of children. In such a case, child labour regulation can actually benefit the entire business sector in the long run. For yet another example, individual banks may benefit from lending more aggressively. But when all of them do the same, they may all suffer in the end, as such lending behaviours may increase the chance of systemic collapse, as we have seen in the 2008 global financial crisis. Restricting what banks can do, then, may actually help them in the long run, even if it does not immediately benefit them (*see Thing 22*).

It is not just that regulation can help firms by preventing them from undermining the basis of their long-term sustainability. Sometimes, regulations can help businesses by forcing firms to do things that may not be in their individual interests but raise their collective productivity in the long run. For example, firms often do not invest enough in training their workers. This is because they are worried about their workers being poached by other firms 'free-riding' on their training efforts. In such a situation, the government imposing a requirement for worker training on all firms could actually raise the quality of the labour force, thereby ultimately benefiting all firms. For another example, in a developing country that needs to import technologies from abroad, the government can help business achieve higher productivity in the long run by banning the importation of overly obsolete foreign technologies that may enable their importers to undermine competitors in the short run but will lock them into dead-end technologies.

Karl Marx described the government restriction of business freedom for the sake of the collective interest of the capitalist class as it acting as 'the executive committee of the bourgeoisie'. But you don't need to be a Marxist to see that regulations restricting freedom for individual firms may promote the collective interest of the entire business sector, not to speak of the nation as a whole. In other words, there are many regulations that are pro- rather than anti-business. Many regulations help preserve the common-pool resources that all firms share, while others help business by making firms do things that raise their collective productivity in the long run. Only when we recognize this will we be able to see that what matters is not the absolute amount of regulation, but the aims and contents of those regulations.

Thing 19
Despite the fall of communism, we are still living in planned economies

What they tell you

The limits of economic planning have been resoundingly demonstrated by the fall of communism. In complex modern economies, planning is neither possible nor desirable. Only decentralized decisions through the market mechanism, based on individuals and firms being always on the lookout for a profitable opportunity, are capable of sustaining a complex modern economy. We should do away with the delusion that we can plan anything in this complex and ever-changing world. The less planning there is, the better.

What they don't tell you

Capitalist economies are in large part planned. Governments in capitalist economies practise planning too, albeit on a more limited basis than under communist central planning. All of them finance a significant share of investment in R&D and infrastructure. Most of them plan a significant chunk of the economy through the planning of the activities of state-owned enterprises. Many capitalist governments plan the future shape of individual industrial sectors through sectoral industrial policy or even that of the national economy through indicative planning. More importantly, modern capitalist economies are made up of large, hierarchical corporations that plan their activities in great detail, even across national borders. Therefore, the question is not whether you plan or not. It is about planning the right things at the right levels.

Upper Volta with rockets

In the 1970s, many Western diplomats called the Soviet Union 'Upper Volta with rockets'. What an insult – that is, to Upper Volta (renamed Burkina Faso in 1984), which was being branded the quintessential poor country, when it wasn't even near the bottom of the world poverty league. The nickname, however, succinctly summarized what was wrong with the Soviet economy.

Here was a country that could send men into space but had people queuing up for basic foodstuffs such as bread and sugar. The country had no problem churning out intercontinental ballistic missiles and nuclear submarines, but could not manufacture a decent TV. It is reported that in the 1980s the second-biggest cause of fires in Moscow was – believe it or not – exploding TVs. The top Russian scientists were as inventive as their counterparts in capitalist countries, but the rest of the country did not seem able to live up to the same standard. What was going on?

In pursuit of the communist vision of a classless society based on collective ownership of the 'means of production' (e.g., machines, factory buildings, roads), the Soviet Union and its communist allies aimed for full employment and a high degree of equality. Since no one was allowed to own any means of production, virtually all enterprises were run by professional managers (with minor exceptions such as small restaurants and hairdressers), preventing the emergence of visionary entrepreneurs, like Henry Ford or Bill Gates. Given the political commitment to high equality, there was a clear cap on how much a business manager, however successful, could get. This meant that there was only a limited incentive for business managers to turn the advanced technologies that the system was clearly capable of producing into products that consumers actually wanted. The policy of full employment at all costs meant that managers could not use the ultimate threat – that of sacking – to discipline workers. This contributed to sloppy work and absenteeism; when he was trying to reform the Soviet economy, Gorbachev frequently spoke of the problem of labour discipline.

Of course, all this did not mean that no one in communist countries was motivated to work hard or to run a good business. Even in capitalist economies, we don't do things just for the money (*see Thing 5*), but communist countries relied, with some success, much more on the less selfish sides of human nature. Especially in the early days of communism, there was a lot of idealism about building a new society. In the Soviet Union, there was also a huge surge of patriotism during and shortly after the Second World War. In all communist countries there were many dedicated managers and workers who did things well out of professionalism and self-respect. Moreover, by the 1960s, the ideal egalitarianism of early communism had given way to realism and performance-related pay had become the norm, mitigating (although by no means eliminating) the incentive problem.

Despite this, the system still failed to function well because of the inefficiency of the communist central planning system, which was supposed to be a more efficient alternative to the market system.

The communist justification of central planning was based on some quite sound logic. Karl Marx and his followers argued that the fundamental problem with capitalism was the contradiction between the social nature of the production process and the private nature of ownership of the means of production. With economic development – or the development of productive forces, in Marxist jargon – the division of labour between firms develops further and as a result the firms become increasingly more dependent on each other – or the social nature of the production process is intensified. However, despite the growing interdependence among firms, the Marxists argued, ownership of the firms firmly remains in separate private hands, making it impossible to coordinate the actions of those interdependent firms. Of course, price changes ensure that there is some *ex post* coordination of firm decisions, but its extent is limited and the imbalance between demand and supply, created by such (in non-Marxist terms) 'coordination failures', accumulates into periodic economic crises. During an economic crisis, the argument went, a lot of valuable resources are wasted. Many unsold products are thrown away, machines that used to produce now-unwanted things are scrapped, and workers who are capable and willing to work are laid off due to the lack of demand. With the development of capitalism, the Marxists predicted, this systemic contradiction would become larger and consequently economic crises would become more and more violent, finally bringing the whole system down.

In contrast, under central planning, the Marxist argued, all means of production are owned by the whole of society and as a result the activities of interdependent production units can be coordinated *ex ante* through a unified plan. As any potential coordination failure is resolved before it happens, the economy does not have to go through those periodic crises in order to balance supply and demand. Under central planning, the economy will produce only exactly what is needed. No resource will lie idle at any time, since there will be no economic crisis. Therefore, the central planning system, it was argued, will manage the economy much more efficiently than the market system.

That, at least, was the theory. Unfortunately, central planning did not work very well in practice. The main problem was that of complexity. The Marxists may have been right in thinking that the development in productive forces, by increasing interdependence among different segments of capital, makes it more *necessary* to plan centrally. However, they failed to recognize that it also makes the economy more complex, making it more *difficult* to plan centrally.

Central planning worked well when the targets were relatively simple and clear, as seen in the success of early Soviet industrialization, where the main task was to produce a relatively small number of key products in large quantities (steel, tractors, wheat, potatoes, etc.). However, as the economy developed, central planning became increasingly difficult, with a growing number of (actual and potential) diverse products. Of course, with economic development, the ability to plan also increased thanks to improvements in managerial skills, mathematical techniques of planning and computers. However, the increase in the ability to plan was not sufficient to deal with the increase in the complexity of the economy.

One obvious solution was to limit the variety of products, but that created huge consumer dissatisfaction. Moreover, even with reduced varieties, the economy was still too complex to plan. Many unwanted things were produced and remained unsold, while there were shortages of other things, resulting in the ubiquitous queues. By the time communism started unravelling in the 1980s, there was so much cynicism about the system that was increasingly incapable of delivering its promises that the joke was that in the communist countries, 'we pretend to work and they pretend to pay us'.

No wonder central planning was abandoned across the board when the ruling communist parties were ousted across the Soviet bloc, following the fall of the Berlin Wall. Even countries such as China and Vietnam, which ostensibly maintained communism, have gradually abandoned central planning, although their states still hold high degrees of control over the economy. So, we all now live in market economies (well, unless you live in North Korea or Cuba). Planning is gone. Or is it?

There is planning and there is planning

The fact that communism has disappeared for all practical purposes does not mean that planning has ceased to exist. Governments in capitalist economies also plan, albeit not in the same comprehensive way that the central planning authorities in communist countries did.

Even in a capitalist economy, there are situations – a war, for example – in which central planning is more effective. For example, during the Second World War, the economies of the major capitalist belligerents, the US, the UK and Germany, were all centrally planned in everything but name.

But, more importantly, many capitalist countries have successfully used what is known as 'indicative planning'. This is planning that involves the government in a capitalist country setting some broad targets concerning key economic variables (e.g., investments in strategic industries, infrastructure development, exports) and working with, not against, the private sector to achieve them. Unlike under central planning, these targets are not legally binding; hence the adjective 'indicative'. However, the government will do its best to achieve them by mobilizing various carrots (e.g., subsidies, granting of monopoly rights) and sticks (e.g., regulations, influence through state-owned banks) at its disposal.

France had great success in promoting investment and technological innovation through indicative planning in the 1950s and 60s, thereby overtaking the British economy as Europe's second industrial power. Other European countries, such as

Finland, Norway and Austria, also successfully used indicative planning to upgrade their economies between the 1950s and the 1970s. The East Asian miracle economies of Japan, Korea and Taiwan used indicative planning too between the 1950s and the 1980s. This is not to say that all indicative planning exercises have been successful; in India, for example, it has not. Nevertheless, the European and East Asian examples show that planning in certain forms is not incompatible with capitalism and may even promote capitalist development very well.

Moreover, even when they do not explicitly plan the entire economy, even in an indicative way, governments in most capitalist economies make and implement plans for certain key activities, which can have economy-wide implications (*see Thing 12*).

Most capitalist governments plan and shape the future of some key industries through what is known as 'sectoral industrial policy'. The European and East Asian countries which practised indicative planning all also practised active sectoral industrial policy. Even countries that have not practised indicative planning, such as Sweden and Germany, have practised sectoral industrial policy.

In most capitalist countries, the government owns, and often also operates, a sizeable chunk of the national economy through state-owned enterprises (SOEs). SOEs are frequently found in the key infrastructure sectors (e.g., railways, roads, ports, airports) or essential services (e.g., water, electricity, postal service), but also exist in manufacturing or finance (more stories about SOEs can be found in the chapter 'Man Exploits Man' of my book *Bad Samaritans*). The share of SOEs in national output could be as high as 20 per cent-plus, in the case of Singapore, or as low as 1 per cent, in the case of the US, but the international average is around 10 per cent. As the government plans the activities of SOEs, this means that a significant part of the average capitalist economy is directly planned. When we consider the fact that SOEs usually operate in sectors with disproportionate impacts on the rest of the economy, the indirect effect of planning through SOEs is even greater than what is suggested by the share of SOEs in national output.

Moreover, in all capitalist economies, the government plans the national technological future by funding a very high proportion (20–50 per cent) of research and development. Interestingly, the US is one of the most planned capitalist economies in this regard. Between the 1950s and the 1980s, the share of government funding in total R&D in the supposedly free-market US accounted for, depending on the year, between 47 per cent and 65 per cent, as against around 20 per cent in Japan and Korea and less than 40 per cent in several European countries (e.g., Belgium, Finland, Germany, Sweden).[1] The ratio has come down since the 1990s, as military R&D funding was reduced with the end of the Cold War. However, even so, the share of government in R&D in the US is still higher than in many other capitalist economies. It is notable that most of the industries where the US has an international technological lead are the industries that have been receiving major government R&D funding through military programmes (e.g., computers, semiconductors, aircraft) and health projects (e.g., pharmaceuticals, biotechnology).

Of course, since the 1980s the extent of government planning in most capitalist economies has declined, not least because of the rise of pro-market ideology during this period. Indicative planning has been phased out in most countries, including in the ones where it had been successful. In many, although not all, countries, privatization has resulted in a falling share of SOEs in national output and investment. The share of government funding in total R&D funding has also fallen in virtually all capitalist countries, although not by very much in most cases. However, I would argue, despite the relative decline of government planning in the recent period, there is still extensive, and increasing, planning in the capitalist economies. Why do I say that?

To plan or not to plan – that is not *the question*

Suppose that a new CEO arrived in a company and said: 'I am a great believer in market forces. In this fast-changing world, we should not have a fixed strategy and should maintain maximum possible flexibility. So, from now on, everyone in this company is going to be guided by ever-changing market prices, and not by some rigid plan.' What do you think would happen? Would his employees welcome a leader with a vision fit for the twenty-first century? Would the shareholders applaud his market-friendly approach and award him with a pay rise?

He wouldn't last a week. People would say he does not have leadership qualities. He would be accused of lacking the 'vision thing' (as George Bush Sr once put it). The top decision-maker, it would be pointed out, should be willing to shape the future of the company, rather than letting it just happen. Blindly following market signals, they would say, is not how you run a business.

People would expect a new CEO to say something like: 'This is where our company is today. That is where I want to take it in ten years' time. In order to get there, we will develop new industries A, B and C, while winding down D and E. Our subsidiary in industry D will be sold off. We will shut down our subsidiary in industry E at home, but some production may be shifted to China. In order to develop our subsidiary in industry A, we will have to cross-subsidize it with the profits from existing businesses. In order to establish a presence in industry B, we have to go into strategic alliance with Kaisha Corporation of Japan, which may involve supplying it with some inputs that we produce at below-market prices. In order to expand our business in industry C, we will need to increase our R&D investment in the next five years. All this may mean the company as a whole making losses in the foreseeable future. If that is the case, so be it. Because that is the price we have to pay in order to have a brighter future.' In other words, a CEO is expected to be a 'man (or a woman) with a *plan*'.

Businesses plan their activities – often down to the last detail. Indeed, that is where Marx got the idea of centrally planning the whole economy. When he talked about planning, there was in fact no real-life government that was practising planning. At the time, only firms planned. What Marx predicted was that the 'rational' planning approach of the capitalist firms would eventually prove superior to the wasteful anarchy of the market and thus eventually be extended to the whole economy. To be sure, he criticized planning within the firm as despotism by capitalists, but he believed that, once private property was abolished and the capitalists eliminated, the rational elements of such despotism could be isolated and harnessed for the social good.

With the development of capitalism, more and more areas of the economy have become dominated by large corporations. This means that the area of the capitalist economy that is covered by planning has in fact grown. To give you a concrete example, these days, depending on the estimate, between one third and one half of international trade consists of transfers among different units within transnational corporations.

Herbert Simon, the 1978 Nobel laureate in economics who was a pioneer of the study of business organizations (*see Thing 16*), put this point succinctly in 1991 in 'Organisations and Markets', one of the last articles he wrote. If a Martian, with no preconceptions, came to Earth and observed our economy, Simon mused, would he conclude that Earthlings live in a *market economy*? No, Simon said, he would almost certainly have concluded that Earthlings live in an *organizational economy* in the sense that the bulk of earth's economic activities is coordinated within the boundaries of firms (organizations), rather than through market transactions between those firms. If firms were represented by green and markets by red, Simon argued, the Martian would see 'large green areas interconnected by red lines', rather than 'a network of red lines connecting green spots'.[2] And we think planning is dead.

Simon did not talk much about government planning, but if we add government planning, modern capitalist economies are even more planned than his Martian example suggests. Between the planning that is going on within corporations and various types of planning by the government, modern capitalist economies are planned to a very high degree. One interesting point that follows from these observations is that rich countries are more planned than poor countries, owing to the more widespread existence of large corporations and often more pervasive (albeit often less visible, on account of its more subtle approach) presence of the government.

The question, then, is not whether to plan or not. It is what the appropriate levels and forms of planning are for different activities. The prejudice against planning, while understandable given the failures of communist central planning, makes us misunderstand the true nature of the modern economy in which government policy, corporate planning and market relationships are all vital and interact in a complex way. Without markets we will end up with the inefficiencies of the Soviet system. However, thinking that we can live by the market alone is like believing that we can live by eating only salt, because salt is vital for our survival.

Thing 20
Equality of opportunity may not be fair

What they tell you

Many people get upset by inequality. However, there is equality and there is equality. When you reward people the same way regardless of their efforts and achievements, the more talented and the harder-working lose the incentive to perform. This is equality of outcome. It's a bad idea, as proven by the fall of communism. The equality we seek should be the equality of opportunity. For example, it was not only unjust but also inefficient for a black student in apartheid South Africa not to be able to go to better, 'white', universities, even if he was a better student. People should be given equal opportunities. However, it is equally unjust and inefficient to introduce affirmative action and begin to admit students of lower quality simply because they are black or from a deprived background. In trying to equalize outcomes, we not only misallocate talents but also penalize those who have the best talent and make the greatest efforts.

What they don't tell you

Equality of opportunity is the starting point for a fair society. But it's not enough. Of course, individuals should be rewarded for better performance, but the question is whether they are actually competing under the same conditions as their competitors. If a child does not perform well in school because he is hungry and cannot concentrate in class, it cannot be said that the child does not do well because he is inherently less capable. Fair competition can be achieved only when the child is given enough food – at home through family income support and at school through a free school meals programme. Unless there is some equality of outcome (i.e., the incomes of all the parents are above a certain minimum threshold, allowing their children not to go hungry), equal opportunities (i.e., free schooling) are not truly meaningful.

More Catholic than the Pope?

In Latin America, people frequently use the expression that some-one is 'more Catholic than the Pope' (*mas Papista que el Papa*). This refers to the tendency of societies in the intellectual periphery to apply doctrines – religious, economic and social – more rigidly than do their source countries.

Koreans, my own people, are probably the world champions at being more Catholic than the Pope (not quite in the literal sense – only around 10 per cent of them are Catholics). Korea is not exactly a small country. The combined population of North and South Koreas, which for nearly a millennium until 1945 used to be one country, is about 70 million today. But it happens to be bang in the middle of a zone where the interests of the giants – China, Japan, Russia and the US – clash. So we have become very adept at adopting the ideology of one of the big boys and being more orthodox about it than he is. When we do commu-nism (up in North Korea), we are more communist than the Russians. When we practised Japanese-style state capitalism (in the South) between the 1960s and the 1980s, we were more state-capitalist than the Japanese. Now that we have switched over to US-style capitalism, we lecture the Americans on the virtues of free trade and shame them by deregulating financial and labour markets left, right and centre.

So it was natural that until the nineteenth century, when we were under the Chinese sphere of influence, we were more Confucian than the Chinese. Confucianism, for those who are not familiar with it, is a cultural system based on the teachings of Confucius – the Latinized name of the Chinese political philosopher, Kong Tze, who lived in the fifth century BC. Today, having seen the economic successes of some Confucian countries, many people think it is a culture particularly well suited to economic development, but it was a typical feudal ideology until it came to be adapted to the requirements of modern capitalism in the second half of the twentieth century.[1]

Like most other feudal ideologies, Confucianism espoused a rigid social hierarchy which restricted people's choice of occupation according to their births. This prevented talented men from lower castes from rising above their station. In Confucianism, there was a crucial divide between the farmers (who were considered to be the bedrock of society) and other working classes. The sons of farmers could sit for the (incredibly difficult) government civil service examination and get incorporated into the ruling class, although this happened rarely in practice, while the sons of artisans and merchants were not even permitted to sit for the exam, however clever they might be.

China, being the birthplace of Confucianism, had the confidence to take a more pragmatic approach in interpreting the classical doctrines and allowed people from merchant and artisanal classes to sit for the civil service examination. Korea – being more Confucian than Confucius – adamantly stuck to this doctrine and refused to hire talented people simply because they were born to the 'wrong' parents. It was only after our liberation from Japanese colonial rule (1910–45) that the traditional caste system was fully abolished and Korea became a country where birth does not set a ceiling to individual achievement (although the prejudice against artisans – engineers in modern terms – and merchants – business managers in modern terms – lingered on for another few decades until economic development made these attractive professions).

Obviously feudal Korea was not alone in refusing to give people equality of opportunity. European feudal societies operated with similar systems, and in India the caste system still operates, albeit informally. Nor was it only along the caste lines that people were refused equality of opportunity. Until the Second World War, most societies refused to let women be elected to public office; in fact they were refused political citizenship altogether and not even allowed to vote. Until recently, many countries used to restrict people's access to education and jobs along racial lines. In the late nineteenth and the early twentieth centuries, the USA prohibited the immigration of 'undesirable' races, especially Asians. South Africa, during the apartheid regime, had separate universities for whites and for the rest (the 'coloureds' and the blacks), which were very poorly funded.

So it has not been long since the majority of the world emerged from a situation where people were banned from self-advancement due to their race, gender or caste. Equality of opportunity is something to be highly cherished.

Markets liberate?

Many of the formal rules restricting equality of opportunity have been abolished in the last few generations. This was in large part because of political struggles by the discriminated against – such as the Chartist demand for universal (male) suffrage in Britain in the mid nineteenth century, the Civil Rights movement by blacks in the US in the 1960s, the anti-apartheid struggle in South Africa in the second half of the twentieth century and the fight by low caste people in India today. Without these and countless other campaigns by women, oppressed races and lower caste people, we would still be living in a world where restricting people's rights according to 'birth lottery' would be considered natural.

In this struggle against inequality of opportunity, the market has been a great help. When only efficiency ensures survival, free-market economists point out, there is no room for racial or political prejudices to creep into market transactions. Milton Friedman put it succinctly in his *Capitalism and Freedom*: 'No one who buys bread knows whether the wheat from which it was made was grown by a Communist or a Republican . . . by a Negro or a white.' Therefore, Friedman argued, the market will eventually drive racism out, or at least reduce it significantly, because those racist employers insisting on employing only white people would be driven out by more open-minded ones who hire the best available talents, regardless of race.

This point is powerfully illustrated by the fact that even the notoriously racist apartheid regime in South Africa had to designate the Japanese 'honorary whites'. There was no way the Japanese executives running the local Toyota and Nissan factories could go and live in townships like Soweto, where non-whites were forced to live under apartheid law. Therefore, the white-supremacist South Africans had to swallow their pride and pretend that the Japanese were whites, if they wanted to drive around in Japanese cars. That is the power of the market.

The power of the market as a 'leveller' is more widespread than we think. As the British writer Alan Bennett's play-turned-movie, *History Boys*, so poignantly shows, students from disadvantaged groups tend to lack intellectual and social confidence and are thus disadvantaged in getting into elite universities – and by extension, better-paying jobs. Obviously, universities do not have to respond to market pressures as quickly as firms have to. However, if some university consistently discriminated against ethnic minorities or working-class kids and took in only people from the 'right' backgrounds despite their inferior quality, potential employers would come to prefer the graduates from non-racist universities. The narrow-minded university, if it is to recruit the best possible students, would have to abandon its prejudices sooner or later.

Given all this, it is tempting to argue that, once you ensure equality of opportunity, free from any formal discrimination other than according to merit, the market will eliminate any residual prejudices through the competitive mechanism. However, this is only the start. A lot more has to be done to build a genuinely fair society.

The end of apartheid and the cappuccino society

While there are still too many people with prejudices against certain races, poor people, lower castes and women, today few would openly object to the principle of equality of opportunity. But at this point, opinions divide sharply. Some argue that equality should end with that of opportunity. Others, including myself, believe that it is not enough to have mere formal equality of opportunity.

Free-market economists warn that, if we try to equalize the outcomes of people's actions and not just their opportunities to take certain actions, that will create huge disincentives against hard work and innovation. Would you work hard if you knew that, whatever you do, you will get paid the same as the next guy who is goofing off? Isn't that exactly why the Chinese agricultural communes under Mao Zedong were such failures? If you tax the rich disproportionately and use the proceeds to finance the welfare state, won't the rich lose the incentive to create wealth, while the poor lose the incentive to work, as they are guaranteed a minimum standard of living whether they work hard or not – or whether they work at all? (*See Thing 21*.) This way, free-market economists argue, everyone becomes worse off by the attempt to reduce inequality of outcome (*see Thing 13*).

It is absolutely true that excessive attempts to equalize outcomes – say, the Maoist commune, where there was virtually no link between someone's effort and the reward that she got – will have an adverse impact on people's work effort. It is also unfair. But I believe that a certain degree of equalization of outcomes is necessary, if we are to build a genuinely fair society.

The point is that, in order to benefit from the equal opportunities provided to them, people require the capabilities to make use of them. It is no use that black South Africans now have the same opportunities as whites to get a highly paid job, if they do not have the education to qualify for those jobs. It is no good that blacks now can enter better (former white-only) universities, if they still have to attend poorly funded schools with underqualified teachers, some of whom can barely read and write themselves.

For most black kids in South Africa, the newly acquired equality of opportunity to enter good universities does not mean that they can attend such universities. Their schools are still poor and poorly run. It is not as if their underqualified teachers have suddenly become smart with the end of apartheid. Their parents are still unemployed (even the official unemployment rate, which vastly underestimates true unemployment in a developing country, is, at 26–28 per cent, one of the highest in the world). For them, the right to enter better universities is pie in the sky. For this reason, post-apartheid South Africa has turned into what some South Africans call a 'cappuccino society': a mass of brown at the bottom, a thin layer of white froth above it, and a sprinkling of cocoa at the top.

Now, free-market economists will tell you that those who do not have the education, the determination and the entrepreneurial energy to take advantage of market opportunities have only themselves to blame. Why should people who have worked hard and obtained a university degree against all odds be rewarded in the same way as someone, coming from the same poor background, who goes into a life of petty crime?

This argument is correct. We cannot, and should not, explain someone's performance only by the environment in which he has grown up. Individuals do have responsibilities for what they have made out of their lives.

However, while correct, this argument is only part of the story. Individuals are not born into a vacuum. The socio-economic environment they operate in puts serious restrictions on what they can do. Or even on what they *want* to do. Your environment can make you give up certain things even without trying. For example, many academically talented British working-class children do not even try to go to universities because universities are 'not for them'. This attitude is slowly changing, but I still remember seeing a BBC documentary in the late 1980s in which an old miner and his wife were criticizing one of their sons, who had gone to a university and become a teacher, as a 'class traitor'.

While it is silly to blame everything on the socio-economic environment, it is equally unacceptable to believe that people can achieve anything if they only 'believe in themselves' and try hard enough, as Hollywood movies love to tell you. Equality of opportunity is meaningless for those who do not have the capabilities to take advantage of it.

The curious case of Alejandro Toledo

Today, no country deliberately keeps poor children from going to school, but many children in poor countries cannot go to school because they do not have the money to pay for the tuition. Moreover, even in countries with free public education, poor children are bound to perform poorly in school, whatever their innate ability may be. Some of them go hungry at home and also skip lunch at school. This makes it impossible for them to concentrate, with predictable results for their academic performance. In extreme cases, their intellectual development may have already been stunted because of a lack of food in their early years. These kids may also suffer more frequently from illness, which makes them skip school more often. If their parents are illiterate and/or have to work long hours, children will have no one to help them with their homework, while middle-class children will be helped by their parents and rich kids may have private tutors. Helped or not, they may not even have enough time for homework, if they have to take care of younger siblings or tend the family goats.

Given all this, as far as we accept that we should not punish children for having poor parents, we should take action to ensure that all children have some minimum amounts of food, healthcare and help with their homework. Much of this can be provided through public policy, as happens in some countries – free school lunches, vaccinations, basic health checks and some help with homework after school by teachers or tutors hired by the school. However, some of this still needs to be provided at home. Schools can provide only so much.

This means that there has to be some minimum equality of outcome in terms of parental income, if poor children are to have anything approaching a fair chance. Without this, even free schooling, free school meals, free vaccinations, and so on, cannot provide real equality of opportunity for children.

Even in adult life, there has to be some equality of outcome. It is well known that, once someone has been unemployed for a long time, it becomes extremely difficult for that person to get back into the labour market. But whether someone loses her job is not entirely determined by the person's 'worth'. For example, many people lose their jobs because they chose to join an industry that looked like a good prospect when they first started but since has been hit hard by a sudden increase in foreign competition. Few American steelworkers or British shipbuilding workers who joined their industries in the 1960s, or for that matter anyone else, could have predicted that by the early 1990s their industries would be virtually wiped out by Japanese and Korean competition. Is it really fair that these people have to suffer disproportionately and be consigned to the scrapheap of history?

Of course, in an idealized free market, this should not be a problem because the American steelworkers and the British shipbuilders can get jobs in expanding industries. But how many former American steelworkers do you know who have become computer engineers or former British shipbuilders who have turned themselves into investment bankers? Such conversion rarely, if ever, happens.

A more equitable approach would have been to help the displaced workers find a new career through decent unemployment benefits, health insurance even when out of a job, retraining schemes and help with job searches, as they do particularly well in Scandinavian countries. As I discuss elsewhere in the book (*see Thing 21*), this can also be a more productive approach for the economy as a whole.

Yes, in theory, a shoeshine boy from a poor provincial town in Peru can go to Stanford and do a PhD, as the former Peruvian President Alejandro Toledo has done, but for one Toledo we have millions of Peruvian children who did not even make it to high school. Of course, we could argue that all those millions of poor Peruvian children are lazy good-for-nothings, since Mr Toledo has proven that they too could have gone to Stanford if they had tried hard enough. But I think it is much more plausible to say that Mr Toledo is the exception. Without some equality of outcome (of parental income), poor people cannot take full advantage of equality of opportunity.

Indeed, international comparison of social mobility corroborates this reasoning. According to a careful study by a group of researchers in Scandinavia and the UK, the Scandinavian countries have higher social mobility than the UK, which in turn has higher mobility than the US.[2] It is no coincidence that the stronger the welfare state, the higher the mobility. Particularly in the case of the US, the fact that low overall mobility is largely accounted for by low mobility at the bottom suggests that it is the lack of a basic income guarantee that is preventing poor kids from making use of the equality of opportunity.

Excessive equalization of outcomes is harmful, although what exactly is excessive is debatable. Nevertheless, equality of opportunity is not enough. Unless we create an environment where everyone is guaranteed some minimum capabilities through some guarantee of minimum income, education and healthcare, we cannot say that we have fair competition. When some people have to run a 100 metre race with sandbags on their legs, the fact that no one is allowed to have a head start does not make the race fair. Equality of opportunity is absolutely necessary but not sufficient in building a genuinely fair and efficient society.

Thing 21
Big government makes people more open to change

What they tell you

Big government is bad for the economy. The welfare state has emerged because of the desire by the poor to have an easier life by making the rich pay for the costs of adjustments that are constantly demanded by market forces. When the rich are taxed to pay for unemployment insurance, healthcare and other welfare measures for the poor, this not only makes the poor lazy and deprives the rich of an incentive to create wealth, it also makes the economy less dynamic. With the protection of the welfare state, people do not feel the need to adjust to new market realities, thereby delaying the changes in their professions and working patterns that are needed for dynamic economic adjustments. We don't even have to invoke the failures of the communist economies. Just look at the lack of dynamism in Europe with its bloated welfare state, compared to the vitality of the US.

What they don't tell you

A well-designed welfare state can actually encourage people to take chances with their jobs and be more, not less, open to changes. This is one reason why there is less demand for trade protectionism in Europe than in the US. Europeans know that, even if their industries shut down due to foreign competition, they will be able to protect their living standards (through unemployment benefits) and get re-trained for another job (with government subsidies), whereas Americans know that losing their current jobs may mean a huge fall in their living standards and may even be the end of their productive lives. This is why the European countries with the biggest welfare states, such as Sweden, Norway and Finland, were able to grow faster than, or at least as fast as, the US, even during the post-1990 'American Renaissance'.

The oldest profession in the world?

Representatives of different professions in a Christian country were debating which profession is the oldest.

The medical doctor said: 'What was the first thing that God did with humans? He performed an operation – he made Eve with Adam's rib. The medical profession is the oldest.'

'No, that is not true,' the architect said. 'The first thing he did was to build the world out of chaos. That's what architects do – creating order out of chaos. We are the oldest profession.'

The politician, who was patiently listening, grinned and asked: 'Who created that chaos?'

Medicine may or may not be the oldest profession in the world, but it is one of the most popular all over the world. However, in no country is it more popular than in my native South Korea.

A survey done in 2003 revealed that nearly four out of five 'top-scoring university applicants' (defined as those within the top 2 per cent of the distribution) in the science stream wanted to study medicine. According to unofficial data, during the last few years, even the least competitive of the country's twenty-seven medical departments (at undergraduate level) has become more difficult to enter than the best engineering departments in the country. It cannot get more popular than that.

The interesting thing is that, even though medicine has always been a popular subject in Korea, this kind of hyper-popularity is new. It is basically a twenty-first-century phenomenon. What has changed?

An obvious possibility is that, for whatever reason (e.g., an ageing population), the relative earnings of medical doctors have risen and the youngsters are merely responding to changes in the incentives – the market wants more able doctors, so more and more able people are going into the profession. However, the relative incomes of medical doctors in Korea have been falling, with the continuous increase in their supply. And it is not as if some new government regulation was introduced that makes it difficult to get jobs as engineers or scientists (the obvious alternative choices for would-be medical doctors). So what is really going on?

What is driving this is the dramatic fall in job security over the last decade or so. After the 1997 financial crisis that ended the country's 'miracle years', Korea abandoned its interventionist, paternalistic economic system and embraced market liberalism that emphasizes maximum competition. Job security has been drastically reduced in the name of greater labour market flexibility. Millions of workers have been forced into temporary jobs. Ironically enough, even before the crisis, the country had one of the most flexible labour markets in the rich world, with one of the highest ratios of workers without a permanent contract at around 50 per cent. The recent liberalization has pushed the ratio up even higher – to around 60 per cent. Moreover, even those with permanent contracts now suffer from heightened job insecurity. Before the 1997 crisis, most workers with a permanent contract could expect, *de facto* if not *de jure*, lifetime employment (as many of their Japanese counterparts still do). Not any more. Now older workers in their forties and fifties, even if they have a permanent contract, are encouraged to make way for the younger generation at the earliest possible chance. Companies cannot fire them at will, but we all know that there are ways to let people know that they are not wanted and thus to make them 'voluntarily' leave.

Given this, Korean youngsters are, understandably, playing safe. If they become a scientist or an engineer, they reckon, there is a high chance that they will be out of their jobs in their forties, even if they join major companies like Samsung or Hyundai. This is a horrendous prospect, since the welfare state in Korea is so weak – the smallest among the rich countries (measured by public social spending as a share of GDP).[1] A weak welfare state was not such a big problem before, because many people had lifetime employment. With lifetime employment gone, it has become lethal. Once you lose your job, your living standard falls dramatically and, more importantly, you don't have much of a second chance. Thus, bright Korean youngsters figure, and are advised by their parents, that with a licence to practise medicine they can work until they choose to retire. If the worst comes to the worst, they can set up their own clinics, even if they do not make much money (well, for a medical doctor). No wonder every Korean kid with a brain wants to study medicine (or law – another profession with a licence – if they are in the humanities stream).

Don't get me wrong. I revere medical doctors. I owe my life to them – I have had a couple of life-saving operations and been cured of countless infections thanks to antibiotics they have prescribed for me. But even I know that it is impossible for 80 per cent of the brainiest Korean kids in the science stream all to be cut out to be medical doctors.

So, one of the freest labour markets in the rich world, that is, the Korean labour market, is spectacularly failing to allocate talent in the most efficient manner. The reason? Heightened job insecurity.

The welfare state is the bankruptcy law for workers

Job security is a thorny issue. Free-market economists believe that any labour market regulation that makes firing more difficult makes the economy less efficient and dynamic. To start with, it weakens the incentive for workers to work hard. On top of that, it discourages wealth creation by making employers more reluctant to hire additional people (for fear of not being able to fire them when necessary).

Labour market regulations are bad enough, it is argued, but the welfare state has made things even worse. By providing unemployment benefits, health insurance, free education and even minimum income support, the welfare state has effectively given everyone a guarantee to be hired by the government – as an 'unemployed worker', if you like – with a minimum wage. Therefore, workers do not have enough incentive to work hard. To make things worse, these welfare states are financed by taxing the rich, reducing their incentives to work hard, create jobs and generate wealth.

Given this, the reasoning goes, a country with a bigger welfare state is going to be less dynamic – its workers are less compelled to work, while its entrepreneurs are less motivated to create wealth.

This argument has been very influential. In the 1970s, a popular explanation of Britain's then lacklustre economic performance was that its welfare state had become bloated and its trade unions overly powerful (which is also partly due to the welfare state, insofar as the latter dulls the threat of unemployment). In this reading of British history, Margaret Thatcher saved Britain by putting unions in their place and reducing the welfare state, even though what actually happened is more complicated. Since the 1990s, this view of the welfare state has become even more popular with the (allegedly) superior growth performance of the US to those of other rich countries with bigger welfare states.[2] When governments in other countries try to cut their welfare spending, they frequently cite Mrs Thatcher's curing of the so-called 'British Disease' or the superior dynamism of the US economy.

But is it true that greater job security and a bigger welfare state make an economy less productive and dynamic?

As in our Korean example, a lack of job security can lead youngsters to make conservative choices with their career, favouring secure jobs in medicine or the law. This may be the right choice for them individually, but it leads to a misallocation of talents and thus reduces economic efficiency and dynamism.

The weaker welfare state in the US has been one important reason why trade protectionism is much stronger there than in Europe, despite a greater acceptance of government intervention in the latter. In Europe (of course, I am ignoring national differences in the details), if your industry declines and you lose your job, it is a big blow but not the end of the world. You will still keep your health insurance and public housing (or housing subsidies), while receiving unemployment benefits (up to 80 per cent of your last pay), government-subsidized retraining and government help in your job search. In contrast, if you are a worker in the US, you'd better make sure you hold on to your current job, if necessary through protectionism, because losing your job means losing almost everything. Unemployment insurance coverage is patchy and of shorter duration than in Europe. There is little public help with retraining and job search. More frighteningly, losing your job means losing your health insurance and probably your home, as there is little public housing or public subsidies for your rent. As a result, worker resistance to any industrial restructuring that involves job cuts is much greater in the US than in Europe. Most US workers are unable to put up an organized resistance, but those who can – unionized workers – will, understandably, do everything they can to preserve the current job distribution.

As the above examples show, greater insecurity may make people work harder, but it makes them work harder in the wrong jobs. All those talented Korean youngsters who could be brilliant scientists and engineers are labouring over human anatomy. Many US workers who could – after appropriate retraining – be working in 'sunrise' industries (e.g., bio-engineering) are grimly holding on to their jobs in 'sunset' industries (e.g., automobiles), only delaying the inevitable.

The point of all the above examples is that, when people know they will have a second (or third or even fourth) chance, they will be much more open to risk-taking when it comes to choosing their first job (as in the Korean example) or letting go of their existing jobs (as in the US– Europe comparison).

Do you find this logic strange? You shouldn't. Because this is exactly the logic behind bankruptcy law, which most people accept as 'obvious'.

Before the mid nineteenth century, no country had a bankruptcy law in the modern sense. What was then called bankruptcy law did not give bankrupt businessmen much protection from creditors while they restructured their business – in the US, 'Chapter 11' now gives such protection for six months. More importantly, it did not give them a second chance, as they were required to pay back all debts, however long it took, unless the creditors gave them a 'discharge' from the duty. This meant that, even if the bankrupt businessman somehow managed to start a new business, he had to use all his new profits to repay the old debts, which hampered the growth of the new business. All this made it extremely risky to start a business venture in the first place.

Over time, people came to realize that the lack of a second chance was hugely discouraging risk-taking by businessmen. Starting with Britain in 1849, countries have introduced modern bankruptcy laws with court-granted protection from creditors during initial restructuring and, more importantly, the power for courts to impose permanent reductions in debts, even against the wishes of the creditors. When combined with institutions like limited liability, which was introduced around the same time (*see Thing 2*), this new bankruptcy law reduced the danger of any business undertaking and thus encouraged risk-taking, which has made modern capitalism possible.

Insofar as it gives workers second chances, we can say that the welfare state is like a bankruptcy law for them. In the same way that bankruptcy laws encourage risk-taking by entrepreneurs, the welfare state encourages workers to be more open to change (and the resulting risks) in their attitudes. Because they know that there is going to be a second chance, people can be bolder in their initial career choices and more open to changing jobs later in their careers.

Countries with bigger governments can grow faster

What about the evidence? What are the relative economic performances of countries that differ in terms of the sizes of their welfare states? As mentioned, the conventional wisdom is that countries with smaller welfare states are more dynamic. However, the evidence does not support this view.

Until the 1980s, the US grew much more slowly than Europe despite the fact that it had a much smaller welfare state. For example, in 1980, public social expenditure as a share of GDP was only 13.3 per cent in the US, compared to 19.9 per cent for the EU's fifteen countries. The ratio was as high as 28.6 per cent in Sweden, 24.1 per cent in the Netherlands and 23 per cent in (West) Germany. Despite this, between 1950 and 1987, the US grew more slowly than any European country. Per capita income grew at 3.8 per cent in Germany, 2.7 per cent in Sweden, 2.5 per cent in the Netherlands and 1.9 per cent in the US during this period. Obviously, the size of the welfare state is only one factor in determining a country's economic performance, but this shows that a large welfare state is not incompatible with high growth.

Even since 1990, when the relative growth performance of the US has improved, some countries with large welfare states have grown faster. For example, between 1990 and 2008, per capita income in the US grew at 1.8 per cent. This is basically the same as in the previous period, but given the slowdown in the European economies, this made the US one of the fastest-growing economies in the 'core' OECD group (that is, excluding the not-fully-rich-yet countries, such as Korea and Turkey).

The interesting thing, however, is that the two fastest-growing economies in the core OECD group during the post-1990 period are Finland (2.6 per cent) and Norway (2.5 per cent), both with a large welfare state. In 2003, the share of public social spending in GDP was 22.5 per cent in Finland and 25.1 per cent in Norway, compared to the OECD average of 20.7 per cent and 16.2 per cent in the US. Sweden, which has literally the largest welfare state in the world (31.3 per cent, or twice as large as that of the US), at 1.8 per cent, recorded a growth rate that was only a shade below the US rate. If you count only the 2000s (2000–8), the growth rates of Sweden (2.4 per cent) and Finland (2.8 per cent) were far superior to that of the US (1.8 per cent). Were the free-market economists right about the detrimental effects of the welfare state on work ethic and the incentives for wealth creation, this kind of thing should not happen.

Of course, by all this I am not suggesting that the welfare state is necessarily good. Like all other institutions, it has its upsides and downsides. Especially if it is based on targeted, rather than universal, programmes (as in the US), it can stigmatize welfare recipients. The welfare state raises people's 'reservation wages' and deters them from taking low-paying jobs with poor working conditions, although whether this is a bad thing is a matter of opinion (personally I think the existence of a large number of 'working poor', as in the US, is as much of a problem as the generally higher unemployment rates we see in Europe). However, if it is well designed, with a view to giving workers a second chance, as it is in Scandinavian countries, it can encourage economic growth by making people be more open to changes and thus making industrial restructuring easier.

We can drive our cars fast only because we have brakes. If cars had no brakes, even the most skilful drivers would not dare to drive at more than 20–30 miles per hour for fear of fatal accidents. In the same way, people can accept the risk of unemployment and the need for occasional re-tooling of their skills more willingly when they know that those experiences are not going to destroy their lives. This is why a bigger government can make people more open to change and thus make the economy more dynamic.

Thing 22
Financial markets need to become less, not more, efficient

What they tell you

The rapid development of the financial markets has enabled us to allocate and reallocate resources swiftly. This is why the US, the UK, Ireland and some other capitalist economies that have liberalized and opened up their financial markets have done so well in the last three decades. Liberal financial markets give an economy the ability to respond quickly to changing opportunities, thereby allowing it to grow faster. True, some of the excesses of the recent period have given finance a bad name, not least in the above-mentioned countries. However, we should not rush into restraining financial markets simply because of this once-in-a-century financial crisis that no one could have predicted, however big it may be, as the efficiency of its financial market is the key to a nation's prosperity.

What they don't tell you

The problem with financial markets today is that they are too efficient. With recent financial 'innovations' that have produced so many new financial instruments, the financial sector has become more efficient in generating profits for itself in the short run. However, as seen in the 2008 global crisis, these new financial assets have made the overall economy, as well as the financial system itself, much more unstable. Moreover, given the liquidity of their assets, the holders of financial assets are too quick to respond to change, which makes it difficult for real-sector companies to secure the 'patient capital' that they need for long-term development. The speed gap between the financial sector and the real sector needs to be reduced, which means that the financial market needs to be deliberately made less efficient.

Three useless phrases

Visitors to Iceland in the 1990s reported that the official tourist guide handed out at Reykjavik airport had, like all other such guides, a 'useful phrases' section. Unlike them, I was told, the Icelandic guide also had a 'useless phrases' section. Apparently it contained three phrases, which were, in English: 'Where is the railway station?', 'It's a nice day today', and 'Is there anything cheaper?'

The railways thing is, surprising though it may be, true – Iceland does not have any railways. About the weather, the guide was perhaps being overly harsh. I haven't lived there, but by all accounts Iceland does seem to have at least a few sunny days a year. As for everything being so expensive, this was also pretty accurate and a consequence of the country's economic success. Labour services are expensive in high-income countries (unless they have a constant supply of low-wage immigrants, as the US or Australia), making everything more expensive than what the official exchange rate should suggest (*see Thing 10*). Once one of the poorest economies in Europe, by 1995 Iceland had developed into the eleventh richest economy in the world (after Luxemburg, Switzerland, Japan, Norway, Denmark, Germany, the United States, Austria, Singapore and France).

Rich as it already was, the Icelandic economy got a turbo-charged boost in the late 1990s, thanks to the then government's decision to privatize and liberalize the financial sector. Between 1998 and 2003, the country privatized state-owned banks and investment funds, while abolishing even the most basic regulations on their activities, such as reserve requirements for the banks. Following this, the Icelandic banks expanded at an astonishing speed, seeking customers abroad as well. Their internet banking facilities made big inroads in Britain, the Netherlands and Germany. And Icelandic investors took advantage of the aggressive lending by their banks and went on corporate shopping sprees, especially in Britain, its former adversary in the famous 'Cod Wars' of the 1950s to 1970s. These investors, dubbed the 'Viking raiders', were best represented by Baugur, the investment company owned by Jón Jóhanneson, the young business tycoon. Bursting on to the scene only in the early 2000s, by 2007 Baugur had become a major force in the British retail industry, with major stakes in businesses employing about 65,000 people, turning over £10 billion across 3,800 stores, including Hamleys, Debenhams, Oasis and Iceland (the temptingly named British frozen-food chain).

For a while, the financial expansion seemed to work wonders for Iceland. Once a financial backwater with a reputation for excessive regulation (its stock market was only set up in 1985), the country was transformed into a vibrant new hub in the emerging global financial system. From the late 1990s, Iceland grew at an extraordinary rate and became the fifth richest country in the world by 2007 (after Norway, Luxemburg, Switzerland and Denmark). The sky seemed to be the limit.

Unfortunately, after the global financial crisis of 2008, the Icelandic economy went into meltdown. That summer, all three of its biggest banks went bankrupt and had to be taken over by the government. Things got so bad that, in October 2009, McDonald's decided to withdraw from Iceland, relegating it to the borderland of globalization. At the time of writing (early

2010), the IMF estimate was that its economy shrank at the rate of 8.5 per cent in 2009, the fastest rate of contraction among the rich countries.

The risky nature of Iceland's financial drive since the late 1990s is increasingly coming to light. Banking assets had reached the equivalent of 1,000 per cent of GDP in 2007, which was double that of the UK, a country with one of the most developed banking sectors in the world. Moreover, Iceland's financial expansion had been fuelled by foreign borrowing. By 2007, net foreign debt (foreign debts minus foreign lending) reached nearly 250 per cent of GDP, up from 50 per cent of GDP in 1997. Countries have gone to pieces with far less exposure – foreign debts were equivalent to 25 per cent of GDP in Korea and 35 per cent of GDP in Indonesia on the eve of the Asian financial crisis in 1997. On top of that, the shady nature of the financial deals behind the Icelandic economic miracle was revealed – very often the main borrowers from the banks were key shareholders of those same banks.

New engine of growth?

Why am I spending so much time talking about a small island with just over 300,000 people that does not even have a train station or a McDonald's, however dramatic its rise and fall may have been? It is because Iceland epitomizes what is wrong with the dominant view of finance today.

Extraordinary though Iceland's story may sound, it was not alone in fuelling growth by privatizing, liberalizing and opening up the financial sector during the last three decades. Ireland tried to become another financial hub through the same strategy, with its financial assets reaching the equivalent of 900 per cent of GDP in 2007. Like Iceland, Ireland also had a bad fall in the 2008 global financial crisis. At the time of writing, the IMF estimate was that its economy contracted by 7.5 per cent in 2009. Latvia, another aspiring financial hub, has had it even worse. Following the collapse of its finance-driven boom, its economy was estimated by the IMF to have shrunk by 16 per cent in 2009. Dubai, the self-appointed financial hub of the Middle East, seemed to hold on a bit longer than its European rivals, but threw in the towel by declaring a debt moratorium for its main state-owned conglomerate in November 2009.

Before their recent falls from grace, these economies were touted as examples of a new finance-led business model for countries that want to get ahead in the era of globalization. As late as November 2007, when the storm clouds were rapidly gathering in the international financial markets, Richard Portes, a prominent British policy economist, and Fridrik Baldursson, an Icelandic professor, solemnly declared in a report for the Iceland Chamber of Commerce that '[o]verall, the internationalisation of the Icelandic financial sector is a remarkable success story that the markets should better acknowledge'.[1] For some, even the recent collapses of Iceland, Ireland and Latvia have not been enough reason to abandon a finance-led economic strategy. In September 2009, Turkey announced that it will implement a series of policies that will turn itself into (yet another) financial hub of the Middle East. Even the government of Korea, a traditional manufacturing powerhouse, is implementing policies aimed at turning itself into the financial hub of Northeast Asia, although its enthusiasm has been dented since the collapse of Ireland and Dubai, after which it was hoping to model the country.

Now, the real trouble is that what countries like Iceland and Ireland were implementing were only more extreme forms of the economic strategy being pursued by many countries – a growth strategy based on financial deregulation, first adopted by the US and the UK in the early 1980s. The UK put its financial deregulation programme into a higher gear in the late 1980s, with the so-called 'Big Bang' deregulation and since then has prided itself on 'light-touch' regulation. The US matched it by abolishing the 1933 Glass-Steagall Act in 1999, thereby tearing down the wall between investment banking and commercial banking, which had defined the US financial industry since the Great Depression. Many other countries followed suit.

What was encouraging more and more countries to adopt a growth strategy based on deregulated finance was the fact that in such a system it is easier to make money in financial activities than through other economic activities – or so it seemed until the 2008 crisis. A study by two French economists, Gérard Duménil and Dominique Lévy – one of the few studies separately estimating the profit rate of the financial sector and that of the non-financial sector – shows that the former has been much higher than the latter in the US and in France during the last two or three decades.[2] According to this study, in the US the rate of profit for financial firms was lower than that of the non-financial firms between the mid 1960s and the late 1970s. But, following financial deregulation in the early 1980s, the profit rate of financial firms has been on a rising trend, and ranged between 4 per cent and 12 per cent. Since the 1980s, it has always been significantly higher than that of non-financial firms, which ranged between 2 per cent and 5 per cent. In France, the profit rate of financial corporations was *negative* between the early 1970s and the mid 1980s (no data is available for the 1960s). However, with the financial deregulation of the late 1980s, it started rising and overtook that of non-financial firms in the early 1990s, when both were about 5 per cent, and rose to over 10 per cent by 2001. In contrast, the profit rate of French non-financial firms declined from the early 1990s, to reach around 3 per cent in 2001.

In the US, the financial sector became so attractive that even many manufacturing companies have turned themselves essentially into finance companies. Jim Crotty, the distinguished American economist, has calculated that the ratio of financial assets to non-financial assets owned by non-financial corporations in the US rose from around 0.4 in the 1970s to nearly 1 in the early 2000s.[3] Even companies such as GE, GM and Ford – once the symbols of American manufacturing prowess – have been 'financialized' through a continuous expansion of their financial arms, coupled with the decline of their core manufacturing activities. By the early twenty-first century, these manufacturing firms were making most of their profits through financial activities, rather than their core manufacturing businesses (*see Thing 18*). For example, in 2003, 45 per cent of GE's profit came from GE Capital. In 2004, 80 per cent of profits of GM were from its financial arm, GMAC, while Ford made all its profits from Ford Finance between 2001 and 2003.[4]

Weapons of financial mass destruction?

The result of all this was an extraordinary growth in the financial sector across the world, especially in the rich countries. The growth was not simply in absolute terms. The more significant point is that the financial sector has grown much faster – no, much, much faster – than the underlying economy.

According to a calculation based on IMF data by Gabriel Palma, my colleague at Cambridge and a leading authority on financial crises, the ratio of the stock of financial assets to world output rose from 1.2 to 4.4 between 1980 and 2007.[5] The relative size of the financial sector was even greater in many rich countries. According to his calculation, the ratio of financial assets to GDP in the UK reached 700 per cent in 2007. France, which often styles itself as a counterpoint to Anglo-American finance capitalism, has not lagged far behind the UK in this respect – the ratio of its financial assets to GDP is only marginally lower than that of the UK. In the study cited above, Crotty, using American government data, calculates that the ratio of financial assets to GDP in the US fluctuated between 400 and 500 per cent between the 1950s and the 1970s, but started shooting up from the early 1980s with financial deregulation, to break through the 900 per cent mark by the early 2000s.

This meant that more and more financial claims were being created for each underlying real asset and economic activity. The creation of financial derivatives in the housing market, which was one of the main causes of the 2008 crisis, illustrates this point very well.

In the old days, when someone borrowed money from a bank and bought a house, the lending bank used to own the resulting financial product (mortgage) and that was that. However, financial innovations created mortgage-backed securities (MBSs), which bundle together up to several thousand mortgages. In turn, these MBSs, sometimes as many as 150 of them, were packed into a collateralized debt obligation (CDO). Then CDOs-squared were created by using other CDOs as collateral. And then CDOs-cubed were created by combining CDOs and CDOs-squared. Even higher-powered CDOs were created. Credit default swaps (CDSs) were created to protect you from default on the CDOs. And there are many more financial derivatives that make up the alphabet soup that is modern finance.

By now even I am getting confused (and, as it turns out, so were the people dealing with them), but the point is that the same underlying assets (that is, the houses that were in the original mortgages) and economic activities (the income-earning activities of those mortgage-holders) were being used again and again to 'derive' new assets. But, whatever you do in terms of financial alchemy, whether these assets deliver the expected returns depends ultimately on whether those hundreds of thousands of workers and small-scale business-owners who hold the original mortgages fall behind their mortgage payments or not.

The result was an increasingly tall structure of financial assets teetering on the same foundation of real assets (of course, the base itself was growing, in part fuelled by this activity, but let us abstract from that for the moment, since what matters here is that the size of the superstructure relative to the base was growing). If you make an existing building taller without widening the base, you increase the chance of it toppling over. It is actually a lot worse than that. As the degree of 'derivation' – or the distance from the underlying assets – increases, it becomes harder and harder to price the asset accurately. So, you are not only adding floors to an existing building without broadening its base, but you are using materials of increasingly uncertain quality for the higher floors. No wonder Warren Buffet, the American financier known for his down-to-earth approach to investment, called financial derivatives 'weapons of financial mass destruction' – well before the 2008 crisis proved their destructiveness.

Mind the gap

All my criticisms so far about the overdevelopment of the financial sector in the last two or three decades are *not* to say that all finance is a bad thing. Had we listened to Adam Smith, who opposed limited liability companies (*see Thing 2*) or Thomas Jefferson, who considered banking to be 'more dangerous than standing armies', our economies would still be made up of the 'Satanic mills' of the Victorian age, if not necessarily Adam Smith's pin factories.

However, the fact that financial development has been crucial in developing capitalism does not mean that all forms of financial development are good.

What makes financial capital necessary for economic development but potentially counterproductive or even destructive is the fact that it is much more liquid than industrial capital. Suppose that you are a factory owner who suddenly needs money to buy raw materials or machines to fulfil unexpected extra orders. Suppose also that you have already invested everything you have in building the factory and buying the machines and the inputs needed, for the initial orders. You will be grateful that there are banks that are willing to lend you the money (using your factory as collateral) in the knowledge that you will be able to generate extra income with those new inputs. Or suppose that you want to sell half of your factory (say, to start another line of business), but that no one will buy half a building and half a production line. In this case, you will be relieved to know that you can issue shares and sell half your shares. In other words, the financial sector helps companies to expand and diversify through its ability to turn illiquid assets such as buildings and machines into liquid assets such as loans and shares.

However, the very liquidity of financial assets makes them potentially negative for the rest of the economy. Building a factory takes at least months, if not years, while accumulating the technological and organizational know-how needed to build a world-class company takes decades. In contrast, financial assets can be moved around and rearranged in minutes, if not seconds. This enormous gap has created huge problems, because finance capital is 'impatient' and seeks short-term gains (*see Thing 2*). In the short run, this creates economic instability, as liquid capital sloshes around the world at very short notice and in 'irrational' ways, as we have recently seen. More importantly, in the long run, it leads to weak productivity growth, because long-term investments are cut down to satisfy impatient capital. The result has been that, despite enormous progress in 'financial deepening' (that is, the increase in the ratio between financial assets and GDP), growth has actually slowed down in recent years (*see Things 7 and 13*).

Thus, exactly because finance is efficient at responding to changing profit opportunities, it can become harmful for the rest of the economy. And this is why James Tobin, the 1981 Nobel laureate in economics, talked of the need to 'throw some sand in the wheels of our excessively efficient international money markets'. For this purpose, Tobin proposed a financial transaction tax, deliberately intended to slow down financial flows. A taboo in polite circles until recently, the so-called Tobin Tax has recently been advocated by Gordon Brown, the former British prime minister. But the Tobin Tax is not the only way in which we can reduce the speed gap between finance and the real economy. Other means include making hostile takeovers difficult (thereby reducing the gains from speculative investment in stocks), banning short-selling (the practice of selling shares that you do not own today), increasing margin requirements (that is, the proportion of the money that has to be paid upfront when buying shares) or putting restrictions on cross-border capital movements, especially for developing countries.

All this is not to say that the speed gap between finance and the real economy should be reduced to zero. A financial system perfectly synchronized with the real economy would be useless. The whole point of finance is that it can move faster than the real economy. However, if the financial sector moves too fast, it can derail the real economy. In the present circumstances, we need to rewire our financial system so that it allows firms to make those long-term investments in physical capital, human skills and organizations that are ultimately the source of economic development, while supplying them with the necessary liquidity.

Thing 23
Good economic policy does
not require good economists

What they tell you

Whatever the theoretical justifications may be for government intervention, the success or otherwise of government policies depends in large part on the competence of those who design and execute them. Especially, albeit not exclusively, in developing countries, government officials are not very well trained in economics, which they need to be if they are to implement good economic policies. Those officials should recognize their limits and should refrain from implementing 'difficult' policies, such as selective industrial policy, and stick to less-demanding free-market policies, which minimize the role of the government. Thus seen, free-market policies are doubly good, because not only are they the best policies but they are also the lightest in their demands for bureaucratic capabilities.

What they don't tell you

Good economists are *not* required to run good economic policies. The economic bureaucrats that have been most successful are usually not economists. During their 'miracle' years, economic policies in Japan and (to a lesser extent) Korea were run by lawyers. In Taiwan and China, economic policies have been run by engineers. This demonstrates that economic success does not need people well trained in economics – especially if it is of the free-market kind. Indeed, during the last three decades, the increasing influence of free-market economics has resulted in poorer economic performances all over the world, as I have shown throughout this book – lower economic growth, greater economic instability, increased inequality and finally culminating in the disaster of the 2008 global financial crisis. Insofar as we need economics, we need different kinds of economics from free-market economics.

Economic miracle without economists

The East Asian economies of Japan, Taiwan, South Korea, Singapore, Hong Kong and China are often called 'miracle' economies. This is, of course, hyperbole, but as far as hyperboles go, it is not too outlandish.

During their Industrial 'Revolution' in the nineteenth century, per capita income in the economies of Western Europe and its offshoots (North America, Australia and New Zealand) grew between 1 per cent and 1.5 per cent per year (the exact number depending on the exact time period and the country you look at). During the so-called 'Golden Age' of capitalism between the early 1950s and the mid 1970s, per capita income in Western Europe and its offshoots grew at around 3.5–4 per cent per year.

In contrast, during their miracle years, roughly between the 1950s and the mid 1990s (and between the 1980s and today in the case of China), per capita incomes grew at something like 6–7 per cent per year in the East Asian economies mentioned above. If growth rates of 1–1.5 per cent describe a 'revolution' and 3.5–4 per cent a 'golden age', 6–7 per cent deserves to be called a 'miracle'.[1]

Given these economic records, one would naturally surmise

that these countries must have had a lot of good economists. In the same way in which Germany excels in engineering because of the quality of its engineers and France leads the world in designer goods because of the talents of its designers, it seems obvious the East Asian countries must have achieved economic miracles because of the capability of their economists. Especially in Japan, Taiwan, South Korea and China – countries in which the government played a very active role during the miracle years – there must have been many first-rate economists working for the government, one would reason.

Not so. Economists were in fact conspicuous by their absence in the governments of the East Asian miracle economies. Japanese economic bureaucrats were mostly lawyers by training. In Taiwan, most key economic officials were engineers and scientists, rather than economists, as is the case in China today. Korea also had a high proportion of lawyers in its economic bureaucracy, especially before the 1980s. Oh Won-Chul, the brains behind the country's heavy and chemical industrialization programme in the 1970s – which transformed its economy from an efficient exporter of low-grade manufacturing products into a world-class player in electronics, steel and shipbuilding – was an engineer by training.

If we don't need economists to have good economic performance, as in the East Asian cases, what use is economics? Have the IMF, the World Bank and other international organizations been wasting money when they provided economics training courses for developing-country government officials and scholarships for bright young things from those countries to study in American or British universities renowned for their excellence in economics?

A possible explanation of the East Asian experience is that what is needed in those who are running economic policy is general intelligence, rather than specialist knowledge in economics. It may be that the economics taught in university classrooms is too detached from reality to be of practical use. If this is the case, the government will acquire more able economic policy-makers by recruiting those who have studied what happens to be the most prestigious subject in the country (which could be law, engineering or *even* economics, depending on the country), rather than a subject that is notionally most relevant for economic policy-making (that is, economics) (*see Thing 17*). This conjecture is indirectly supported by the fact that although economic policies in many Latin American countries have been run by economists, and very highly trained ones at that (the 'Chicago Boys' of General Pinochet being the most prominent example), their economic performance has been much inferior to that of the East Asian countries. India and Pakistan also have many world-class economists, but their economic performance is no match for the East Asian one.

John Kenneth Galbraith, the wittiest economist in history, was certainly exaggerating when he said that 'economics is extremely useful as a form of employment for economists', but he may not have been far off the mark. Economics does not seem very relevant for economic management in the real world.

Actually, it is worse than that. There are reasons to think that economics may be positively harmful for the economy.

How come nobody could foresee it?

In November 2008, Queen Elizabeth II visited the London School of Economics, which has one of the most highly regarded economics departments in the world. When given a presentation by one of the professors there, Professor Luis Garicano, on the financial crisis that had just engulfed the world, the Queen asked: 'How come nobody could foresee it?' Her Majesty asked a question that had been in most people's minds since the outbreak of the crisis in the autumn of 2008.

During the last couple of decades, we were repeatedly told by all those highly qualified experts – from Nobel Prize-winning economists through world-class financial regulators to frighteningly bright young investment bankers with economics degrees from the world's top universities – that all was well with the world economy. We were told that economists had finally found the magic formula that allowed our economies to grow rapidly with low inflation. People talked of the 'Goldilocks' economy, in which things are just right – not too hot, not too cold. Alan Greenspan, the former chairman of the Federal Reserve Board, who presided over the world's biggest and (financially and ideologically) most influential economy for two decades, was hailed as a 'maestro', as the title of the book on him by the journalist Bob Woodward of Watergate fame had it. His successor, Ben Bernanke, talked of a 'great moderation', which came with the taming of inflation and disappearance of violent economic cycles (*see Thing 6*).

So it was a real puzzle to most people, including the Queen, that things could go so spectacularly wrong in a world where clever economists were supposed to have sorted out all the major problems. How could all those clever guys with degrees from some of the best universities, with hyper-mathematical equations coming out of their ears, have been so wrong?

Learning of the sovereign's concern, the British Academy convened a meeting of some of the top economists from academia, the financial sector and the government on 17 June 2009. The result of this meeting was conveyed to the Queen in a letter, dated 22 July 2009, written by Professor Tim Besley, a prominent economics professor at the LSE, and Professor Peter Hennessy, a renowned historian of British government at Queen Mary, University of London.[2]

In the letter, Professors Besley and Hennessy said that individual economists were competent and 'doing their job properly on its own merit, but that they lost sight of the wood for the trees' in the run-up to the crisis. There was, according to them, 'a failure of the collective imagination of many bright people, both in this country and internationally, to understand the risks to the system as a whole'.

A failure of the *collective imagination*? Hadn't most economists, including most (although not all) of those who were at the British Academy meeting, told the rest of us that free markets work best because we are *rational* and *individualistic* and thus know what we want for ourselves (and no one else, possibly except for our immediate families) and how to get it most efficiently? (*See Things 5 and 16.*) I don't remember seeing much discussion in economics about imagination, especially of the collective kind, and I've been in the economics profession for the last two decades. I am not even sure whether a concept like imagination, collective or otherwise, has a place in the dominant rationalist discourse in economics. The great and the good of the economics world of Britain, then, were basically admitting that they don't know what has gone wrong.

But this understates it. Economists are not some innocent technicians who did a decent job within the narrow confines of their expertise until they were collectively wrong-footed by a once-in-a-century disaster that no one could have predicted.

Over the last three decades, economists played an important role in creating the conditions of the 2008 crisis (and dozens of smaller financial crises that came before it since the early 1980s, such as the 1982 Third World debt crisis, the 1995 Mexican peso crisis, the 1997 Asian crisis and the 1998 Russian crisis) by providing theoretical justifications for financial deregulation and the unrestrained pursuit of short-term profits. More broadly, they advanced theories that justified the policies that have led to slower growth, higher inequality, heightened job insecurity and more frequent financial crises that have dogged the world in the last three decades (*see Things 2, 6, 13 and 21*). On top of that, they pushed for policies that weakened the prospects for long-term development in developing countries (*see Things 7 and 11*). In the rich countries, these economists encouraged people to overestimate the power of new technologies (*see Thing 4*), made people's lives more and more unstable (*see Thing 6*), made them ignore the loss of national control over the economy (*see Thing 8*) and rendered them complacent about de-industrialization (*see Thing 9*). Moreover, they supplied arguments that insist that all those economic outcomes that many people find objectionable in this world – such as rising inequality (*see Thing 13*), sky-high executive salaries (*see Thing 14*) or extreme poverty in poor countries (*see Thing 3*) – are really inevitable, given (selfish and rational) human nature and the need to reward people according to their productive contributions.

In other words, economics has been worse than irrelevant. Economics, as it has been practised in the last three decades, has been positively harmful for most people.

How about the 'other' economists?

If economics is as bad as I say it is, what am I doing working as an economist? If irrelevance is the most benign social consequence of my professional actions and harm the more likely one, should I not change my profession to something more socially beneficial, such as electronic engineering or plumbing?

I stick to economics because I believe that it does not have to be useless or harmful. After all, throughout this book I have myself used economics in trying to explain how capitalism really works. It is a particular type of economics – that is, free-market economics as it has been practised in the last few decades – that is dangerous. Throughout history, there have been many schools of economic thinking that have helped us better manage and develop our economies.

To start from where we are today, what has saved the world economy from a total meltdown in the autumn of 2008 is the economics of John Maynard Keynes, Charles Kindleberger (the author of the classic book on financial crises, *Manias, Panics, and Crashes*) and Hyman Minsky (the greatly undervalued American scholar of financial crises). The world economy has not descended into a rerun of the 1929 Great Depression because we absorbed their insights and bailed out key financial institutions (although we have not properly punished the bankers responsible for the mess or reformed the industry yet), increased government spending, provided stronger deposit insurance, maintained the welfare state (that props up the incomes of those who are unemployed) and flushed the financial market with liquidity on an unprecedented scale. As explained in earlier *Things*, many of these actions that have saved the world are ones opposed by free-market economists of earlier generations and of today.

Even though they were not trained as economists, the economic officials of East Asia knew some economics. However, especially until the 1970s, the economics they knew was mostly not of the free-market variety. The economics they happened to know was the economics of Karl Marx, Friedrich List, Joseph Schumpeter, Nicholas Kaldor and Albert Hirschman. Of course, these economists lived in different times, contended with different problems and had radically differing political views (ranging from the very right-wing List to very left-wing Marx). However, there was a commonality between their economics. It was the recognition that capitalism develops through long-term investments and technological innovations that transform the productive structure, and not merely an expansion of existing structures, like inflating a balloon. Many of the things that the East Asian government officials did in the miracle years – protecting infant industries, forcefully mobilizing resources away from technologically stagnant agriculture into the dynamic industrial sector and exploiting what Hirschman called the 'linkages' across different sectors – derive from such economic views, rather than the free-market view (*see Thing 7*). Had the East Asian countries, and indeed most of the rich countries in Europe and North America before them, run their economies according to the principles of free-market economics, they would not have developed their economies in the way they have.

The economics of Herbert Simon and his followers has really changed the way we understand modern firms and, more broadly, the modern economy. It helps us break away from the myth that our economy is exclusively populated by rational self-seekers interacting through the market mechanism. When we understand that the modern economy is populated by people with limited rationality and complex motives, who are organized in a complex way, combining markets, (public and private) bureaucracies and networks, we begin to understand that our economy cannot be run according to free-market economics. When we more closely observe the more successful firms, governments and countries, we see they are the ones that have this kind of nuanced view of capitalism, not the simplistic free-market view.

Even within the dominant school of economics, that is, the neo-classical school, which provides much of the foundation for free-market economics, there are theories that explain why free markets are likely to produce sub-optimal results. These are theories of 'market failure' or 'welfare economics', first proposed by the early twentieth-century Cambridge professor Arthur Pigou, and later developed by modern-day economists such as Amartya Sen, William Baumol and Joseph Stiglitz, to name just a few of the most important ones.

Free-market economists, of course, have either ignored these other economists or, worse, dismissed them as false prophets. These days, few of the above-mentioned economists, except those belonging to the market-failure school, are even mentioned in the leading economics textbooks, let alone properly taught. But the events that have been unfolding for the last three decades have shown that we actually have a lot more positive things to learn from these other economists than from free-market economists. The relative successes and failures of different firms, economies and policies during this period suggest that the views of these economists who are now ignored, or even forgotten, have important lessons to teach us. Economics does not have to be useless or harmful. We just have to learn right kinds of economics.

Conclusion
How to rebuild the world economy

The daunting task ahead of us is to completely rebuild the world economy. Things are not as bad as they were during the Great Depression only because governments have propped up demand through huge deficit spending and unprecedented easing of money supply (the Bank of England has never had a lower interest rate since it was founded in 1644), while preventing bank runs through expansion of deposit insurance and the bailing-out of many financial firms. Without these measures, and the substantial automatic increase in welfare spending (e.g., unemployment benefit), we could be living through a much worse economic crisis than that of the 1930s.

There are people who believe the currently dominant free-market system to be fundamentally sound. They assume that tinkering on the margins will be a sufficient solution to our condition – a bit more transparency here, a tad more regulation there, and a modicum of restraints on executive pay over there. However, as I have tried to show, the fundamental theoretical and empirical assumptions behind free-market economics are highly questionable. Nothing short of a total re-envisioning of the way we organize our economy and society will do.

So what is to be done?

This is not a place to spell out all the detailed proposals required for the reconstruction of the world economy, many of which have been discussed in the foregoing 23 *Things* anyway. Here I will only outline some *principles* – eight of them – that I think we need to have in mind in redesigning our economic system.

★

To begin with: paraphrasing what Winston Churchill once said about democracy, let me restate my earlier position that *capitalism is the worst economic system except for all the others*. My criticism is of free-market capitalism, and not all kinds of capitalism.

The profit motive is still the most powerful and effective fuel to power our economy and we should exploit it to the full. But we must remember that letting it loose without any restraint is not the best way to make the most of it, as we have learned at great cost over the last three decades.

Likewise, the market is an exceptionally effective mechanism for coordinating complex economic activities across numerous economic agents, but it is no more than that – a mechanism, a machine. And like all machines, it needs careful regulation and steering. In the same way that a car can be used to kill people when driven by a drunken driver, or to save lives when it helps us deliver an emergency patient to hospital in time, the market can do wonderful things but also deplorable ones. The same car can be made better by putting in improved brakes, more powerful engines or more efficient fuel, and the same market can be made to perform better through appropriate changes to the attitudes of the participants, their motives and the rules that govern it.

There are different ways to organize capitalism. Free-market capitalism is only one of them – and not a very good one at that. The last three decades have shown that, contrary to the claims of its proponents, it slows down the economy, increases inequality and insecurity, and leads to more frequent (and sometimes massive) financial crashes.

There is no one ideal model. American capitalism is very different from Scandinavian capitalism, which in turn differs from the German or French varieties, not to speak of the Japanese form. For example, countries which find American-style economic inequality unacceptable (which some may not) may reduce it through a welfare state financed by high progressive income taxes

(as in Sweden) or through restrictions on money-making opportunities themselves by, say, making the opening of large retail
stores difficult (as in Japan). There is no simple way to choose
between the two, even though I personally think that the Swedish model is better than the Japanese one, at least in this respect.

So capitalism, yes, but we need to end our love affair with
unrestrained free-market capitalism, which has served humanity
so poorly, and install a better-regulated variety. What that variety would be depends on our goals, values and beliefs.

Second: *we should build our new economic system on the recognition
that human rationality is severely limited.* The 2008 crisis has revealed
how the complexity of the world we have created, especially in
the sphere of finance, has vastly outpaced our ability to understand and control it. Our economic system has had a mighty fall
because it was rewired following the advice of economists who
believe the human ability to deal with complexity is essentially
unlimited.

The new world should be formed with a clear recognition that
we have only limited powers of objective reasoning. It is suggested
that we can prevent another major financial crisis by enhancing
transparency. This is wrong. The fundamental problem is not
our lack of information but our limited ability to process it.
Indeed, if lack of transparency was the problem, the Scandinavian
countries – famously transparent – would not have experienced
a financial crisis in the early 1990s. As long as we continue to
allow unlimited 'financial innovations', our ability to regulate
will always be outstripped by our ability to innovate.

If we are really serious about preventing another crisis like the
2008 meltdown, we should simply ban complex financial instruments, unless they can be unambiguously shown to benefit
society *in the long run*. This idea will be dismissed by some as
outrageous. It's not. We do that all the time with other products

– think about the safety standards for food, drugs, automobiles and aeroplanes. What would result is an approval process whereby the impact of each new financial instrument, concocted by 'rocket scientists' within financial firms, is assessed in terms of risks and rewards to our system as a whole in the long run, and not just in terms of short-term profits for those firms.

Third: while acknowledging that we are not selfless angels, *we should build a system that brings out the best, rather than worst, in people.*

Free-market ideology is built on the belief that people won't do anything 'good' unless they are paid for it or punished for not doing it. This belief is then applied asymmetrically and reconceived as the view that rich people need to be motivated to work by further riches, while poor people must fear poverty for their motivation.

Material self-interest is a powerful motive. The communist system turned out to be unviable because it ignored, or rather wanted to deny, this human driver. This does not, however, prove that material self-interest is our only motive. People are *not* as much propelled by material self-interest as free-market textbooks claim. If the real world were as full of rational self-seeking agents as the one depicted in those textbooks, it would collapse under the weight of continuous cheating, monitoring, punishment and bargaining.

Moreover, by glorifying the pursuit of material self-interest by individuals and corporations, we have created a world where material enrichment absolves individuals and corporations of other responsibilities to society. In the process, we have allowed our bankers and fund managers, directly and indirectly, to destroy jobs, shut down factories, damage our environment and ruin the financial system itself in the pursuit of individual enrichment.

If we are to prevent this kind of thing happening again, we should build a system where material enrichment is taken seriously but is not allowed to become the only goal. Organizations – be they corporations or government departments – should be designed to reward trust, solidarity, honesty and cooperation among their members. The financial system needs to be reformed to reduce the influence of short-term shareholders so that companies can afford to pursue goals other than short-term profit maximization. We should better reward behaviour with public benefits (e.g., reducing energy consumption, investment in training), not simply through government subsidies but also by bestowing it with a higher social status.

This is not just a moral argument. It is also an appeal to enlightened self-interest. By letting short-term self-interest rule everything we risk destroying the entire system, which serves no one's interest in the long run.

Fourth: *we should stop believing that people are always paid what they 'deserve'.*

People from poor countries are, individually, often more productive and entrepreneurial than their counterparts in rich countries. Should they be given equal opportunity through free immigration, these people can, and will, replace the bulk of the workforce in rich countries, even though that would be politically unacceptable and undesirable. Thus seen, it is the national economic systems and immigration control of the rich countries, rather than their lack of personal qualities, that keep poor people in poor countries poor.

Emphasizing that many people stay poor because they do not have true equal opportunity is not to say that they deserve to remain poor insofar as they have had equal opportunity. Unless there is some equalizing in outcome, especially (although not exclusively) so that all children can have more than minimum nutrition and parental attention, the equality of opportunity provided by the market mechanism will not guarantee truly fair competition. It will be like a race where no one has a head start but some people run with weights on their legs.

At the other end of the spectrum, executive pay in the US has gone into the stratosphere in the last few decades. US managers have increased their relative pay by at least ten times between the 1950s and today (an average CEO used to get paid thirty-five times an average worker's salary then, while today he is paid 300–400 times that), but that is not because their productivity has risen ten times faster than that of their workers. Even excluding stock options, US managers are paid two and a half times what their Dutch counterparts are or four times what their Japanese counterparts are, despite no apparent superiority in their productivity.

Only when we are free to question the hand of cards that the market has dealt us will we be able to find ways to establish a more just society. We can, and should, change the rules of the stock market and the corporate governance system in order to restrain excessive executive pay in limited liability companies. We should not only provide equal opportunity but also equalize, to an extent, the starting points for all children for a truly meritocratic society. People should be given a real, not superficial, second chance through unemployment benefits and publicly subsidized retraining. Poor people in poor countries should not be blamed for their poverty, when the bigger explanations lie in the poverty of their national economic systems and immigration control in the rich countries. Market outcomes are not 'natural' phenomena. They can be changed.

Fifth: *we need to take 'making things' more seriously.* The post-industrial knowledge economy is a myth. The manufacturing sector remains vital.

Especially in the US and the UK, but also in many other countries, industrial decline in the last few decades has been treated as an inevitability of a post-industrial age, if not actively welcomed as a sign of post-industrial success.

But we are material beings and cannot live on ideas, however great the knowledge economy may sound. Moreover, we have always lived in a knowledge economy in the sense that it has always been a command over superior knowledge, rather than the physical nature of activities, that has ultimately decided which country is rich or poor. Indeed, most societies are still making more and more things. It is mainly because those who make things have become so much more productive that things have become cheaper, in relative terms, than services that we think we don't consume as many things as before.

Unless you are a tiny tax haven (a status that is going to become more and more difficult to maintain, following the 2008 crisis), such as Luxemburg and Monaco, or a small country floating on oil, such as Brunei or Kuwait, you have to become better at making things in order to raise your living standard. Switzerland and Singapore, which are often touted as post-industrial success stories, are in fact two of the most industrialized economies in the world. Moreover, most high-value services are dependent (sometimes even parasitic) on the manufacturing sector (e.g., finance, technical consulting). And services are not very tradable, so an overly large service sector makes your balance of payments situation more precarious and thus your economic growth more difficult to sustain.

The myth of the post-industrial knowledge economy has also misdirected our investments. It has encouraged excessive emphasis on, for example, formal education, whose impact on economic growth turns out to be highly complex and uncertain, and on the spread of the internet, whose productivity impacts are actually quite modest.

Investment in 'boring' things like machinery, infrastructure and worker training needs to be encouraged through appropriate changes in tax rules (e.g., accelerated depreciation for machinery), subsidies (e.g., to worker training) or public investment (e.g., redirection into infrastructural development). Industrial policy needs to be redesigned to promote key manufacturing sectors with high scope for productivity growth.

Sixth: *we need to strike a better balance between finance and 'real' activities.*

A productive modern economy cannot exist without a healthy financial sector. Finance plays, among other things, the crucial role of resolving the mismatch between the act of investment and the bearing of its fruits. By 'liquidizing' physical assets whose characteristics cannot be changed quickly, finance also helps us to reallocate resources quickly.

However, in the last three decades, finance has become the proverbial tail that wags the dog. Financial liberalization has made it easier for money to move around, even across national borders, allowing financial investors to become more impatient for instant results. As a consequence, both corporations and governments have been forced to implement policies that produce quick profits, regardless of their long-term implications. Financial investors have utilized their greater mobility as a bargaining chip in extracting a bigger share of national income. Easier movement of finance has also resulted in greater financial instability and greater job insecurity (which is needed for delivering quick profits).

Finance needs to be slowed down. Not to put us back to the days of debtors' prison and small workshops financed by personal savings. But, unless we vastly reduce the speed gap between finance and the real economy, we will not encourage long-term investment and real growth, because productive investments often take a long time to bear fruit. It took Japan forty years of protection and government subsidies before its automobile industry could be an international success, even at the lower end of the market. It took Nokia seventeen years before it made any profit in the electronics business, where it is one of the world leaders today. However, following the increasing degree of financial deregulation, the world has operated with increasingly shorter time horizons.

Financial transaction taxes, restrictions on cross-border movement of capital (especially movements in and out of developing countries), greater restrictions on mergers and acquisitions are some of the measures that will slow down finance to the speed at which it helps, rather than weakens or even derails, the real economy.

Seventh: *government needs to become bigger and more active.*

In the last three decades, we have been constantly told by free-market ideologues that the government is part of the problem, not a solution to the ills of our society. True, there are instances of government failure – sometimes spectacular ones – but markets and corporations fail too and, more importantly, there are many examples of impressive government success. The role of the government needs to be thoroughly reassessed.

This is not just about crisis management, evident since 2008, even in the avowedly free-market economies, such as the US. It is more about creating a prosperous, equitable and stable society. Despite its limitations and despite numerous attempts to weaken it, democratic government is, at least so far, the best vehicle we have for reconciling conflicting demands in our society and, more importantly, improving our collective well-being. In considering how we can make the best out of the government, we need to abandon some of the standard 'trade-offs' bandied about by free-market economists.

We have been told that a big government, which collects high income taxes from the wealthy and redistributes them to the poor, is bad for growth, as it discourages wealth creation by the rich and makes lower classes lazy. However, if having a small government is good for economic growth, many developing countries that have such a government should do well. Evidently this is not the case. At the same time, the Scandinavian examples, where a large welfare state has coexisted with (or even encouraged) good growth performance, should also expose the limits to the belief that smaller governments are always better for growth.

Free-market economists have also told us that active (or intrusive, as they put it) governments are bad for economic growth. However, contrary to common perception, virtually all of today's rich countries used government intervention to get rich (if you are still not convinced about this point, see my earlier book, *Bad Samaritans*). If designed and implemented appropriately, government intervention can increase economic dynamism by augmenting the supply of inputs that markets are bad at supplying (e.g., R&D, worker training), sharing risk for projects with high social returns but low private returns, and, in developing countries, providing the space in which nascent firms in 'infant' industries can develop their productive capabilities.

We need to think more creatively how the government becomes an essential element in an economic system where there is more dynamism, greater stability and more acceptable levels of equity. This means building a better welfare state, a better regulatory system (especially for finance) and better industrial policy.

Eighth: *the world economic system needs to 'unfairly' favour developing countries.*

Because of the constraints imposed by their democratic checks, the free-market advocates in most rich countries have actually found it difficult to implement full-blown free-market reform. Even Margaret Thatcher found it impossible to consider dismantling the National Health Service. As a result, it was actually developing countries that have been the main subjects of free-market policy experiments.

Many poorer countries, especially in Africa and Latin America, have been forced to adopt free-market policies in order to borrow money from free-market-loving international financial organizations (such as the IMF and the World Bank) and rich-country governments (that also ultimately control the IMF and the World Bank). The weakness of their democracies meant that free-market policies could be implemented more ruthlessly in developing countries, even when they hurt a lot of people. This is the ultimate irony of all – people needing most help were worst hit. This tendency was reinforced by the strengthening of global rules over the last couple of decades on what governments can do to protect and develop their economies (more necessary in the poor countries) through the establishment and/or strengthening of organizations such as the WTO, the BIS and various bilateral and regional free-trade and investment agreements. The result has been a much more thorough implementation of free-market policies and much worse performance in terms of growth, stability and inequality than in developed countries.

The world economic system needs to be completely overhauled in order to provide greater 'policy space' for the developing countries to pursue policies that are more suitable to them (the rich countries have much greater scope to bend, or even ignore, international rules). The developing countries need a more permissive regime regarding the use of protectionism, regulation of foreign investment and intellectual property rights, among others. These are policies that the rich countries actually used when they were developing countries themselves. All this requires a reform of the WTO, abolition and/or reform of existing bilateral trade and investment agreements between rich and poor countries, and changes in the policy conditions attached to loans from international financial organizations and to foreign aid from the rich countries.

Of course, these things are 'unfairly favourable' to the developing countries, as some rich countries would argue. However, developing countries already suffer from so many disadvantages in the international system that they need these breaks to have a hope of catching up.

The eight principles all directly go against the received economic wisdom of the last three decades. This will have made some readers uncomfortable. But unless we now abandon the principles that have failed us and that are continuing to hold us back, we will meet similar disasters down the road. And we will have done nothing to alleviate the conditions of billions suffering poverty and insecurity, especially, but not exclusively, in the developing world. It is time to get uncomfortable.

Notes

THING 1

1 On how tariff (hampering free trade in goods) was another important issue in the making of the American Civil War, see my earlier
book *Kicking Away the Ladder – Development Strategy in Historical
Perspective* (Anthem Press, London, 2002), pp. 24–8 and references
thereof.

THING 2

1 A. Smith, *An Inquiry into the Nature and Causes of the Wealth of Nations*
(Clarendon Press, Oxford, 1976), p. 741.

2 N. Rosenberg and L. Birdzell, *How the West Grew Rich* (IB Tauris
& Co., London, 1986), p. 200.

3 A. Glyn, *Capitalism Unleashed – Finance, Globalisation, and Welfare*
(Oxford University Press, Oxford, 2004), p. 7, fig. 1.3.

4 J. G. Palma, 'The revenge of the market on the rentiers – Why neo-
liberal reports on the end of history turned out to be premature',
Cambridge Journal of Economics, 2009, vol. 33, no. 4, p. 851, fig. 12.

5 See W. Lazonick and M. O'Sullivan, 'Maximising shareholder value:
A new ideology for corporate governance', *Economy and Society*, 2000,
vol. 29, no. 1, and W. Lazonick, 'The buyback boondoggle', *Business
Week*, 24 August 2009.

6 Lazonick, op. cit.

THING 4

1 R. Sarti, 'Domestic service: Past and present in Southern and Northern Europe', *Gender and History*, 2006, vol. 18, no. 2, p. 223, table 1.

2 As cited in J. Greenwood, A. Seshadri and M. Yorukoglu, 'Engines of liberation', *Review of Economic Studies*, 2005, vol. 72, p. 112.

3 C. Goldin, 'The quiet revolution that transformed women's employment, education, and family', *American Economic Review*, 2006, vol. 96, no. 2, p. 4, fig. 1.

4 I. Rubinow, 'The problem of domestic service', *Journal of Political Economy*, 1906, vol. 14, no. 8, p. 505.

5 The book is H.-J. Chang and I. Grabel, *Reclaiming Development – An Alternative Economic Policy Manual* (Zed Press, London, 2004).

6 K. Ohmae, *The Borderless World: Power and Strategy in the Interlinked Economy* (Harper & Row, New York, 1990).

THING 5

1 An accessible summary of the academic literature on the complexity of human motivations can be found in B. Frey, *Not Just for the Money – Economic Theory of Personal Motivation* (Edward Elgar, Cheltenham, 1997).

2 The example is an elaboration of the one used by K. Basu, 'On why we do not try to walk off without paying after a taxi-ride', *Economic and Political Weekly*, 1983, no. 48.

THING 6

1 S. Fischer, 'Maintaining price stability', *Finance and Development*, December 1996.

2 A study by Robert Barro, a leading free-market economist, concludes that moderate inflation (10–20 per cent) has low negative effects on growth, and that, below 10 per cent, inflation has no effect at all. See R. Barro, 'Inflation and growth', *Review of Federal Reserve Bank of St Louis*, 1996, vol. 78, no. 3. A study by Michael Sarel, an IMF economist, estimates that below 8 per cent inflation has little impact on growth – if anything, he points out, the relationship is positive below that level – that is, inflation helps rather than hinders growth. See M. Sarel, 'Non-linear effects of inflation on economic growth', *IMF Staff Papers*, 1996, vol. 43, March.

3 See: M. Bruno, 'Does inflation really lower growth?', *Finance and Development*, 1995, vol. 32, pp. 35–8; M. Bruno and W. Easterly, 'Inflation and growth: In search of a stable relationship', *Review of Federal Reserve Bank of St Louis*, 1996, vol. 78, no. 3.

4 In the 1960s, Korea's inflation rate was much higher than that of five Latin American countries (Venezuela, Bolivia, Mexico, Peru and Colombia) and not much lower than that of Argentina. In the 1970s, the Korean inflation rate was higher than that found in Venezuela, Ecuador and Mexico, and not much lower than that of Colombia and Bolivia. The information is from A. Singh, 'How did East Asia grow so fast? – Slow progress towards an analytical consensus', 1995, UNCTAD Discussion Paper, no. 97, table 8.

5 There are many different ways to calculate profit rates, but the relevant concept here is returns on assets. According to S. Claessens, S. Djankov and L. Lang, 'Corporate growth, financing, and risks in the decades before East Asia's financial crisis', 1998, Policy Research Working Paper, no. 2017, World Bank, Washington, DC, fig. 1, the returns on assets in forty-six developed and developing

countries during 1988–96 ranged between 3.3 per cent (Austria) and 9.8 per cent (Thailand). The ratio ranged between 4 per cent and 7 per cent in forty of the forty-six countries; it was below 4 per cent in three countries and above 7 per cent in three countries. Another World Bank study puts the average profit rate for non-financial firms in 'emerging market' economies (middle-income countries) during the 1990s (1992–2001) at an even lower level of 3.1 per cent (net income/assets). See S. Mohapatra, D. Ratha and P. Suttle, 'Corporate financing patterns and performance in emerging markets', mimeo., March 2003, World Bank, Washington, DC.

6 C. Reinhart and K. Rogoff, *This Time is Different* (Princeton University Press, Princeton and Oxford, 2008), p. 252, fig. 16.1.

THING 7

1 On Lincoln's protectionist views, see my earlier book *Kicking Away the Ladder* (Anthem Press, London, 2002), pp. 27–8 and the references thereof.

2 This story is told in greater detail in my earlier books: *Kicking Away the Ladder* is a heavily referenced and annotated academic – but by no means difficult-to-read – monograph, focused particularly on trade policy; *Bad Samaritans* (Random House, London, 2007, and Bloomsbury USA, New York, 2008) covers a broader range of policy areas and is written in a more user-friendly way.

THING 8

1 For further evidence, see my recent book *Bad Samaritans* (Random House, London, 2007, and Bloomsbury USA, New York, 2008), ch. 4, 'The Finn and the Elephant', and R. Kozul-Wright and

P. Rayment, *The Resistible Rise of Market Fundamentalism* (Zed Books, London, 2007), ch. 4.

THING 9

1 K. Coutts, A. Glyn and B. Rowthorn, 'Structural change under New Labour', *Cambridge Journal of Economics*, 2007, vol. 31, no. 5.
2 The term is borrowed from the 2008 report by the British government's Department for BERR (Business, Enterprise and Regulatory Reform), *Globalisation and the Changing UK Economy* (2008).
3 B. Alford, 'De-industrialisation', *ReFRESH*, Autumn 1997, p. 6, table 1.
4 B. Rowthorn and K. Coutts, 'De-industrialisation and the balance of payments in advanced economies', *Cambridge Journal of Economics*, 2004, vol. 28, no. 5.

THING 10

1 T. Gylfason, 'Why Europe works less and grows taller', *Challenge*, 2007, January/February.

THING 11

1 P. Collier and J. Gunning, 'Why has Africa grown slowly?', *Journal of Economic Perspectives*, 1999, vol. 13, no. 3, p. 4.
2 Daniel Etounga-Manguelle, a Cameroonian engineer and writer, notes: 'The African, anchored in his ancestral culture, is so convinced that the past can only repeat itself that he worries only superficially about the future. However, without a dynamic perception of the future, there is no planning, no foresight, no scenario building; in

other words, no policy to affect the course of events' (p. 69). And then he goes on to say that 'African societies are like a football team in which, as a result of personal rivalries and a lack of team spirit, one player will not pass the ball to another out of fear that the latter might score a goal' (p. 75). D. Etounga-Manguelle, 'Does Africa need a cultural adjustment program?' in L. Harrison and S. Huntington (eds.), *Culture Matters – How Values Shape Human Progress* (Basic Books, New York, 2000).

3 According to Weber, in 1863, around a quarter of France's population did not speak French. In the same year, 11 per cent of schoolchildren aged seven to thirteen spoke no French at all, while another 37 per cent spoke or understood it but could not write it. E. Weber, *Peasants into Frenchmen – The Modernisation of Rural France, 1870-1914* (Stanford University Press, Stanford, 1976), p. 67.

4 See H-J. Chang, 'Under-explored treasure troves of development lessons – lessons from the histories of small rich European countries (SRECs)' in M. Kremer, P. van Lieshout and R. Went (eds.), *Doing Good or Doing Better – Development Policies in a Globalising World* (Amsterdam University Press, Amsterdam, 2009), and H-J. Chang, 'Economic history of the developed world: Lessons for Africa', a lecture delivered in the Eminent Speakers Programme of the African Development Bank, 26 February 2009 (can be downloaded from: http://www.econ.cam.ac.uk/faculty/chang/pubs/ChangAfDBlecturetext.pdf).

5 See H-J. Chang, 'How important were the "initial conditions" for economic development – East Asia vs. Sub-Saharan Africa' (ch. 4) in H-J. Chang, *The East Asian Development Experience: The Miracle, the Crisis, and the Future* (Zed Press, London, 2006).

6 For comparison of the quality of institutions in today's rich countries when they were at similar levels of development with those found in today's developing countries, see H-J. Chang, *Kicking Away the Ladder* (Anthem Press, London, 2002), ch. 3.

THING 12

1 For a user-friendly explanation and criticism of the theory of comparative advantage, see 'My six-year-old son should get a job', ch. 3 of my *Bad Samaritans* (Random House, London, 2007, and Bloomsbury USA, New York, 2008).

2 Further details can be found from my earlier books, *Kicking Away the Ladder* (Anthem Press, London, 2002) and *Bad Samaritans*.

THING 13

1 The sixteen countries where inequality increased are, in descending order of income inequality as of 2000, the US, South Korea, the UK, Israel, Spain, Italy, the Netherlands, Japan, Australia, Canada, Sweden, Norway, Belgium, Finland, Luxemburg and Austria. The four countries where income inequality fell were Germany, Switzerland, France and Denmark.

2 L. Mishel, J. Bernstein and H. Shierholz, *The State of Working America, 2008/9* (Economic Policy Institute, Washington, DC, 2009), p. 26, table 3.

3 According to the OECD (Organization for Economic Development and Cooperation), before taxes and transfers, the US, as of mid 2000s, had a Gini coefficient (the measure of income inequality, with 0 as absolute equality and 1 as absolute inequality) of 0.46. The figures were 0.51 for Germany, 0.49 for Belgium, 0.44 for Japan, 0.43 for Sweden and 0.42 for the Netherlands.

THING 14

1 L. Mishel, J. Bernstein and H. Shierholz, *The State of Working America, 2008/9* (Economic Policy Institute, Washington, DC, 2009), table 3.2.
2 Ibid., table 3.1.
3 'Should Congress put a cap on executive pay?', *New York Times*, 3 January 2009.
4 Mishel et al., op. cit., table 3.A2. The thirteen countries are Australia, Belgium, Canada, France, Germany, Italy, Japan, the Netherlands, New Zealand, Spain, Sweden, Switzerland and the UK.
5 Ibid., table 3.A2.
6 L. A. Bebchuk and J. M. Fried, 'Executive compensation as an agency problem', *Journal of Economic Perspectives*, 2003, vol. 17, no. 3, p. 81.

THING 15

1 OECD, 'Is informal normal? – Towards more and better jobs in developing countries', 2009.
2 D. Roodman and J. Morduch, 'The impact of microcredit on the poor in Bangladesh: Revisiting the evidence', 2009, working paper, no. 174, Center for Global Development, Washington, DC.
3 M. Bateman, *Why Doesn't Microfinance Work?* (Zed Books, London, 2010).

THING 16

1 Mansion House speech, 19 June 2009.
2 For a very engaging and user-friendly presentation of the researches

on the irrational side of human nature, see P. Ubel, *Free Market Madness: Why Human Nature is at Odds with Economics – and Why it Matters* (Harvard Business School Press, Boston, 2009).

THING 17

1 J. Samoff, 'Education for all in Africa: Still a distant dream' in R. Arnove and C. Torres (eds.), *Comparative Education – The Dialectic of the Global and the Local* (Rowman and Littlefield Publishers Inc., Lanham, Maryland, 2007), p. 361, table 16.3.

2 L. Pritchett, 'Where has all the education gone?', *The World Bank Economic Review*, 2001, vol. 13, no. 3.

3 A. Wolf, *Does Education Matter?* (Penguin Books, London, 2002), p. 42.

4 In the eighth grade, the US overtook Lithuania, but was still behind Russia and Hungary; fourth-grader score for Hungary and eighth-grader scores for Latvia and Kazakhstan are not available.

5 The other European countries were, in order of their rankings in the test, Germany, Denmark, Italy, Austria, Sweden, Scotland and Norway. See the website of the National Center for Educational Statistics of the US Department of Education Institute of Education Sciences, http://nces.ed.gov/timss/table07_1.asp.

6 The other rich countries were, in order of their rankings in the test, Japan, England, the US, Australia, Sweden, Scotland and Italy. See the above website.

7 The most influential works in this school of thought were Harry Braverman's *Labor and Monopoly Capital: The Degradation of Work in the Twentieth Century* (Monthly Review Press, New York, 1974) and Stephen Marglin's 'What do bosses do?', published in two parts in *The Review of Radical Political Economy* in 1974 and 1975.

8 Wolf, *op. cit.*, p. 264.

9 On the issue of sorting and many other insightful observations on the role of education in economic development, see Wolf, *op. cit.*

THING 18

1 R. Blackburn, 'Finance and the fourth dimension', *New Left Review*, May/June 2006, p. 44.

THING 19

1 The share of federal government in total R&D spending in the US was 53.6 per cent in 1953, 56.8 per cent in 1955, 64.6 per cent in 1960, 64.9 per cent in 1965, 57.1 per cent in 1970, 51.7 per cent in 1975, 47.2 per cent in 1980, 47.9 per cent in 1985 and 47.3 per cent in 1989 (estimated). See D. Mowery and N. Rosenberg, 'The U.S. National Innovation System' in R. Nelson (ed.), *National Innovation Systems* (Oxford University Press, New York and Oxford, 1993), p. 41, table 2.3.
2 H. Simon, 'Organizations and markets', *Journal of Economic Perspectives*, 1991, vol. 5, no. 2, p. 27.

THING 20

1 On how the Confucian culture was *not* a cause of East Asian economic development, see 'Lazy Japanese and thieving Germans', ch. 9 in my book *Bad Samaritans* (Random House, London, 2007, and Bloomsbury USA, New York, 2008).
2 M. Jäntti et al., 'American exceptionalism in a new light: a comparison of intergenerational earnings mobility in the Nordic countries, the United Kingdom and the United States', The Warwick Economic Research Paper Series, Department of Economics, University of Warwick, October 2005.

THING 21

1 OECD is the Organization for Economic Cooperation and Development. It is the club of the rich countries, with several members describing whom as 'rich' may be debatable, such as Portugal, Korea, Czech Republic, Hungary, Slovak Republic, Poland, Mexico and Turkey (in descending order of per capita income). Of these, Portugal and Korea are the richest, with around $18,000 per capita income (in 2006), and Turkey the poorest, with per capita income of $5,400 (in 2006). The next poorest OECD member after Portugal and Korea is Greece, which has a per capita income over $24,000. In 2003 (the latest year for which the OECD has the data), public social spending accounted for 5.7 per cent of GDP in Korea. The highest was Sweden, with 31.3 per cent. The OECD average was 20.7 per cent. See *OECD Factbook 2008: Economic, Environmental and Social Statistics*.

2 In 2003 (the latest year for which the OECD has the data), public social spending accounted for 16.2 per cent of GDP in the US, compared to the OECD average of 20.7 per cent and the EU15 average of 23.9 per cent. Among the OECD member states, only Korea (5.7 per cent) and Mexico (6.8 per cent) – two countries that are usually not considered fully developed – had a lower ratio. Ibid.

THING 22

1 R. Portes and F. Baldursson, *The Internationalisation of Iceland's Financial Sector* (Iceland Chamber of Commerce, Reykjavik, 2007), p. 6.

2 G. Duménil and D. Lévy, 'Costs and benefits of neoliberalism: A class analysis', in G. Epstein (ed.), *Financialisation and the World Economy* (Edward Elgar, Cheltenham, 2005).

3 J. Crotty, 'If financial market competition is so intense, why are financial firm profits so high? – Reflections on the current "golden

age" of finance', Working Paper, no. 134, PERI (Political Economy Research Institute), University of Massachusetts, Amherst, April 2007.

4 The information for GE is from R. Blackburn, 'Finance and the fourth dimension', *New Left Review*, May/June 2006, p. 44. J. Froud et al., *Financialisation and Strategy: Narrative and Numbers* (Routledge, London, 2006), estimates that the ratio could be as high as 50 per cent. The Ford number comes from the Froud et al. study and the GM number from the Blackburn study.

5 J. G. Palma, 'The revenge of the market on the rentiers – Why neoliberal reports of the end of history turned out to be premature', *Cambridge Journal of Economics*, 2009, vol. 33, no. 4.

THING 23

1 Your per capita income will double in ten years, if you are a 'miracle' economy growing at 7 per cent. If you are a 'golden age' economy growing at 3.5 per cent per year per capita, it will take around twenty years to double your per capita income. In those twenty years, per capita income of the miracle economy will have quadrupled. In contrast, it will take around seventy years for an 'industrial revolution' economy, growing at 1 per cent in per capita terms, to double its per capita income.

2 The letter can be downloaded from the website, http://media. ft.com/cms/3e3b6ca8-7a08-11de-b86f-00144feabdco.pdf.

Index